CONFEDERATE DAUGHTERS

Coming of Age
during the Civil War

Victoria E. Ott

SOUTHERN ILLINOIS UNIVERSITY PRESS
Carbondale

11 10 09 08   4 3 2

Library of Congress Cataloging-in-Publication Data
Ott, Victoria E., 1971–
  Confederate daughters : coming of age during the Civil
War / Victoria E. Ott.
      p. cm.
  Includes bibliographical references and index.
  ISBN-13: 978-0-8093-2828-4 (alk. paper)
  ISBN-10: 0-8093-2828-3 (alk. paper)
  1. United States—History—Civil War, 1861–1865—
Women. 2. United States—History—Civil War, 1861–
1865—Social aspects. 3. Young women—Confederate
States of America—Social conditions. 4. Women, White—
Confederate States of America—Social conditions.
5. Teenage girls—Confederate States of America—Social
conditions. 6. Group identity—Confederate States of
America—History. 7. Nationalism—Confederate States
of America—History. 8. Confederate States of America—
Social conditions. 9. Young women—Southern States—
History—19th century. 10. Teenage girls—Southern
States—History—19th century. I. Title.

E628.O88 2008
973.7′1—dc22   2007020904

*To Thomas Oliver Ott III and the memory of
Margaret Franklin Ott*

Contents

Illustrations

Acknowledgments

THIS BOOK IS THE RESULT of the generous and tireless support of many people and institutions. My work began at the University of Tennessee, where I received a considerable amount of financial assistance from the Department of History, including the Charles O. Jackson Fellowship, made possible by the Jackson Family; the Bernadotte-Schmitt research stipend; and the Lee Verstanding Scholarship. Moreover, the department offset the cost of attending several history conferences during which I presented portions of my research. Outside the university, I received significant financial support from the Virginia Historical Society's Mellon Fellowship program, the Society of Colonial Dames of Tennessee's graduate student scholarship, and Phi Alpha Theta's Doctoral Scholarship.

Throughout the process of research and writing, I benefited from the expertise of several talented people. I was fortunate to have found a wonderful group of scholars who were willing to mentor me throughout the writing process and who encouraged me to seek publication. I am forever indebted to Stephen V. Ash. Our lively discussions on the Civil War challenged me to think critically about the social experiences of war and inspired me to pursue a research topic on female youths. Always dedicated, he reminded me to take a balanced approach to the lives of women in the Civil War South and pushed me to write in a way that would draw the reader into the narrative. His careful guidance as a teacher as well as his model of exemplary scholarship in the social history of the Civil War South serves as a lifelong example for my own career. I am thankful for the efforts of Allison Ensor; to Lorri Glover, who urged me to think creatively about gender as a tool of analysis and to approach my subject with confidence; and to Robert J. Norrell, who provided crucial feedback for turning my research into a book. I tested my ideas about young women's identity formation by participating in a seminar hosted by the University of Tennessee's Center for the Study of War and Society. The faculty, students, and interested public who attended the session offered important insights on how I could strengthen my argument and provided direction in uncovering additional primary sources. I also received guidance from other scholars at professional conferences. In particular, my work benefited from the inspiring exchanges with Anya Jabour at the Southern Association of Women Historians meeting in Richmond, Virginia, and Angela Boswell's comments on a paper that I presented at the Mid-Atlantic Conference on History in Fayetteville, Arkansas.

At Birmingham-Southern College, I appreciate the collegial environment that supports my efforts to continue my work. The college's Summer Stipend Program allowed me, in my first year as a faculty member, to pursue additional archival trips. Faculty members graciously offered their time to attend a presentation of my research into young women's reminiscences of the war and offered advice for revisions. The helpful guidance of my colleagues from across the disciplines demonstrates the important role the liberal arts can play in scholarly development. I am especially grateful to the members of the history department—Guy Hubbs, Randy Law, Mark Lester, Matt Levey, and Bill Nicholas—for their sound advice, constant encouragement, and friendship.

This book was also made possible by the dedicated editorial and production staff at Southern Illinois University Press. Sylvia Frank Rodrigue expressed an early interest in my topic. I also appreciate the professionalism and guidance of Barb Martin and Kathy Kageff. The keen editorial skills of Keith Poulter made the copyediting process a rather smooth and enjoyable experience. I appreciate also the high standards of Lola Starck, who managed the reproduction of the images. Additionally, this book benefited considerably from the readers who reviewed drafts of the manuscript for SIU Press and offered significant direction for revisions.

At the University of Central Florida, I met two scholars who transformed my life. Shirley Leckie convinced me to take my interest in examining women's lives seriously. Thanks to her encouragement, my curiosity about the female past grew into a lifelong pursuit to tell its story. I am likewise fortunate to have worked with Carole Adams in Central Florida's women's studies program, during which time she took me under her wing and introduced me to the nature of the historical profession. She invited me to what became my first women's history conference and included me in the process of academic program development. Moreover, Carole became a great friend who taught me the value of social activism.

This work would certainly never have come to fruition without the constant support of my friends and family or, as I refer to them collectively, my "cheering section." Included in this group are Valerie Emanoil, Lynn Sherrill, Nancy Schurr, David Phipps, Véronique Vanblaere, Mary Donna Luckey, and my brother, John Ott. I am also thankful that I found a supportive partner and best friend in my husband, John Vanover. He encouraged me to pursue my passion for historical investigation, while offering much-needed diversions from the rigors of research and writing. This book is dedicated to my parents, Thomas Oliver Ott III and the late Margaret Franklin Ott, who taught me to think independently, to be compassionate toward others, and to find the humor in life.

CONFEDERATE
DAUGHTERS

Introduction

IN THE FINAL YEAR OF THE CIVIL WAR, Emma Florence
LeConte, age seventeen, looked at her surroundings with a sense of despair.
Gone were the carefree days of her childhood. Now the pale riders of war,
destruction, and fear consumed her life. Her family was split apart, the
men having left to fight or to retrieve other family members from danger.
The imminent Union invasion of her hometown of Columbia, South
Carolina, threatened to separate her from the home of her fond childhood
memories. As a young woman coming of age in the Confederacy, LeConte,
like many of her age group, expressed anger and frustration over a war that
forced her to mature faster than had traditionally been expected:

> Truly we girls, whose lot in life is to grow up in these times, are
> unfortunate. No pleasure, no enjoyment . . . nothing but the stern
> realities of life. These which should come later are made familiar
> to us at an age when only gladness should surround us. . . . I have
> seen little of the light heartedness and exuberant joy that people talk
> about as the natural heritage of youth.[1]

LeConte's keen observations of the effects of war on female youths
provide a glimpse into the disruptive nature of war in the lives of the
South's daughters. Yet, LeConte's diary as a whole is not solely a story of
women's wartime experiences. Rather, in the private pages of her intimate
journal, LeConte exposes the reasons why southerners, at least those of her
age, gender, and status, supported a war to defend the cause of Southern
independence. It was through the lens of youth that LeConte and her
peers understood the Confederate cause. As members of slaveholding
families ranging from middling, urban households to the vast plantation
districts, teenage daughters understood that slave ownership was tightly

bound to their financial and social standing, and embraced the feminine ideals that separated them from the non-slaveholding yeomanry and poor white women. From their earliest recollections, southern daughters had prepared to assume one day their place upon the proverbial pedestal of the "southern lady." These female youths, moreover, were born and raised in a period of American history when regional debates over slavery reached their height. Consequently, they knew nothing of the Old South of their mothers and older female kin when slaveholders existed with little threat to their "peculiar institution." Yet, young women looked to the past with a romantic gaze, hoping to return to the idyllic Old South of former generations of southern women. Thus, as the region stood on the brink of war in early 1861, daughters believed that not only was their way of life at stake but so was their ability to live up to the ideals of southern slaveholding women set before them.

This is a study of Confederate identity and the efforts of young women to create and sustain a new nationhood. Both contemporaries of the era as well as historians have done much work on the subject of Confederate nationalism. What these studies reveal is a common set of languages and themes used to validate secession and support the creation of a national structure. These languages and themes helped white southerners who supported secession replace their identity as Americans with a Confederate sense of self. The most significant aspect of the nationalistic rhetoric was the connection with the Revolutionary past. Secessionists saw roots of their nation in the struggle for independence, and compared their conflict with the Union with that against the British monarchy in 1776. Moreover, as historian Anne Sarah Rubin points out, southerners believed that in creating a new nation, they had become "guardians of Revolutionary ideals," those that trumpeted independence from a tyrannical government. Southerners also infused their Revolutionary language with constitutional symbolism. They touted the Confederacy as the protector of the constitution and the freedoms it was intended to ensure. Religion played a significant role as well. Southerners believed themselves to be the people chosen by God to create a better nation, one that could withstand the influences of immoral and greedy outsiders. The notion that the Confederacy itself was a matter of divine providence, however, would come into question in the wake of battlefield defeats later in the war. Nonetheless, their newspapers, schoolbooks, and church sermons continually placed these themes at the forefront of discussions concerning the new nation. Supporters of the Confederacy accepted the rhetoric as the basis of their nationalistic identity, a point made clear in their private conversations, correspondences, and journals. While secessionist men concerned themselves with the particulars of erecting a national structure, namely the institutions and departments needed to run a country, the majority of white southerners played a role in the creation of Confederate nationhood.[2]

Equally important in examining the creation of this identity was the reason why white southerners threw their support behind the new nation. While whites downplayed, or, at times, even ignored slavery as a central issue, protecting the South's "peculiar institution" remained an essential feature in their motivation to separate from the Union. They understood that their economic interests lay in the continuation of slavery as a form of labor. The agrarian-based society was dependent upon a cheap and plentiful workforce and they found this in the chattel slavery that had taken root in the region by the late seventeenth century. Slavery also played a key role in the political identity of the South. The acquisition of new territories in the 1840s made possible by the Mexican War precipitated one of the most heated sectional debates since the Nullification Crisis of the 1830s. Southerners saw the expansion of slavery into those new lands as essential to the continuation of their economic and political interests. Northerners, however, believed that slavery violated the doctrines of free labor and thus should be excluded from those territories. The Compromise of 1850 provided a temporary fix to the regional strife, but the issue of the Kansas-Nebraska territories once again placed slavery at the center of the political contests between slave and free labor. Through a series of events—including Bleeding Kansas and the Supreme Court's decision in *Dred Scott vs. Sanford* (1857)—that culminated in the election of Abraham Lincoln in 1860, many southerners came to believe that their best course was to secede from the Union and create their own separate nation.[3]

Cultural concerns also factored prominently into the creation of a Confederate identity. Southerners understood their society in terms of race and one's relationship to slavery. Racial identity formed the basis of the social order and determined one's power within it. Slaveholders and non-slaveholders alike wielded great authority over African Americans both free and enslaved. Those who owned slaves, however, exerted a greater influence over antebellum culture, setting the standards for gentility and honor. And any threat to the institution of slavery threatened to undermine their class identity and their standing in the community. Non-slaveholding southerners also stood to lose something, for their higher status in the social order depended upon the subjugation of African Americans. And even those non-slaveholders who felt little connection to slaveholding society, could identify with the desire to defend the region against the invasion of northern outsiders and, eventually, northern armies. Gender also played a significant role in defining the social structure. The dependency of white women helped to buttress the patriarchal or paternalistic power of white men both in and outside the home. As the regional tensions began to take shape, slaveholding southerners came to see that their culture, along with their economic and political interests, was in jeopardy. To ensure the continuation of their elevated status in the social order, along with the gender ideals that informed men and women's roles, whites turned to the Confederacy and the creation of a new national identity. Adolescent, southern daughters, the subject of this study, were equally concerned with the cultural, economic, and political issues that defined the here and now. But, unlike the adult population, these young women had yet to realize their potential as adults.[4]

This desire to preserve tradition became the impetus for southern daughters to participate in the nationalistic movement. Born between 1843 and 1849, a time of mounting regional tensions, and members of slaveholding, secessionist families, these young women demonstrated extraordinary agency as they sought to protect the cultural script promised to them once they reached maturity. Their dilemma raises key questions that point to the uniqueness of their experience. What did they stand to gain by the Confederacy's success and what did they stand to lose in defeat? How did young women conceptualize their role in the Confederacy as their parents assumed the adult responsibilities in creating the national structure and identity? In what ways did they define their roles according to the rhetorical image of Confederate women and to the reality of wartime circumstances? Did their support for the war, like so many of the older generation of women, begin to wane as the conflict took its toll on communities? Finally, I turn to the issue of war and memory in asking how this generation participated in the creation of Lost Cause mythology. Moreover, what do their reminiscences of the Confederate experience reveal to us about their worldview in the New South era? To reach the answers, I chose to follow the lives of eighty-five young women who left written records of their experiences during this period of change. From their story of secession, war, and defeat emerges a broader understanding of the participants in the creation of Confederate nationalism.[5]

Southern daughters who came of age in the Confederacy clung tenaciously to the gender ideals and racial order of the slaveholding culture. As children in the Old South, they learned from their mothers, clergy, and educators to accept the ideals that lauded female devotion to domesticity, purity, piety, and submissiveness. These cultural expectations likewise informed the daily lives of female youths. At school, educators inculcated the values of respectability, and emphasized marriage and motherhood as the fulfillment of female duty. Mothers were careful to train their young charges in the benevolent duty outside the home that society regarded as the natural extension of women's domestic and familial roles. Adolescent daughters responded to this period of training with a mixture of excitement and frustration. As youths attempting to form their own identity, they often clashed with parents who sought to enforce the standards of respectable behavior. Yet they perceived their entrance into bellehood as a time of freedom and viewed their eventual marriage with much enthusiasm. The regional tensions stemming from the debate over slavery's expansion into the territories, however, loomed ominously over the South in the 1850s. This debate, coupled with the growing abolitionist movement had the potential to undermine the economic security and social status of the family with which adolescent daughters identified. Worse still, the possible end to slavery threatened to disrupt the life course that their parents, teachers, and clergy had laid out for them from the beginning of their adolescence.

The cries for secession raised by the fire-eaters, then championed throughout slaveholding communities, provided a glimmer of hope for the continuation of their culture and security for their future. As a result, daughters joined with their mothers to donate their labor and material resources to the southern cause. Described by historians as Confederate womanhood, southern society encouraged all women to support the cause through work as well as material and familial sacrifice. Mothers and daughters worked together in soldiers' aid societies and attended public gatherings celebrating the departure of local companies. They also experienced the same disruptions in the household stemming from the dearth of material resources, loss of slaves, and absence of male kin from the home. But, young women's age and position in the family shaped the way in which this group experienced these transformations on the home front. As a result, they created their own sense of duty to the southern cause that reflected their stage of development and role within the family. Their interpretation of Confederate womanhood paved the way for young women to enter a new realm of political and civic participation as well as to navigate the disruptions to their households and personal relationships that war caused. They transformed their courtships, familial roles, and social activities from their antebellum form into expressions of patriotic support for a cause that they believed would ensure the survival of the social order and, in turn, protect their future as women of the slaveholding class. This sense of duty worked in tandem with their need to preserve the slave South to sustain their support for the Confederacy, even through four years of war. Young women did question the validity of the conflict, especially as they faced the death of family members and financial ruin, but they held tightly to the ideals of the Confederate mission.[6]

Southern daughters' conceptualization of female duty concentrated on the family and resonated outward to the community. They shared war work with their mothers, especially in the soldiers' aid societies. Nevertheless, through their dress, social engagements, and relationships, young women expressed their loyalty in ways that reflected their age. Providing for the home and family amid financial hardships and loss of slaves also became means of demonstrating their political allegiance within the confines of their private lives. They regarded their domestic work and contributions to the household economy as crucial elements in sustaining the family through four long years of war. Southern daughters, amid the disruptions of their family lives, found a source of continuity with the Old South through their courtships and, in some cases, marriages. Rather than accept the irregularity of suitors as a form of self-sacrifice, as some historians suggest, young women reoriented their relationships to suit the wartime disruptions. In this environment, they found a greater level of freedom in their interaction with the opposite sex. Despite the liberalization of their courtships, young women never questioned the result. They remained committed to the traditional path for women, that they would one day marry and create a family in which they would assume the place of wife, mother, and slave mistress—roles identified with preceding generations of southern slaveholding women.

The defeat of the Confederacy ended young women's hopes of preserving the antebellum past. In the postwar era, they searched for ways to give meaning to their wartime experiences while reconciling themselves to the political, economic, and social changes that lay ahead. Young women found a way to come to terms with the defeat and the demise of the slave system by means of a cultural effort to memorialize the Confederacy. In the narrative of the Lost Cause, this generation of women offered their own veneration of the southern cause using the image of the Confederate belle that they created in their personal recollections. Moreover, they used their writings to articulate a worldview that lauded a return to prewar gender roles and the reassertion of white supremacy in the wake of emancipation.

The stage of development serves as a useful tool in explaining how individuals and groups processed disruptive events precipitated by war and the cultural consequences of that process. William Tuttle, in his study of children in World War II, notes that "what is important is not only what happens in a child's life but also when in the child's life—that is, at what age—the event occurs." That is, children's stage of physical and mental development influences the methods they use to cope with disruptions to their daily routines. He concludes that the shared age category in conjunction with the shared experience of war can create a generational identity that reaches maturity in adulthood and is visible in a common worldview. Historian Rebecca Klatch takes this argument a step further by examining a generation in a particular stage of its psychological and physical development. In her analysis of young adults during the 1960s, she argues that a generation represents a category similar to class in that all its members share certain experiences. "During depressions, wars, and other periods of rapid change," Klatch asserts, "crucial group experiences act as 'crystallizing agents,' binding people of the same age into 'generation-units.'"[7]

My study applies this understanding of life stages to the lives of southern daughters coming of age in the Confederate South. These young women share several common characteristics that bind them together as a group, allowing for larger generalizations about their self-perceptions and worldviews. I have selected young women aged between twelve and eighteen when the war commenced, because they were either entering or were well into the formative stage of their adolescent identity (see appendix, table 3). Historians debate the sociological classification of teenagers and the point at which American society began to separate adolescence from childhood. John and Virginia Demos contend that the term was not in use between 1800 and 1875. Most of the contemporary literature concerning child rearing, furthermore, expressed little concern for that period of youth. The term came into use after the restructuring of the family during early twentieth-century industrialization and urbanization. Evidence from the antebellum era, however, refutes the notion that adolescence, as a stage of development, is anachronistic. Personal and public records indicate that mothers, fathers, educators, and even young women themselves distinguished the teenage years as an interim stage between childhood and adulthood.[8]

A distinction between child and adolescent, especially with regard to young women, emerged in the first half of the nineteenth century. As a teenage daughter matured physically and mentally, society regarded her as different from a child. Certain events such as menstruation marked the beginning of a girl's growth into womanhood. This growth culminated in her marriage, typically in her early twenties. Mothers and other female kin also made the distinction between child and young woman by directing her in new tasks once she reached the age of twelve or thirteen. The teenage daughter assumed new responsibilities in the home and became increasingly involved in church and social events.[9]

Distinctions between child and adolescent also appeared in education. A young woman's education changed once she reached her teenage years. During his daughter's childhood, a father typically oversaw her learning and expected her to study the same subjects taught to boys. Historian Anya Jabour found that William Wirt of Virginia, for example, directed his children's education in a variety of topics such as English, French, natural philosophy, and history. Parents of the slaveholding class also had the luxury of affording private tutors and governesses to educate their young daughters. With the onset of adolescence, however, they underwent a change in the location as well as subject matter of their education. When Wirt's daughter, Laura, reached her teenage years, for example, he decided that her education needed to include more female-directed domestic tasks. This sort of shift ensured that daughters received a well-rounded education and that they cultivated the conventional skills associated with southern womanhood, such as cooking, sewing, and entertaining. Despite the lack of formal recognition of an "adolescent stage" in the Old South, parents saw a need to alter their daughter's education as they became teenagers.[10]

Appearance and mannerisms also helped to distinguish between adolescence and adulthood. As teenagers, young women typically wore their hair down or in a fashionable short style. Their dress was less formal and conservative, with fewer shawls and more ribbons and ornaments. When a young woman reached eighteen, society considered her a young adult. To signify this transition, she began to wear her hair up and assumed the title of "Miss." For example, Susan Bradford of Pine Hill plantation in Tallahassee, Florida, noted in 1865 that as a mature woman, she "must dress accordingly" and since her older sister had married, the now eighteen-year-old Susan could assume the title of "Miss Bradford." Alice Lucas of Charlottesville, Virginia, wrote in 1864 that upon her eighteenth birthday people addressed her as "Miss Lucas" rather than by her first name. Although the term "adolescent" did not appear until much later, on the eve of the Civil War distinctions between a female child and teenager existed in the realm of family life, church, education, and self-identity. In this study, therefore, I refer to this generation of females as adolescents.[11]

In addition to age, regional identity also tied this generation together. The young women included in this study come from varying locales in the slaveholding South. In 1860, slightly over half of the sample were resident in states of the Upper South, with a majority of those in Virginia and one living in the border state of Maryland, while the remainder lived in the Deep South (see appendix, table 2). Of those included, nearly all resided on plantations in rural areas. Only a small number lived in urban centers, namely New Orleans, Atlanta, Charleston, and Columbia, when the war commenced. Despite their geographic differences, the young women expressed a strong cultural identification with the South and ardent support for the Confederacy. All of the young women in this study come from families who either supported secession or came to support it after Abraham Lincoln's call for troops after the events at Fort Sumter. They echoed the sentiments of politicians who couched their defense of the Confederacy in terms of preserving the constitutional rights and liberties of southerners. Throughout the war, they openly expressed their patriotism and immersed themselves in various forms of war work. Reconstruction did very little to diminish the primacy of regionalism in their identity. The presence of federal officials, Republican governments, and economic hardships contributed to a strong sense of southern distinctiveness.

Their membership in middling or elite slaveholding families also contributed to their common identity. The number of slaves owned, in addition to the families' personal and real property values, served as tangible markers separating them from yeomen and non-slaveholding families. Southern daughters from homes with twenty or fewer slaves comprised over 50 percent of the sample while the remainder came from families with twenty-one or more slaves (see appendix, table 1). Based on those families with real property value listed in the census, about 45 percent had a worth of 21,000 dollars or higher while nearly 57 percent of families owned personal property, including slaves, worth 21,000 dollars or more (see appendix, tables 4 and 5). Such wealth helped bind these young women together as members of a common socioeconomic class. More specifically, they shared the same privileges and material markers of youthful females from wealthy families. Their parents, for example, had the financial means to provide their daughters with a formal education that emphasized both academic training and preparation for their entrance into genteel society. They attended identical social functions where they mingled with other members of their economic class. Daughters of the slaveholding circles enjoyed vacations and extended visitations from close family and friends. Their family's wealth also permitted these young women to follow common fashion trends. Such distinctions of gentility were specific to the class of slaveholding families, setting their daughters apart from those of yeomen and poor, landless white families with limited financial resources.[12]

As members of the southern gentry, the young women of this generation understood and accepted the cultural values of honor identified with the slaveholding class. Both men and women shared in the ideals of honor but they understood them in gendered terms. Men defined masculine honor as a code of conduct that determined a man's self-worth and community reputation. His ability to provide financial support and physical protection to his dependents, including slaves, in the home bolstered his reputation as a patriarch. This image extended outside the household, where community members viewed such men as fitted to assume leadership positions. Women conceptualized honor in terms of their duty to the home and family. Their reputation depended greatly on their ability to fulfill their many roles as mother, wife, moral guardian, and slave mistress, ensuring that their work remained tied to the household. The financial security of middling and elite slaveholding women also permitted them to refrain from wage earning work, an area deemed inappropriate for women of their class status. But, women's domestic work extended into the community, where they took on a number of benevolent activities such as providing charity to destitute families, raising funds for the church, and conducting Sunday school lessons. The interrelatedness of male honor and female conduct placed great pressure on women to live up to the standards of respectability that emphasized female submission, domesticity, and morality. Female honor, however, did not emerge solely in the context of male reputation. Women understood that their adherence to the rhetoric of southern womanhood contributed to their own status in the slaveholding South. Their value and worth as determined by their public reputation derived from their roles in the home and the extension of those roles into the community. Thus, women's stake in their adherence to female respectability equaled that of their male kin.[13]

The sources used in this study come from the young women themselves and, when applicable, their family members, beaux, and friends. Focusing on private rather than public documents as the major sources allowed me to step into the minds of this age group so as to understand their loyalism to the Confederacy and its effects on their identity. Thus, the primary focus is on the narrative rather than quantitative evidence. Diaries offer the most valuable source in this process because they provide a window on everyday lives. Mothers often encouraged daughters to keep a diary as a way to practice writing skills. While many young women maintained a diary for only a few years, some continued writing even as wives and mothers. The letters between adolescent females and their family members are another important source. These letters reveal young women's reaction to both war and home front activities. Published private memoirs are another fruitful source for historians exploring home front experiences. Using sources written after the fact is problematic, of course. Their recollections are shaped by cultural biases, often sacrificing accuracy for ideology. However, memoirs can serve as useful tools of analysis. They provide details of daily life that reveal volumes concerning the material culture of the home front and personal relationships of young women. Memoirs likewise illuminate the worldview of young women who were attempting to come to terms with defeat. The memory of war that they constructed allows us to delve deeper into the cultural battle that women waged to shape the memory of the Confederacy and war.

Although I focus on the story of these young women, I constructed a brief quantitative profile of my subject group using census and archival records. The 1850 and 1860 population schedules offered information on the wealth, age, residency, and occupation of the male head of household for most of the youths in this study. The slave schedules from those same decades provided information on their slaveowning status. I was unable to locate about 14 percent of the young women in the census records and thus turned to archival records for information concerning date of birth, residency, and, when possible, their slaveowning status. I likewise uncovered the date of marriage for 40 percent of my subject group using information from archival sources. Inconsistencies in marriage records precluded a much larger sample. Finally, I drew some conclusions about the birth rate of those who became mothers, using the 1880 population schedule.[14]

I found that I could best tell the story of these young women through a chronological framework, while focusing on the common themes that defined their experiences before, during, and after the war. Chapter one surveys adolescent females in the late antebellum period. It explores social prescriptions for elite daughters, looking specifically at their preparation for their roles as wives and mothers in the slaveholding class. In the second chapter, I examine young women's political identity in the secession crisis and war eras. As their fathers and brothers left for the battlefield in defense of their nation's honor, southern daughters believed their duty was to assist in that defense, to ensure the safe return of their kin, and to preserve the future of the slaveholding South. This assistance came in the form of outspoken patriotism and volunteerism in community activities deemed appropriate for female youths. Wartime loyalty also politicized the household, as self-sacrifice became a part of their daily routines. The third chapter explores this theme by focusing on how young women, in an effort to sustain the family throughout the war, became self-sufficient daughters in the household. By adjusting to new domestic duties as they confronted the loss of slaves and sought paid work outside the home to combat financial hardships, they were doing their part to preserve the family's status. Chapter four concentrates on young women's efforts to transform courtship and marriage during the war into sources of cultural continuity. While the male population often fluctuated, leaving a dearth of potential suitors at times, southern daughters created ingenious ways of ensuring opportunities for marriage. In the final chapter, I examine young women's efforts to construct a memory of their Confederate experience. This examination of the personal and published recollections of everyday women illustrates how age became a determining factor in their attempts to create a metanarrative of the war that exalted the Lost Cause while allowing them to stand apart from the older generation of women.

When Emma Florence LeConte wrote that she knew little of the "light-heartedness of youth," she expressed a feeling shared by many of her slave-holding peers. Forced to grow up in a time of great economic, political, and social change, this generation of young women shared an experience that shaped their identity as they reached adulthood in the postwar era. Their diaries, correspondence, and memoirs reveal that daughters of slave-holding, secessionist families believed that nothing short of their future was at stake. Even as they mourned the loss of male kin and confronted financial ruin, these female youths clung to the hope that the Confederacy would emerge victorious, thus securing their status in southern society. As hope faded into despair, and youth blossomed into womanhood, southern daughters came to terms with defeat by merging Old South feminine values with their wartime experiences.

1

"Our Bright Youth"

IN JUNE 1859, less than two years before the start of the Civil War, Susan Bradford, aged thirteen, was paying little attention to the brewing sectional conflict between the North and South. Bradford, of Pine Hill plantation near Tallahassee, Florida, spent her summer break from school aiding in the preparations for her sister's wedding. As the daughter of Edward Bradford, former territorial governor of Florida and a prominent planter, Susan enjoyed the extravagant display that marked the marriage ceremonies of the Old South's elite. She noted in her diary the numerous wedding presents and elaborate dresses as well as the many guests who came from all over the area to attend her sister's wedding. Although her father had schooled her in the politics of the sectional conflict, the excitement over the wedding overshadowed any political concerns she had. Only in passing did Bradford mention the conflict during the wedding festivities after overhearing her older male kin engaged in "a serious talk" about the future of the South.[1]

Bradford, like many of her female peers, focused mainly on the normal activities of daily life. Not until 1860, when talk of secession circulated throughout the South, did young women realize that a dark storm was brewing on the horizon. The clouds of secession seemed but a passing concern to many young women whose youthful activities occupied most of their attention. Their education, relationships, religious faith, and social engagements comprised the center of their universe, serving as the basis of female youth culture among slaveholding society. It is at this point in their lives that we begin our exploration of what southern daughters stood to gain by the Confederacy's success. By throwing their support behind secession and the war effort, young women hoped to maintain not only a lifestyle to which they had grown accustomed but also a future they had come to expect.[2]

Traditional notions of female duty and respectability served as a guiding force in young women's upbringing in the late antebellum era. Social prescriptions for these youths encouraged preparation for their eventual roles as wives, mothers, and slave mistresses. School and church inculcated the values of feminine duty to the home and family while promoting strict guidelines for their behavior, and their social engagements and courtships reinforced traditional views on gender expectations. These areas of teenage life, specifically family, church, social activities, and education, promoted a self-perception that supported conventional ideas of proper southern womanhood among the middling and elite classes of slaveholders. Training future women of the slaveholding South likewise entailed teaching adolescent females how to interact with slaves. Parents oversaw their daughters' association with slaves both inside and outside the home and expected them to follow the prescribed model of race relations. Their domestic training, however, gave them very little practical experience in the day-to-day management of a home and its dependents. Yet as rigid and confining as their education in the ideals of southern womanhood was, adolescent females nevertheless relished the freedom that came with being young and single and found independence from social restrictions, even if just briefly, in the youth culture of the antebellum South. Their church, school, and family life, areas that informed this age-based culture, all provided avenues for social interaction and gave daughters a degree of control in their activities and relationships. On the eve of the Civil War, young women's indoctrination into the racial and gendered order of the Old South was complete, and they anticipated the day when they would fill the ranks of their mothers and grandmothers.

Education was a primary tool for preparing adolescent daughters for their future duties of wife. During childhood, most women either attended a neighborhood school or received private tutoring. Most fathers expressed concern over their daughters' formal education and, when able, supervised their studies outside the classroom. As girls matured, however, parents wanted them not only to continue their formal education but paid closer attention to their cultivation of domestic skills and religious morality. Mothers and older female kin therefore assumed a

Fig. 1. Georgia Female College, 1842. Library of Congress, Prints and Photographs Division [LC-USZ62–1915]

larger role in the education of young women as they approached adolescence. Schools and churches reinforced this transition to a more domestic and religious education.[3]

A key part of a young woman's education was the female academy or seminary. In the 1830s, these institutions spread to meet the demands for female education beyond the primary level. With the intensification of the separate-spheres ideology in the early 1800s, middle- and upper-class parents increasingly looked to higher education as a means of both inculcating notions of female duty and developing intellectual abilities. By the 1850s, most adolescent females from slaveholding families attended a seminary or academy. They entered the school around the age of twelve or thirteen and graduated at seventeen or eighteen. While many young women attended a school in their community, many others went to an academy far from home, sometimes rooming and boarding with relatives or family friends who lived nearby. Parents paid dearly to send their daughters to such schools: by the 1850s, up to $200 a year for tuition, room, and board. Schools sent out periodic report cards to students and parents. At the end of the school year, students participated in public examinations with community members present. Here they exhibited projects in sewing and craft work, gave musical recitals, showed off their knowledge of various subjects such as math and science, and read their best composition pieces or poems. The day of examination was exciting for young women, who, besides displaying their skills, had the chance to interact with the community.[4]

The curriculum consisted of a variety of subjects dealing with intellectual and "ornamental" subjects. The liberal arts were at the core of a female education. Young women took classes in the classics, language, grammar, rhetoric, literature, composition, math, and science, which together would presumably instill good character in the student and give her the intellectual capabilities to fulfill her future roles as wife and mother. According to Elizabeth Ridley, of Southampton, Virginia, a typical schedule of studies included "Scholar's Companion, Translation of French in the 'Life of Washington,' History and Astronomy one day and Comstock's Philosophy and Rhetoric the other. Well's Grammar, and conjugate French verbs in Olendorf's Grammar." Ridley and her peers spent their evenings engaged in spelling, writing, and reading. Ornamental subjects included embroidery, needlework, crafts, and music, this last being the most popular. Such topics were intended to encourage specialty skills for the domestic setting with little consideration for more practical forms of sewing that would produce clothing.[5]

Most young women did not expect to put their education to use beyond their traditionally prescribed roles in the home and society. Even those such as Sarah Wadley, who enjoyed the intellectual challenges of her education that included such subjects as arithmetic and Latin, in most cases did not consider a career. Class and gender prescriptions in the late-antebellum South shaped a young woman's expectations about life after graduation. Most parents looked to education as a means to make their daughters a more desirable mate. Few daughters of slaveholding families, furthermore, had professional goals, for taking work outside the home would blur the line separating them from poorer white and slave women.[6]

Educators were careful to connect female education with ideas of female duty to the family and community. In *Hints on Female Education*, published in 1851, educational expert Elias Marks encouraged teachers to approach their female students with an eye to their future responsibilities. "The education of either sex," Marks advised, "is to be directed to the respective duties which each is destined to perform on the great theatre of existence. Woman is the associate, the companion, the friend, the counselor of man. She should, in every respect, be qualified for the important duties which she is destined to perform." According to educators, a proper education inculcated the traditional academic subjects balanced by a nurturing of the student's morality and social graces. Educators and parents alike viewed such education as "the legitimate source of the moral character and political happiness of a people." According to Marks, the quality of society began "at the shrine of domestic virtue and domestic intelligence," which he identified as the domain of women.[7]

Other educators also shared Marks's views on the role of female education in teaching the values of familial duty. Three decades earlier, educator J. Burton encouraged students to approach their education as a tool in sustaining the moral character of their families. "Your influence in society, either as daughters, as wives, or as mothers," Burton asserted, "is so extensive that it must be extremely political, to direct it aright." Some of Burton's advice, however, not only emphasized young women's future roles but also the ways in which their present status, as daughters and sisters, could buttress the good name of their family. He pointed to conduct as the primary means of protecting their family's reputation, advising students "the happiness of parents depends, in a great measure, on the conduct of their offspring." Only through proper conduct, he asserted, would a young woman fulfill her "filial duty." James Garnett, an educator at a Virginia school for young women, echoed Burton's connections between behavior and respectability in a series of lectures to his students by urging his female charges to "practise *while young*, the manners of ladies." He saw the developmental stage between childhood and womanhood as pivotal in young women's indoctrination into southern notions of respectability. "Now is the time to acquire not only your manners, but your morals," Garnett implored, "*now* is the irrevocable period (if neglected) to learn by practice, all those admirable courtesies of social life, comprehended in the term manners . . . to secure for us the esteem, the admiration, and the love of mankind."[8]

Educators looked to history as inspiration for their female students in attaining societal expectations. Burton, for example, searched the words of the French political philosopher Baron de Montesquieu, whose writings on democracy and the separation of powers influenced the authors of the United States Constitution, to illustrate the societal importance of female morality and domesticity. "Montesquieu, speaking of the influence of the female sex on public manners," he offered, "says that the safety of a state depends upon the virtues of the women." Such influence, according to Burton, required "a sedateness of behaviour" for the public welfare. Conversely, he argued that for those women who failed to exert a moral influence, their public leaders "have endeavoured to correct that false taste." Burton added that the political successes of ancient Greece resulted from the "chastity and economical virtues of its women."[9]

Schools also provided a setting for young women to rebel against authority. Parents emphasized submission in preparing their daughters for domestic life, and they expected little challenge to their rules and guidance. However, once they were at school and away from their parents' influence, some young women challenged school authorities. Historian Brenda Stevenson argues that rebelling against school teachers constituted a symbolic challenge to parents' power. Still, while many young women behaved in ways that seemed rebellious, they quickly submitted to their teachers. Susan Bradford illustrated this point when she played a prank at the end of her algebra class. After completing the last lesson in the textbook, Bradford threw the book out the window. Her teacher immediately censured her and ordered her to retrieve the book, whereupon Bradford remorsefully brought it back to the schoolroom. Educators also attempted to correct young women's deportment by noting their conduct on report cards, thus informing parents about their daughters' behavior. For example, Myra Inman noted that a classmate at the Cleveland Masonic Female Institute in East Tennessee received bad marks for "prompting" a friend. As a result, her parents made her "stay in" when they went out to visit friends and family members on a Friday evening.[10]

Student life at academies and seminaries, although rigidly structured, did offer young women a chance to socialize with their female peers. Many formed strong friendships while attending school and these bonds commonly lasted through adolescence and into adulthood. Young women who attended school away from home found that friendships with classmates served as a kind of substitute for familial relationships, partially filling the void created by the absence of family members. These friendships also created a social outlet for daughters who felt confined by the rules of the academy. Walks after school or conversations at night allowed young women to form female bonds but also to socialize away from the watchful eye of school authorities. Friendships also provided solace for young women during times of sadness. Olin Davis, the daughter of a Methodist minister in Virginia, described how one of her classmates suddenly left the school to attend to her sick aunt. When the aunt died, Davis and the other female students rallied around the young woman by writing letters that offered comfort and advice on dealing with the death.[11]

A young woman's education took place in the home as well as in the classroom setting. Daughters received limited training in the practical skills expected of wives, mothers, and slave mistresses. Within the home, mothers and older female kin taught young women domestic skills. Rather than teach the overall management of a household, however, they typically taught female youths a few specific tasks. Before the war, very few adolescent daughters managed a home, and then only on those rare occasions when both mother and older female siblings were away. In most cases when a mother visited relatives, her younger daughters merely increased their share of household duties. Fourteen-year-old Martha "Nannie" Davis, of Virginia, was an example: after her mother left for Richmond, Virginia, Martha helped with housekeeping but was not allowed the responsibility of managing the household and servants. Most regular domestic duties included taking care of their rooms, picking flowers, helping make preserves, and sewing. Some young women experienced difficulty in their domestic training; one was Sarah Wadley, who concluded after her failure to make a dress that "it is quite hard work for me." Many others had a knack for it and found it to be a form of entertainment that filled their day. Myra Inman, for example, set aside time each day with her sisters to work on sewing. At thirteen, she learned how to make an apron, sew tucks in skirts, and make a quilt. She also practiced sewing by making a shirt for George, one of the family's household slaves. Most young women honed their cooking skills by preparing specialty foods and baked goods. Susan Bradford learned how to make French rolls with the help of her older cousin. Young women also learned to prepare full meals for their family. On one occasion, Myra Inman "cooked a meal of victuals" for her mother and sisters. For the most part, however, food preparation was left to household slaves and older female family members.[12]

Parents also taught their daughters about the significance of interpersonal relations, with particular attention to hierarchical relationships of the slaveholding household and deference to a patriarchal figure. The strong maternal influence in a young woman's life produced close relationships between mothers and daughters. From an early age, daughters turned to their mothers for emotional as well as physical comfort. When a young woman reached adolescence, her relationship with her mother took on another dimension. A mother provided the primary training for her daughter's future domestic and maternal roles and directed her in a number of household chores. Daughters likewise looked to their mothers as social and cultural mentors, seeking their advice on dress, manners, courtship, and other aspects of southern womanhood. Myra Inman went on visits, attended church meetings, and shopped with her mother, thus witnessing firsthand the social and moral responsibilities of a slaveholding woman. Daughters felt a deep sense of devotion to their mothers but always within the context of the hierarchy that characterized slaveholding families. Young women understood that the division of power in the home favored fathers over mothers; nonetheless, they respected their mother's authority and yielded to her decisions.[13]

The frequent absence of men from the household kept many young women from forging the same close bond with their father they shared with their mother. Susan Bradford's father, a politician, traveled often while seeing to his legislative duties. Bettie Alexander of Monroe County, Virginia, saw her father on several occasions leave to attend to plantation business in Texas, spending two months at a time away from home. Even when their fathers were at home, young women spent the majority of their day in the company of women, learning domestic skills, visiting, or at school. Although often separated from their fathers, young women developed affectionate relationships with them. Their financial dependence on their fathers tied young women to their paternal figures in other ways. They depended on their fathers' income to achieve the material standards of slaveholding society. From popular fashion to their boarding school education, young women were inextricably dependent upon a paternal figure to provide for them in such a way that they could fit in with their peer group. Doing so opened up a world of social engagements and courtship opportunities among the middling and elite classes. But the bond between fathers and daughters also came from genuine feelings. Most fathers doted on their young daughters and enjoyed attending to their material needs, And most adolescent daughters responded with love and affection.[14]

Despite the context of their relationships, parents expected deference to their authority from their children. Mothers and fathers regardless of their regional and historical context have always expected obedient children. Nevertheless, in the Old South it served a cultural purpose of reinforcing paternalism as a moral justification for the exploitative system of slavery. The image of the benevolent master caring for the material and spiritual well-being of his slaves in exchange for their submission served to ease the conscience of slave owners. It also provided a rhetorical defense against the abolitionist critique that emphasized the cruelty of the slave system. The paternalistic nature of the slaveowner extended to all dependents in the household regardless of race, gender, or age. Just as he wielded power over his slaves, the master expected the same submission from those inside his family. The financial support and physical protection the male head of household provided to his family served as a justification for his authority and likewise the submission of all members. While the wife and children may at times have questioned or even chafed under his dominance, they did so privately. Few members openly challenged his authority. To do so meant risking their material well-being as well as their image to the outside community.[15]

Mothers and fathers expected adherence to this value even while their daughters attended school away from home. John Henry Hankins, a Virginia planter, for example, disapproved of his daughter taking guitar lessons. Rather, he sent word that "she had better take on the organ" and postpone a guitar class until her last session of school. Young women also acknowledged parental authority even when attending boarding school meant being away from the watchful eyes of parents. They wrote frequently to their mothers and fathers, especially when homesick, and sought their advice on education, dress, and social conduct. Parents could rely on educators to reinforce their authority in the school setting. Burton believed that demonstrating deference to parents was important to ensuring familial honor. "Your parents are entitled to your first respects," Burton advised in his lectures, "they should be conferred on those, who act a parent's part; and who interest themselves in your welfare and happiness." Underscoring this reciprocity in the parent-child relationship, Burton reminded his students "parents are bound in duty to maintain their children. It is likewise the duty of children to reverence their parents."[16]

Perhaps the most egalitarian relationship a young woman had in her family life was that with her sisters. In many ways, the closeness between sisters surpassed that between husbands and wives and between children and their parents. By providing an escape from the rigid hierarchy of the patriarchal household, sisterhood offered fulfillment and comfort for young women in a world that valued males more than females. Susan Bradford, for example, admired her older sister and looked to her for advice. Her relationship with her sister also gave Bradford a social outlet. Isolated on a large plantation in Florida, the young woman never forged close female friendships like those of her peers away at school. Myra Inman developed deep affection for her sister Rhoda, who was close to her in age. The two young women spent most of their free time sewing in the parlor and talking about their social activities and expectations for the future. When Inman began attending social functions, Rhoda accompanied her, often offering advice on proper conduct. Although marriage separated younger and older sisters physically, they generally remained close. Bettie Alexander was devastated by her sister's departure after marrying but maintained their bond through correspondence.[17]

The bonds forged with brothers varied considerably from the sororal relationship. The rhetoric of the separate spheres for men and women that proliferated advice manuals to parents and educators emphasized differences in the upbringing of brothers and sisters. Young women, for example, spent their days in the domestic setting engaged in sewing, reading, correspondence, and visitations with friends and family. Parents and educators, however, encouraged sons to participate in activities such as hunting, fishing, debate clubs, and literary societies that would prepare them for their roles as head of household and inculcate a sense of community responsibility. Brothers and sisters did find opportunities to create close relationships through their play as young children or shared social engagements as they got older. Yet, the separate education for men and women often created a physical distance between brothers and sisters that tested the strength of their bonds. Correspondence and frequent visits nonetheless allowed them to continue their relationships. While Virginia Hankins's brother James attended the Hanover Academy in Virginia, she wrote letters to him frequently. The letters continued after James eventually enrolled at the University of Virginia. Elizabeth

Ridley and her brother also corresponded regularly while he attended the Brookland School in Virginia. Most letters contained family news or neighborhood gossip. Yet they also provided means for siblings to reveal details of their personal lives they wished to keep hidden from parents. Ridley's brother, for example, described an encounter with some young women who attended a meeting of his literary society: "After the society was over we (some of us at least) went into the parlor and were introduced to the ladies. . . . The ladies played on the piano and sung [*sic*] and we had a general conversation until about 11 o'clock when we all retired. . . . I had a very pleasant time."[18]

On the other hand, the training of sons in the ideals of manhood meant they would often assert an authoritative role in their relationships with sisters. Older brothers especially took on a fatherly tone in their letters, offering advice on matters such as social conduct and educational pursuits. While away at school, James Hankins responded to his sister's complaints that her education would lead her nowhere. "You say because you are of the other sex," he wrote, "the use of study will avail nothing." James encouraged Virginia in her studies not as a means for financial reward or public notoriety but rather as a means to ensuring her reputation as a respectable woman. He likened her education to that of Clio, the Greek goddess who recorded history. "Her name signified honor and reputation," he asserted, "Be you like her Dear Sister and like her laurels shall encircle your brow." After hearing complaints that his sisters took little interest in their education, Elizabeth Ridley's brother threatened to "take you all in hand" when he returned from school. Sisters likewise sought the guidance of their brothers. Olin Davis wrote her brother frequently about her courses while he was away, and even solicited his suggestions for a topic for the paper assigned in her composition class.[19]

Along with token domestic skills and interpersonal relations, young women's education also involved spiritual development. The tenets of southern womanhood emphasized the religious duties of women, and parents and educators encouraged daughters' moral training in the church. Mothers especially viewed benevolent activities and Bible studies as indispensable training for female moral guardianship of the home. In evangelical denominations the pinnacle of a young woman's religious training was her conversion experience, which signified (among other things) her acceptance of "moral responsibility." Parents expected their daughters who attended school away from home to participate in religious activities, and schools generally required religious education and church attendance. The school routine usually included prayer at the beginning and end of each day. On Sundays, students attended a church of their choice or that of their school master or mistress. Some female seminaries offered evening Bible lectures for students. Many schools, furthermore, required students to attend revivals and camp meetings held in the community. Louisiana Hankins, for example, expressed concerns over her daughter's moral development while away at school. She approved of Virginia attending a confirmation ceremony of friends but added, "how happy your mother would have been if my daughter had been one of their numbers." Nonetheless, Virginia's mother felt assured that her daughter was following her instructions in seeking out "good and pious" friends.[20]

Young women demonstrated an acceptance of their duty as moral guardian in their daily routines. Whether living at or away from home, they studied the Bible, attended church, and joined in other religious gatherings. A popular activity for young women was attending camp meetings or revivals held by churches in the community. They also taught Sunday school and participated in church charitable work. Olin Davis, for example, joined female church members in raising money for benevolent work; her church organized the Washington Street Fair, in which women of all ages made craftwork and food to sell. These activities were not solely religious but also social, offering opportunities for young women to get together with their peers. Davis enjoyed her participation in the fair because it allowed her to mingle with her friends as well as meet potential suitors. Young women also asserted their moral duty by offering spiritual advice to family members. After several pleas from his sister not to neglect his faith while attending the University of Virginia, James Hankins grew frustrated. "I have no time to answer your letter with my philosophy of religion," he responded, "in regard to the religious doctrine you wish to inculcate into my brain . . . I fear you have too much zeal . . . it may be converted into fanaticism." Nevertheless he concurred with her notions that "a wise submission to Providencial [*sic*] will and reliance on the protection of Almighty God are the greatest and most divine attributes of mankind."[21]

The frequency of death tested the faith of young women as it did the faith of all antebellum southerners. Seventeen-year-old Catherine Louisa

McLaurin, for example, lost a family member and four former school-mates to illness in a single year. Spiritual fortitude helped reconcile young women to the death of a loved one. Those of faith found comfort in the belief that they would one day reunite with deceased loved ones in heaven. Time-honored funeral rituals and traditions, moreover, served as cathartic events that allowed them a release of emotions. Sarah Wadley, age fifteen, noted after her aunt passed away in 1860 that her death "has done me good, I feel nearer to heaven since she has gone there and I have learned now to feel resigned at her loss."[22]

Perhaps the most significant aspect of a young woman's upbringing was her training in courtship expectations and rituals. By the early nineteenth century, the ideals of romantic affection and companionate marriage had supplanted notions of patriarchal authority and order in the personal relationships between men and women. Young women sought a suitor from their peer group, those who were among their socioeconomic class, but also considered physical attraction and emotion appeal as criteria for courtships.[23]

Although companionship and romantic affection shaped young women's decision to marry, parents asserted some authority over their daughters'

Fig. 2. The Four Seasons of Life: Youth. "The Season of Love." Library of Congress, Prints and Photographs Division [LC-USZ62–2093]

choice in a mate. Parental concern for a young woman's courtships stemmed from the significance of marriage in sustaining familial status. Mothers and fathers expected their daughters to seek their advice on when and with whom they should engage in a courtship. Arranged marriages were no longer a common practice; however, parents asserted a degree of influence over their daughters' choices. As Jabour points out, young women drew their potential beaux from "within a pool of prospective mates which was defined by parents, relatives, and neighbors." Sarah Wadley, for example, noted her father's concern over whom she would wed. He made it clear that he would tolerate her marrying a minister but preferred someone who could turn her mind "from metaphysics," to which he felt she was "too much inclined." He directed her also to wait until she was twenty before committing to marriage. Most parents, in fact, encouraged their daughters to wait until they completed their education or were in their early twenties. Educators also weighed in on discussions of female conduct in their courtship activities, usually echoing the advice of parents to adhere to notions of respectability. James Garnett lectured to the young women at Elm-Wood School in Virginia that marriage "should never be precipitately entered," and thus they should choose suitors "with parental approbation on both sides." Burton also warned students that they "may be disposed to make an improper and imprudent choice" and should seek "parental counsel" when pursuing a courtship. A daughter who ignored her parents' advice and sought an inappropriate suitor, according to Burton, behaved "unwisely as well as undutifully."[24]

Parents pushed their daughters to seek a young man from their same class group who embodied the standards of respectability. Such a status typically derived from the blood ties of a potential beau as well as his economic aspirations, education, and mannerisms. Educators supported parental expectations of a proper match. "It may be necessary to caution you against the ill consequences, of fixing your affections hastily . . . until you are well acquainted with his temper, principles, and habits," advised Burton. For Burton, the choices of his female students depended on the ability of both to perform their duties within their gender-defined spheres. "It is the province of the male sex," he asserted, "to encounter with the cares and perplexities, which are incident to their respective conditions, occupations and professions in life" whereas it was the female role to "sooth those anxieties" in the domestic realm. In doing so, Burton argued, "men are enabled to support them better." Garnett urged his students to seek a spouse who demonstrated the personal traits of respectability. "Good temper . . . and good morals," he offered, "should be the indispensable basis of this union [marriage]."[25]

While most southern daughters sought a suitor based on romantic attraction, they adhered to class and gender ideals when narrowing down their choices. Rarely did a daughter venture out of her class group in seeking a potential mate. Most feared that such divergence from the norm would threaten ancestral lineage, thus potentially diminishing a family's reputation. Moreover, marrying in their class group assured the continuance of material comforts to which they had grown accustomed. Notions of masculine duty likewise permeated young women's decision in choosing a beau. Often she would cease a courtship with a beau who garnered little respect from his community. If her suitor lacked the ambition or financial means to meet her expectations, a young woman quickly ended the relationship.[26]

Southern norms concerning the conduct of single women shaped the rituals of courting couples. An act of indiscretion could damage a young woman's social standing and render her unable to marry within the middling and elite classes. Most parents were concerned with leaving their daughters alone with a male companion. Although mothers and fathers understood that their daughters would test the boundaries of appropriate behavior at times, they did everything possible to discourage it. Young women, for example, traveled only with a male escort. Some, like Mary Conway Shields, of Jefferson County, Mississippi, were required to have a chaperone when attending dances, parties, and community functions. When young men visited their daughter at home, parents rarely left them unsupervised; usually a family member or friend remained in the room for the sake of propriety. Occasionally, a young man brought two or three friends along when calling, to forestall gossip among neighbors. A daughter away at school or visiting relatives was subject to the same strict standards of conduct around male peers. When she needed an escort to a social function, she often called on male friends of the family or relatives who lived in the area. Female students received visits from young men but school officials supervised their activities and limited the time they spent together. Although they were under the watchful eye of the school master or mistress, young men and women found ways to circumvent the rigid rules. For example, on some occasions when a young man would call on a female relative at the school, she introduced him to some of her friends, which usually received less attention from school officials.[27]

Yet some families in the South had adopted more relaxed rules governing visitations. Following the custom of northern families, those from southern elite households began leaving young men and women alone. Privacy to engage in candid conversations and explore emotional ties allowed youths to decide the suitability of their companion and make informed decisions about their prospects. This freedom was acceptable to parents as long as their daughters' choice in a suitor fit within the class and gender norms of the slaveholding South.[28]

Young women's behavior with the opposite sex was everywhere subject to parental scrutiny. Parents and teachers discouraged coquetry, a form of flirtation practiced by many young women of courtship age. Such conduct was associated with courtship rituals, but parents feared it could cross the line into impropriety or a poor choice of suitor. Others feared that flirtations could threaten a young man's reputation in society by distracting him from individual ambitions. "Your influence, at this period of life," an educator warned, "may . . . be injurious to the young part of the other sex, by enticing them from those pursuits, which might be profitable to their country, and glorious to themselves." Rather than engage in flirtatious behavior, young women should "inspire young men with maxims of honour, virtue, and event patriotism" in their courting activities. Garnett believed that a young woman who engaged in coquetry risked gaining a reputation for misleading men. "Stripped of all disguise, it [coquetry] is neither more, nor less, than an artful mixture of hypocrisy, fraud, treachery, and falsehood," he contended.[29]

While elite young southern women felt constrained to live up to their parents' standards of courtship and marriage, they viewed the courtship period as a time of freedom. Some delayed marriage as long as possible, either because they enjoyed pursuit by beaux or because they had doubts about marriage and motherhood. Sarah Wadley confided in her diary that she intended "to pass a single life," explaining that "my health, or more properly my constitution is too feeble to sustain the burden which a wife and mother must bear." Catherine Louisa McLaurin, age seventeen, expressed similar doubts about marriage after she visited with an older female friend who was a newlywed. "[I]f getting married has such a bad effect upon all girls as it has on her," she wrote, "then all should hold fast their hands."[30]

Most young women enjoyed the power they wielded over courtship decisions, often pursuing several relationships before marrying. Despite warnings to avoid flirtatious behavior, coquetry was common, and declarations of affection filled the discussions and letters between young men and women. Southern daughters, especially early in their adolescence, however, generally refrained from making any serious commitment to a suitor. Myra Inman, for example, reveled in the attention she received from potential beaux. At the age of fourteen, she began attending social engagements in hopes of leading to courtships, giving little consideration of marriage. Rather she relished the attention from her male peers including a serenade from a group of young men. Inman and most other young women savored the period between childhood and marriage as a time of freedom, unburdened by the familial responsibilities that lay ahead after marriage.[31]

Social activities gave young women an opportunity to interact with young men and practice social skills. At church functions, community

Fig. 3. Fall Games. The Apple-Bee. *Harper's Weekly,* November 26, 1859. Library of Congress, Prints and Photographs Division [LC-USZ62–5370]

get-togethers, parties, balls, and dances, they could visit with male peers without risking their reputation in the community. Family leisure activities also gave daughters an opportunity for social interaction. Sarah Wadley recorded in her diary that during the summer of 1860 she went with her family to Cohuttah Springs in Murray County, Georgia, where along with several male and female friends she filled her days with games such as blind man's bluff and her evenings with dances and parties.[32]

Even when well trained in social graces, young women anguished over their ability to interact properly with young men. Many feared that if they were awkward, peers would brand them a wallflower or would exclude them from activities. Sarah Wadley wrote of her insufficient skills in socializing with young men: "How often have I regretted, so foolishly, that I had not been educated to speak words without meaning and to practice gracefully all those coquettish airs which form such an important part of conversation between ladies and gentlemen." Social graces, young women agreed, were indispensable to one who sought courtship and marriage.[33]

Adolescent daughters also placed great emphasis on attractive dress, even though most parents and educators encouraged them to dress plainly, avoiding "gaudy" or loud clothing. Their ability to sew often aided efforts to secure the latest fashion in dresses and hats. Myra Inman, for example, embroidered designs on sleeves and waistbands to lend a more stylish appearance to her dresses. Even the latest hairstyles concerned young women after they reached adolescence. To distinguish themselves from children, many changed their hair. Mary Conway Shields, for example, recalled that when she reached fifteen she began to wear her hair down like many of her female friends. Most young women were insecure about their appearance and believed that if their peers thought them unattractive, they would have few opportunities for socializing and courtship. For instance, Sarah Wadley took offense when a young gentleman flippantly remarked that her large nose and heavy eyebrows were "sure signs of a fine mind"; she interpreted his comment as an attempt "to console me for my ugliness."[34]

While parents paid close attention to their daughters' educational, domestic, spiritual, and social development, they also considered indoctrination into the slave system as an essential part of the developmental process. Parents expected that their daughters would one day marry into a slaveholding family and assume their place as the mistress of the "big house." At an early age, women absorbed the prevailing wisdom that emphasized the necessity and propriety of slavery. Parents taught their daughters that the South's peculiar institution was the foundation of their socioeconomic status and that the slaves performed the necessary labor to maintain the household. Moreover, their reputation in the larger community stemmed from their membership in the slaveholding class. In essence, the privileged existence of middling and elite daughters depended upon from the slave system.[35]

Adolescent females, like their mothers, had an ambivalent attitude toward African Americans: they simultaneously cared for them and feared them. They were both paternalistic and racist, believing that as an "inferior" race, blacks needed care and direction to survive. Paternalism, according to pro-slavery advocates, was a reciprocal relationship in which a master provided nurturance and protection in return for the slave's submission and labor. Slaveholding parents brought up young women to regard slaves, particularly those in the home, as part of the "family, white and black" but, at the same time inculcated the racist belief that African Americans derived from a backward and uncivilized race.[36]

Most young women viewed slavery as a benevolent institution that provided care for a people whom they saw as dependent on assistance. Especially during the holidays, they participated in gift-giving and other events that emphasized the familial nature of the master-slave relationship. Mary Conway Shields, for example, noted that at Christmas-time in 1859 she and her family gave gifts to the numerous field and house slaves at Pecano, the family's plantation in Louisiana. Shields's parents gave her fruit and toys to distribute to the slave children. The relationship between adolescent females and older slaves reinforced the paternalistic ethos. Girls' first contact with slaves was with the nurses who cared for them as children. Louisa Sheppard noted the closeness she felt with her nurse, Ellen, who helped care for Sheppard after her mother died during childbirth. After she reached adolescence, Sheppard often went to Ellen to hear stories about her mother.[37]

Although parents encouraged paternalism, they attempted to maintain some separation between their daughters and bondspeople and closely supervised their activities with slaves. When Susan Bradford's father held his annual barbeque for the house and field slaves, he refused to allow his daughter to attend or even watch the event from afar. Discouraged by their parents from getting too close to slaves, daughters learned little about their overall management. Many women who married therefore found themselves ill-prepared to assume the role of slave mistress. Parents also tried to preserve some distance between their daughters and slaves who were close to them in age. Girls played with such slaves, but learned at an early age to treat black playmates differently from white playmates. Parents encouraged daughters to take on the role of mistress when interacting with slaves their age. One who followed the rule was Susan Bradford, who, upon learning of some misbehavior by Frances, a female slave close to her in age, commented that "I tried hard to raise Frances with good principles. . . . It was such a disappointment to me."[38]

By the time young women reached adolescence they had accepted the gender and racial ideals of the slaveholding South. In this stage of development their parents, educators, and clergy worked together to indoctrinate them into the ideals of southern womanhood, ideals that placed heavy demands on their daily lives and relationships. Their educational experience that took place in the home and school environment prepared them to take on the roles of mothers, wives, and slave mistresses in hopes of carrying on the culture of the slaveholding community. The gender rhetoric became an essential feature of their preparation for adulthood. Young women understood and adopted the feminine ideologies that placed high value on the domesticity, benevolence, and submission of women as adults. Moreover, they learned that their courtship choices played a significant role in assuring the continuation of their class identity, and, in spite of the importance of romantic affection in choosing a suitor, they were willing to choose from a pool of eligible men from within their socioeconomic group. An equally important issue was inculcating the racial assumptions of the slaveholding class. While they perceived slaves as part of the family white and black, they accepted that African Americans occupied a lower position in the social order. Yet young women were not without a voice in their choices over their friends, courtships, and relationships with slaves. Their female peer culture—forged in their schools, social engagements, and personal relationships—offered young women a level of freedom from the strictures of the slaveholding culture, and, in the process, an opportunity to assert their own identity as young, southern belles.

Even as Susan Bradford participated joyfully in her sister's wedding festivities, she was aware of the brewing North-South political crisis.

She perceived the activities of abolitionists and the attempts to limit the spread of slavery as a threat to her family's stability. Bradford perhaps understood the seriousness of the political situation better than most of her peers because of her father's close ties to southern politics and his desire to teach his daughter about political and civic affairs. But, even those young women uninterested in such matters could not fail to see the omens of a coming storm.

2

The Politicized Belle

IN THE UNION-OCCUPIED CITY OF KNOXVILLE, Tennessee, a federal officer approached nineteen-year-old Ellen Renshaw House about her apparent patriotism for the Confederate cause. He asked if she believed that "reconstructing the Union" would ever be possible. She called the idea "simply ridiculous," and argued that "southern children hated the Yankee nation from the time they were born, and the hatred grew with their growth and strengthened with their strength." This and similar declarations by House soon earned her a measure of notoriety among the occupiers. Eventually, a Union general sent word to her parents that she would be banished from town unless she tempered her behavior. She insisted, however, that "the only thing I have ever done was to wave to our poor fellows as they were going north to prison."[1]

In actuality, House had done more than just wave to Confederate soldiers. She worked with others in Knoxville to collect blankets and other goods for prisoners of war, visited prisoners in the hospital, and brazenly spoke her mind to Union soldiers. House went too far, however, when she insulted the wife of an officer. Officials retaliated by ordering her to leave Knoxville. Although her mother wanted to go with her, House chose to go by herself, eventually making her way to Eatonville, Tennessee, where she continued to aid the Confederate war effort.[2]

Although House was eventually sent away for her actions, her age and gender allowed her to defy the enemy and aid the Confederacy for over a year. Seventeen when the war broke out, she had matured into a young adult by the time the Yankees occupied Knoxville in 1863; but she was still considered a young woman, unmarried and under the protection of her family. She used this fact to escape punishment, until the occupiers' patience ran out altogether. The decision to exile House, furthermore, shows that the occupiers recognized the political power of young women and held them accountable for their actions. House too understood the political significance of her support for the war and flaunted her banishment like a badge of honor. Although few young women received such severe punishment for their patriotism, House's sentiments exemplified the extent to which teenage daughters would defend the southern cause.

House and her peers heeded the calls for Confederate patriotism and joined their mothers in the civic world of war work. Their loyalism, however, stemmed from reasons quite different from those of the older generations of women. Unlike their mothers and other female kin, these youths awaited the realization of the roles that parents, educators, and clergy taught them to expect, and the outcome of the war would help them achieve it. To shirk their duty to the Confederate cause for which so many of their male kin were dying thus would threaten to derail their plans for the future. This effort to ensure a traditional path to womanhood encouraged civic involvement and outspoken support for the Confederate cause. As a result, women coming of age in wartime found their own political voice. Their youth permitted a degree of freedom in their patriotic expressions much greater than that permitted their mothers and older female kin. Their mothers saw their primary responsibility as being to the survival and protection of the family while their daughters, because of their age and position in the family, were free from such concerns. They manifested their political engagement through their knowledge of military battles and leaders, their clothing, their social activities, their relationships with peers, and their interactions with Union soldiers. While these young women gained a new political identity by participating in public events and speaking out in defense of the Confederacy, they were not seeking to overturn the conventions of the antebellum past but rather to conserve them.

The environment that permitted young women to participate in politics and civic affairs was one in which the lines between public and private life were blurred. Historians have shown that the war often heightened women's civic activism and created new spaces in which they could express their political beliefs. The politically charged atmosphere that war produced allowed public affairs to invade the domestic arena, while the civic domain became a place of informal political exchanges. Likewise, within the home, women often hosted social activities during which they

expressed their political views. Women's political participation took place
in the domestic setting where they engaged in war work, hosted patriotic
gatherings, and discussed their support for the Confederacy. Similarly,
their duties within the home informed their civic participation outside
the household. Their work in the soldiers' aid societies and hospitals became locations for women to utilize their responsibilities in the home and
family for the good of the cause. In this atmosphere in which domestic
and civic concerns were intertwined, southern daughters found it easy to
demonstrate their loyalism.[3]

Young women's introduction into the world of politics began with the
secession crisis. They were born during the territorial debates of the 1840s
and witnessed the sectional tensions come to a head as they reached their
teenage years in the 1850s. Calls for secession went out in those years, but
adolescent daughters' reactions to the formation of an independent South
depended on family loyalty, which varied considerably throughout the
region. Most families with large slaveholdings supported the calls for an
independent South that followed Abraham Lincoln's election in 1860.
Even a portion of non-slaveholders shared with the slaveholding class an
ideological defense of secession rooted in the South's racial and gender
ordering. The willingness of yeomen to defend secession and southern
independence derived from what historian Lacy Ford describes as "the
old 'country-republican' ideal of personal independence" based on the
idea that racial hierarchy sustained by slavery afforded them a higher
position in the rank of society. The yeomen were willing to defend this
ideal because they too had come to depend upon it. On the other hand,
historians have demonstrated that a shared belief in equality based on
the dependency of African Americans and women tied the two classes
together in defense of slavery. Yet many citizens who owned fewer or no
slaves, especially in areas outside the plantation districts, resisted secession
until Lincoln's proclamation calling for troops to put down the southern
rebellion following the Confederate attack on Fort Sumter in April 1861.
Others remained loyal to the Union throughout the duration of the war
even with the threat of social ostracism and physical harm. Those who
did often went underground in a network of Unionists to secure their
safety and that of their loved ones.[4]

The gentry and yeomanry, however, shared little beyond a common
ideological perspective in their support of the Confederacy. For slaveholding

southerners, preserving the institution of slavery secured a higher place for them in the socioeconomic ladder. By throwing their support to the southern cause, they helped to secure the wealth that they had bound up in the ownership of slaves. Moreover, protecting the status quo permitted middling and elite slaveholders to retain their public reputation and rank in southern society. Southern daughters of slaveholding families understood the significance of secession in these terms. Parents made sure that their daughters learned the pro-slavery position on the sectional conflict and its implications for slave owners. Mothers and fathers discussed secession with their daughters and encouraged them to read articles and books supporting their position. While these young women absorbed the sentiments of their families, they became active participants in their political education. They sought their own information on the political issues and regularly engaged in discussions with family and friends, often articulating a well-thought out position on the topics of secession and war.[5]

Many daughters in the lower South aligned with their parents on the secession issue before the 1860 election. A member of the slaveholding class in Monroe, Louisiana, Sarah Wadley's father endorsed secession and made sure his daughter understood why. After several conversations with him, Wadley laid blame for the sectional tensions on northerners who "have sowed the seeds of dissension and insurrection among us, those seeds are fast ripening and a bloody harvest seems impending. . . . [T]hey shout Freedom and Union, but they would take away our freedom and give it to the negroes." Susan Bradford received a similar indoctrination in the ideals of secession. As a member of a politically notable family, Bradford spent her childhood immersed in the pro-slavery arguments. In 1858, Bradford's father began teaching his daughter about "the deep feeling of dislike and mistrust . . . between the North and the South." To underscore his point, Mr. Bradford gave her a book by John C. Calhoun on states' rights. By 1860, it was clear the youth had internalized her father's secessionist views. After reading an article on the 1860 election, she concluded that the Republican candidates "have two objects in view, the freeing of the Negroes and the downfall of the South."[6]

The issue of slavery played a central role in young women's developing allegiance to the southern cause. The 1859 raid on Harper's Ferry, Virginia, in which an armed band of abolitionists led by John Brown seized a federal armory in hopes of sparking a slave rebellion, led many to believe that a defense of southern interests was needed. Although Brown's plan failed, the raid fueled white southerners' fear of a northern conspiracy against slavery and led them to question the loyalty of African Americans to their masters. These same fears persisted throughout the course of the sectional debates and into the war. When Louisa McCord, of Columbia, South Carolina, returned from an extended trip overseas, she learned of the attempted revolt. As she listened to her brother and mother discuss the possibility of a similar incident in their community, McCord, whose household and plantation consisted of over one hundred slaves, became anxious about her family's safety. News of Harper's Ferry was not McCord's first encounter with abolitionism. During her tour of Europe, the young woman came across a copy of Harriet Beecher Stowe's *Uncle Tom's Cabin*, which she referred to as a "mass of falsehood."[7]

Susan Bradford found the news of Harper's Ferry distressing and grew increasingly anxious about the status of slavery in her own home. The Bradford family owned a plantation in Leon County, Florida. Secluded in a rural portion of the state, Susan pondered how the 142 slaves living on the Bradford estate would react to the events at Harper's Ferry. "The horrible, horrible time that has come to us," she wrote in her diary, "our world seems turned topsy-turvy." Bradford admitted that the attempts at insurrection in Virginia had led the family to "trust none of the dear black folks who, before this, we had relied on at every turn." She was afraid to speak to the slaves "for fear it will prove just what should have been left unsaid," and wondered anxiously if "the people we have always loved [will] put the torch to our homes and murder us when we seek to escape." As she closed her entry, Bradford expressed her belief that the violence she expected from the family slaves was "what John Brown was urging them to do." Clearly, news of a plot to incite insurrection had forced Bradford to ponder her own relationship with the slaves. Her fears also nurtured a feeling of distrust toward outsiders, which she directed toward a northern governess hired to teach her in the home. Bradford eventually tried to have her dismissed. "She is not like anyone we have had before," she wrote, "I do not believe she has even taught school in her life." The governess finally left to return home before the war commenced.[8]

The election of Lincoln and secession of southern states that followed heightened concerns about slave insurrections. Some southerners feared that the election of an anti-slavery candidate would incite rebellion among their slaves. As the country moved toward war, slaveholding families were plagued by the fear that their servants would take advantage of the disruptive environment to turn on their masters and mistresses. Sarah "Sally" Clayton recalled that anxieties ran high as talk of war circulated among Atlanta citizens. The young woman and many of her female peers grew increasingly fearful that the slaves of the city would attempt an uprising. Rumors of possible insurrections continued to the point that one evening on their way to a concert, Sally and her friends crouched down in the carriage "like frightened hares" out of fear of an attack. Myra Inman recorded in her diary that a story of potential slave revolt had sparked some of her neighbors in Cleveland, Tennessee, to arm themselves. Anxiety over slave rebellions intensified among young women left at home without the protection of their mothers and fathers. In the occupied city of New Orleans, Clara Solomon felt vulnerable to slave unrest with her father away on business. She confided to her diary that she feared the slaves more than the Union army. Oranie Virginia Snead recalled that after Union soldiers raided her community in Fluvanna County, Virginia, she grew increasingly concerned about the slaves. "We realized that we were in the lines of the enemy," she wrote, "and worse still on a large plantation of negroes suddenly inflated with the prospect of freedom."[9]

The election of Lincoln encouraged young women to support southern independence. As states of the lower South rushed to organize secession conventions, young women joined the patriotic frenzy. Susan Bradford's father, a delegate to the Florida convention in Tallahassee in January of 1861, encouraged his daughter to attend. She spent much of her time listening as he explained the proceedings and echoed secessionist arguments. Louisa McCord found secession activities in the state capital too interesting to ignore. Before Lincoln's election, she had given little thought to the sectional tensions that absorbed her parents' attention. But now, as Columbians celebrated the state's decision to secede, she joined the swirl of political activity. She along with her female peers, for example, donned a blue badge with a palmetto emblem to show support. Others in the upper South spoke openly of their support for secession as their states contemplated the issue. During the secession conventions in Virginia, Cloe Tyler Whittle of Norfolk believed that her state had no recourse but to leave the Union after events at Fort Sumter. The president's request, she wrote, was "appalling," and after it was confirmed, she recorded this demand in her diary: "Secession—Immediate—Secession."[10]

In some households, families disagreed on the secession issue, leaving their children conflicted on the matter. Mary Conway Shields of Jefferson County, Mississippi, for example, noted that her mother ardently advocated secession from an early date and spoke frequently about its benefits to slaveholders. Shields's father, however, refused to support southern independence until Lincoln's April 1861 request for troops. Because of the conflicting sentiments in her home, Shields wavered on the issue until her brother left for the Confederate army. With her closest sibling off to war, Shields became a champion of the Confederate cause and felt proud that her brother was fighting. Young women on occasion also expressed regret over the disintegration of the Union. Although Sarah Wadley ardently supported Louisiana's decision to secede, she felt sorry, too: "how sad to think that we are united no longer, that we are no more natives of one common country." "[N]ecessary as is the separation," she remarked, "how can we think of it without grief?"[11]

As southerners plunged into war, the home became a setting for adolescent daughters' indoctrination in the Confederate cause. Daughters of southern politicians, such as Susan Bradford, found that wartime politics were a regular topic in the home. Many times Bradford's family used the dinner table as a forum for political discussions in which her father allowed her to participate. Louise Wigfall, whose father was a senator, spent several evenings listening to her father's guests debate issues concerning the Confederate government. The Ridley household in Southampton, Virginia, teemed of Confederate patriotism after their state's secession. Thirteen-year-old Elizabeth Ridley watched as her father led the organization of a "vigilance committee in the neighborhood" before joining the Confederate army for service.[12]

Letters from family members immersed adolescent daughters in the language of the Confederate cause. In a November 1860 letter to his sister, James Hankins expressed his hope that Virginia would remain in the Union despite Lincoln's election. Yet he made clear that the source of the regional conflict lay in the North and their perceived attacks on the slave system. Like many slaveholding men, James came to view the southern cause as the defense of their republican rights and liberties. "Murderous demagogues," he wrote, "in a spirit of blasphemy hugs this trying time close in their slimy embrace and . . . hisses between his clenched teeth destruction upon the peace of his fellow citizens and the welfare of his country." He blamed such "fanaticism" on the rhetoric of northern politicians whom he described as "blacks from hell."[13]

Evangelical churches also encouraged political involvement among southern daughters, by serving as a medium of war news and by providing a spiritual defense of secession and war. Louisa McCord of Charleston, South Carolina, recalled that young women often attended prayer meetings where they received news of battlefield defeats and victories. Sarah Wadley found the church useful in understanding the ideological basis for the Confederacy, having heard a persuasive sermon on what she called "the mistaken piety of abolitionists." Wadley, like many other young women of the slaveholding South, absorbed the scriptural and historical defense of slavery that churches promoted; her preacher regarded the institution as "sanctioned by both the bible, and by ancient usage." Susan Bradford extracted a different message from the church services she attended. She felt a stronger sense of southern patriotism after her preacher prayed for the delegates to the Florida secession convention. The service left her with a feeling of responsibility to help the South in its quest for independence: "it made everyone feel . . . as if some share of the responsibility rested on each one of us."[14]

Educators instilled a sense of political responsibility and patriotism in their young charges. Many daughters continued their schooling in the early part of the war, and classrooms became a forum for political expression and education. Immediately after secession, many southern schools reoriented their curriculum to reflect the ideological arguments of the Confederacy. The *Daily Richmond Enquirer* reported that southern publishing houses were releasing their own versions of textbooks, including the *Southern Confederacy Arithmetic*. By 1863, the Confederate government had taken steps to organize a separate teachers' association. One of the primary purposes of the organization was to help teachers adopt textbooks "for the instruction of youth prepared by Southern men, who alone can rightly understand the wants of our people." In addition to textbook adoption, teachers often assigned compositions and debates with the theme of the North-South conflict. Readings included topics on the American Revolution that invited comparisons to the Confederate cause. Myra Inman, for example, argued after reading *The Life of Marion*, a history of patriot soldier Francis Marion, that the American Revolution was similar to the Civil War because both represented a struggle for republican rights and independence. Learning of the various battles and Confederate leaders and following the movements of the armies also took the place of traditional classroom subjects. Sallie Clayton, a student at the Atlanta Female Institute, volunteered for an assignment that required mapping the lines of the armies. To the amazement of her teacher, Clayton exhibited extensive knowledge of the major campaigns.[15]

School activities promoted expression of Confederate patriotism. At the request of their headmaster, Sarah Lowe and her classmates at the Huntsville Female Academy sewed a banner that she presented to the local company of volunteers before they left for the front. Lowe's teachers also encouraged the students to attend patriotic public addresses. Sally Clayton's teacher had students perform military drills and required them to compete in a march against a cavalry company. Such activities absorbed much of the time and energy of female students. Lowe, for example, confided in her diary that she had trouble studying with "so much war news to occupy our minds" as well as numerous public events.[16]

While young women internalized the message taught them by parents, clerics, and educators, they expressed some ambivalence toward war. Daughters recognized that war meant the departure of their fathers, brothers, and other male kin for the front. That the cause they so strongly supported would break up their families led many to question the desirability of war. When Susan Bradford's relative quipped that her newborn nephew was another soldier to fight for the South, Bradford was shocked and responded that "war and bloodshed seem very terrible to me." After some of her family members left for the front, Catherine McLaurin secretly hoped that God would stop the war. As her uncle's company left for battle, Louisa McCord remarked, "we felt as if life itself had gone . . . the misery of all that was to come seemed to settle down upon us." Cordelia Lewis Scales felt some guilt over her feelings when her brothers volunteered: "I know it is not right for me to feel sorry that they are gone, and I am glad they have acted so, still I cannot say that I give them up without a murmur."[17]

Young women who watched their beaux leave for battle also expressed ambivalence. Nettie Fondren of Thomasville, Georgia, had maintained a courtship with Robert Mitchell before he left to serve in the Confederate military. Throughout his absence, the couple corresponded regularly, sharing their fears about his safety in battle and the fate of the Confederate cause. She told her betrothed that although the "national horizon is dark and threatening" he should remain committed to the cause. "Onward! Onward!" she urged him, "until the vile invader is driven from our sunny South." Yet a few months later, she expressed horror over "the bloodshed, strife and suffering" caused by war and wondered "what will be the end of it all."[18]

Many adolescent daughters comforted themselves by denying the likelihood of a lengthy conflict or focusing more on patriotic events at home. In 1860, Bettie Alexander of Monroe County, Virginia, expressed fear of war but at the same time dismissed it as "all talk." Not long after the war began, several of Susan Bradford's relatives enlisted in the army, which caused much anxiety among her female kin. Bradford's hope was that "the war . . . [would] not last long." Her mother also tried to comfort her and her sisters by assuring them that "there would be no fighting—just talk of war and reconciliation would follow." Some refused to let it bother them—a luxury that their youth and class allowed them. Annie Jeter of New Orleans recalled that while parents prepared for war, the youths of the city turned to social activities. "We young folk," she wrote, "could not realize the horror of war and were as gay as ever with dances and parties, some farewell ones given for soldiers." Louisa McCord felt excited over secession in South Carolina but admitted that she took a lighthearted approach to the matter; she knew, however, that to her parents "it was serious enough."[19]

Nonetheless, southern daughters had little choice but to come to terms with their fathers and brothers fighting in the war and the import of familial duty allowed them to do so. Those who enlisted often described their service as an honorable duty essential to the defense of the Confederacy and, thus, to the defense of the home and family. Historian James McPherson in his study of Civil War soldiers demonstrates the centrality of duty as the motivation for military service. Duty, according to McPherson, was as a "binding moral obligation involving reciprocity" in which one had a responsibility to serve the country "under whose protection one had lived." To avoid their patriotic duty threatened to tarnish a man's public reputation and that of his family. Fathers and brothers were careful to discuss their service with family members in these terms. Although Virginia had yet to secede from the Union, James Hankins, for example, expressed to his sister his willingness to fight for what he saw as the defense of southern honor. "I have joined the troop or applied," he wrote his sister, "and am ready to fight for the old Brother of us all. . . . The North has thrown the gauntlet, the South takes it up . . . and Virginia . . . will be found in the front ranks of the brave Southern phalanx which fights to uphold Southern honor, Southern chivalry, and Southern independence." After participating in his first battle while serving in a North Carolina regiment, George Whitaker Wills wrote home to his sister that his commanding officer had praised him for "our valor in the recent battle." For Wills, the recognition of his achievement came when the officer noted that the men had "crowned our heads with honor" by acting bravely on the battlefield. He continued to call on the rhetoric of duty when the Confederacy experienced defeat in the eastern theatre in 1863. His duty, he asserted, was to "keep up the name of our State." Even as he faced illness due to the strains of camp life, he refused to seek a furlough, noting that others here doing duty as unwell as myself and therefore think still I should be here!"[20]

The idea of serving the Confederate cause to defend the home and family provided a level of comfort to those young women wrought with despair over the safety of their loved ones. Elizabeth Ridley wrote several letters to her brother expressing concern for his security, to which he responded that she "ought to feel proud that you have a brother in the war. . . . [I]f I die, you know it is a 'glorious thing' to die in defense of one's country." Samuel Sanders, a doctor from Cheraw, South Carolina, realized that his decision to serve as an officer for the 21st South Carolina Infantry deeply saddened Mary Jane, his young daughter. Although Mary Jane was away at boarding school when her father left, she expressed the emotional stress she endured knowing his life would be in danger. Sanders attempted to assuage his daughter's fears by relying on the notion that defense of the Confederacy would ultimately preserve the reputation of the family and ensure its survival. "The honor of the family is involved," he wrote, "at the close of this war, to have it said, and to have my children know, that I was not ready to do my whole duty in throwing off the despicable yoke which is oppressing us." Sanders approached the issue of death as the risk one takes in fulfilling one's duty "as a Christian gentleman, when necessary, for my wife and children." To Sanders, invoking the exemption laws for military service would mean to "evade my responsibility in this crisis for the sake of personal safety." "A man who will not offer up his life for his family when necessary," he added, "takes a very low view of his Christian duty and does dishonor to his wife and children." Sanders also couched his sense of duty in terms of upholding his revolutionary heritage, hoping to inculcate the value of sacrifice for the southern cause in preserving tradition. "I would be disgraced if I staid at home, and unworthy of my revolutionary ancestors," Sanders contended. In trying to comfort Mary Jane's fears, Sanders reassured his daughter that "my Heavenly Father will take care of me, in the path of duty."[21]

By the start of the war, young women had clearly absorbed the ideals of independence inculcated by their parents, educators, and clergy. Likewise, they accepted wartime sacrifices as extensions of familial duty. Yet young women interpreted the meaning of secession and war using the lens of their youth and gender, resulting in a devotion to the Confederate cause rooted in a desire to maintain a sense of continuity with the past of their mothers and grandmothers. It was in this context that southern daughters began to shape their notions of female self-sacrifice—the basis of Confederate womanhood. As their fathers, brothers, and beaux left for the war, young women joined in war work with their mothers and expressed their willingness to sacrifice for the cause. Virginia Hankins, for example, demonstrated her loyalism by refusing to attend some social occasions while her brother served in a Virginia regiment. She wrote him that she "could not mingle in such scenes at such times" and thus was willing to forego an invitation to a party. Knowing that her brother was standing guard in his camp "watching the enemy," she chose to stay home, noting that "as I could not watch with you I prayed for you." For adolescent daughters like Hankins, who were still in the process of forming their self-perceptions, their concept of patriotic duty whether through sacrifice, war work, or outspoken support left a lasting impression on their feminine identity. The connection between patriotic involvement and familial reputation gave way to a new sense of civic and political responsibility that young women saw as inseparable from their sense of self. Samuel Sanders encouraged his daughter to view their separation in terms of political duty. "Don't distress yourself about my volunteering for the war," he offered, "You must be a patriotic daughter, ready to devote everything for the cause of our poor bleeding country."[22]

Young women viewed participation in home front activities as a substitute, albeit a poor one, for fighting alongside their male counterparts. They saw it as their responsibility to serve their nation, but they recognized and bemoaned the limitations their gender placed on them. Elizabeth Collier of Goldsboro, North Carolina, for example, expressed her frustration over being unable to fight: "I am but a feeble woman, would God I were a man." Fifteen-year-old Louise Wigfall wrote her brother that she wished she could fight with him, but had to resign herself merely to playing "Dixie" on the piano when entertaining guests. While most women, young and old, never considered serving in the military a serious option, others donned short haircuts, adopted aliases, and enlisted in the Confederate army. Historians argue that the motivations behind their enlistment stem from those similar to their male counterparts. Some saw it as an opportunity to earn a better income or experience an adventure away from home. Still, others offered their service out of a sense of patriotic duty to the Confederate cause. There were some, however, whose reasons stemmed from their gender identity. Those who found the gender system too oppressive welcomed the freedom that a male identity brought with it, while a number of women who went to the front did so out of a desire to remain with their husbands and other loved ones. Female soldiers were more common (though still rare) in the Union army than in that of the Confederacy However, there are some instances of southern women disguising themselves, including Melvernia Elverina Peppercorn who enlisted in 1862 and Nancy Corbin of Tennessee. Both young women chose to enlist out of a sense of patriotic duty but also because it allowed them to remain close to their loved ones. In the case of Nancy Corbin, military service permitted a larger degree of freedom from the watchful eye of her father who guarded her interaction with male soldiers on the home front closely. But, for the majority of young women of the slaveholding class, stepping out of the confines of their gender would possibly hinder their expectations for marriage and motherhood. Serving in the military seemed too much of a challenge to their cultural norms and they resolved to donate their time and energy toward female associations.[23]

Swept up in the home front enthusiasm, most young women worked with their mothers and older female kin in patriotic activities. Like the older generation of southern women, adolescent daughters participated in such efforts out of a sense of responsibility to provide material support for the cause. Nettie Fondren described what she saw as the duty of all women on the home front: "If ever there was on Earth an elevated task for women it is working for the brave men whose lives are offered up for us, and on whom the salvation of our country actively depends." Elizabeth Waties Allston shared that sense of responsibility. "[W]hen we know that this is a new country born into the world," she wrote, "it behooves everyone to exert themselves to the utmost to make men great and our women good. . . . [E]veryone can do something."[24]

When organizing the soldiers' aid societies in Virginia, the women of the state encouraged the younger members of the female population to join with them. Several women of Richmond, Virginia, for example, organized an association and sent out a general call to all women of the city to participate. The Soldiers' Aid Society of Virginia was started in June of 1861, consisting of delegates from churches in the city, and was divided into several committees for the purpose of providing aid to soldiers. The organization included a nursing committee to provide service in the city's hospitals and a funds committee to collect and administer donations for supplies for troops and hospitals. The growth of Richmond's military population, however, taxed the resources of the organization to the point where they published in the *Daily Richmond Enquirer* a general call of all women to help. "We felt . . . we should need the cooperation of our sisters," they implored, "and therefore address a circular, first to those of our own State, suggesting that in every county and every community societies should be formed at once, which suggestion is meeting with a hearty response."[25]

The efforts of their peers along with southern society's encouragement of young women's war work helped in recruiting female youths into these community organizations. In one instance, a young woman of Charleston, South Carolina, writing under the title of "the Daughter of a Nullifier," sent out her own challenge to female peers to contribute items for Confederate soldiers. "While everybody else is volunteering his or her services, to aid in this great cause of Southern independence," she wrote, "I would not be idle." She further added that "my every pulse beats secession" and likened her patriot spirit to that of Joan of Arc. Southern newspapers also promoted the efforts of female youths in the sewing societies by emphasizing the romantic potential of such war work. The *Natchez Daily Courier*, for example, tried to recruit young women to crochet a "woolen helmet" for their soldier-beau. "Upon a bitter cold night," the author proclaimed, "when the soldier is on guard, as he draws his helmet over his head he will thank his lady-love for her acceptable present, and bless her for thinking so kindly of him." Two months later, the same paper reported that three young women had pledged to make a wardrobe of clothes for three soldiers as long as "the soldiers whom they select will consent to marry them when the war is over."[26]

Mothers and older female kin encouraged daughters to join relief societies and oversaw their participation. Sallie Clayton, for example, became involved in a hospital association in which mothers and daughters worked together to roll bandages, pick lint, and sew. The collective efforts of women of all age groups provided a way for young women to continue their maternal-centered education during the war but also allowed them to learn organizational skills. With the help of other women, Annie Jeter learned to knit a sock a day. Sarah Wadley learned valuable skills when she was elected secretary of her mother's sewing society. Although Wadley had trepidations about assuming an office she knew little of, her mother guided her and even reproached her when she took haphazard notes at the meetings. Her mother's direction paid off when Wadley spent one evening of "considerable labour" documenting the donations and reviewing meeting minutes. Adolescent daughters also became apprentices to their mothers in fund-raising activities. Under the guidance of older female members, young women visited neighbors and friends to solicit donations for relief organizations. Louisa McCord's mother asked her to collect money to help the local sewing society make a flag. Ellen Renshaw House, along with her father and sister, visited neighbors to ask for blankets for Confederate prisoners of war. House went so far as to organize her friends to collect clothes and other items for prisoners. Young women heeded the call to enlist their services in organizations headed by their mothers and older female kin. In the case of Clarksville, Virginia, however, the younger female population created their own separate organization. The Young Ladies' Aid Society of Clarkesville focused much of its energy on receiving donations from the community and passing them on to the state society. On one occasion, the group collected $104.38 from members of the community.[27]

Some southern daughters found producing clothing for Confederate soldiers a difficult task, given the parameters of their antebellum education.

Young women's prewar training in sewing focused primarily on needle-work. The demands placed on women to provide socks, shirts, and other articles forced female youths to learn more practical sewing skills quickly. Some found the requirement rather challenging. The *Charleston Mercury* reported in October of 1861 that several young women in the city were hard at work sewing and knitting to outfit the soldiers. "Visit them," the article stated, "when you will, they meet you knitting in hand." But, the author added that the items produced failed to "indicate a very exact knowledge of the human anatomy," alluding to the lack of skills among the younger women. In describing a sock one had made, the author concluded that it "was intended for the foot of the entire Southern Confederacy."[28]

The many military and private hospitals throughout the South provided other opportunities for civic involvement. Daughters often accompanied their mothers when they served as nurses. In a letter to the editor of the *Charleston Mercury*, one group of young women, calling themselves the "Daughters of the 'Spunky Little State,'" announced that their female peers had taken to volunteering their services to "enact the part of Florence Nightengale [sic]," a female nurse during the Crimean War. They challenged other young women of the city to take up the same cause and to provide assistance to Confederate soldiers "at the forts." Although teenage daughters often volunteered in the hospitals, parents made sure to shield their female youths from many forms of nursing. Seeing unclothed or semi-clad soldiers, they feared, would place their daughters in danger of impropriety. Moreover, parents were careful to protect them from the death, disease, and grotesque nature of the hospitals. Consequently, young women participated in nursing mainly by providing food and other ma-terials to the hospitals. Judith Ann Robertson of Chesterfield, Virginia, for example, went with her mother to several hospitals but was permitted only to distribute food and milk to the soldiers. When hospitals were short-handed, however, young women sometimes found opportunities to do more. Louisa Sheppard assisted her mother in her nursing duties in the wayside hospital established in their home. On one occasion, when her mother was busy with other patients, she asked Louisa to sit with an unattended soldier and "attend to his minor wants." Louisa wrote a let-ter for him and brought him food and water, but avoided more intimate nursing duties.[29]

While daughters followed their female elders into local aid societies and hospitals, they engaged in their own community activities centered in their peer culture. The patriotic movements in the early stages of the war transformed the social gatherings of teenage girls into forms of political expression separate from the world of adults. Their ties to female friends and family members close in age helped to form the associations needed to initiate such activities. In July 1861, for example, Clara Solomon and several female friends attended a picnic to raise funds for the destitute families of volunteers. A popular activity among young women was sewing a flag to present to the local company of volunteers. Susan Bradford was filled with pride when she and other young women from her community gathered to sew a flag. She noted that "everyone, did our part in the work, even if the stitches were few, when the fingers unskilled." Sally Clayton and her female peers proclaimed their support for the southern cause when they presented a flag that read "Never, Never, Never." Informal tributes became common forms of political expression. Mary Fries of Salem, North Carolina, wrote that when a military company marched through her town, she and other young women threw bouquets to the men. Sarah Lowe and her classmates at the Huntsville Female Academy received permission from the headmaster on several occasions to greet a company passing through town. These gatherings afforded opportunities for social interactions and meeting a potential beau, but they were also suitable forms of political expression for teenage girls.[30]

Young women publicly proclaimed their loyalism by hosting community performances. Concerts in which they sang "Dixie" and "The Bonnie Blue Flag" became popular activities for communities. Young women played a large role in organizing the events and sent the proceeds to the local soldiers' aid society. Other performances involved tableaux with patriotic themes. In one such performance, Cordelia Lewis Scales played "Volunteer" on the guitar while a young man costumed as a soldier stood beside her. Sallie Clayton and her peers participated in a similar scene entitled "Young Ladies with the Blues," posing alongside the "Fulton Blues," a mock company consisting of boys too young to serve. The *Natchez Daily Courier* reported that a number of young women planned to host a series of tableaux to raise funds for the "the benefit of the soldiers now in the army." In comparison to other fundraising efforts, the female youths of Natchez had considerable success with their event, raising $600 to donate to the Confederate aid societies.[31]

Female youths also transformed their normal concerns with fashion and dress into forms of political expression. Before the war, they had regarded dress purely as a matter of taste and distinction, but as they were swept up in the tide of patriotism, their clothing were statements of Confederate nationalism that gained them public recognition. When seventeen-year-old Cloe Tyler Whittle went to a neighbor's house to celebrate Virginia's secession, she wore what she called her "Secession Dress," remarking that "it shows what women can do, when all that is in their power is to put a few brass buttons up the front of their dress." Sallie Clayton and her classmates at the Atlanta Female Institute also expressed support for southern independence when they became "the first to appear in Georgia cotton" at the state fair. Sallie McEwen of Franklin, Tennessee, made a military uniform so she could join a mock company that included her friends and classmates. Annie Jeter, along with her female peers, made Confederate flags to wear as aprons and wore cotton blossoms in her hair at a concert to benefit soldiers. Young women encountered few obstacles from their peers or older community members. Transforming the traditional concerns of female youths into statements of loyalty still remained within the parameters of gender convention. They avoided radical clothing, such as the pantaloons adopted by some women in the North, or dress deemed inappropriate for their age. As long as they continued to uphold the dictates of respectability, young women were free to use their clothing as political expressions even if the public nature of their actions garnered attention from soldiers.[32]

In areas under Union occupation, female patriotic dress became a powerful vehicle for expressing loyalism while avoiding charges of treason or social impropriety. In one instance, the popular trend of wearing hoopskirts became a contentious issue in the occupied city of Memphis, Tennessee. The *New Orleans Era* reported that the young women chose to avoid hoopskirts as "a badge of secesh principles." Their decision to abandon the fashion stemmed from their desire to find a subtle way of disobeying Union authority and proclaiming their continued allegiance to the Confederacy. Eliminating hoopskirts had been a common practice among young women in some areas who saw the trend as a frivolous display of luxury in times when Confederacy needed their support. In Natchez, Mississippi, for example, the local paper reprinted a call for young women to go without the hoops, citing that "we think that all ladies might dispense with them these hard times, as they are a mere matter of 'form.'" But for the female youths of Memphis, abandoning the trend grew out of a sense of defiance. "Although hooped skirts are plentiful at Memphis," the reported mentioned, "the rebel women have agreed among themselves not to wear them. It is their secret sign—their badge—their rebel flag. No longer allowed to flaunt past our brave fellows with their emblems of treason pinned to their dresses and bonnets, they have hit upon this plan." To illustrate this point, the author described one episode when a Union soldier approached a young woman to find out why her peers no longer wore the hoops. According to the article, she responded "you Yankees can't make us wear hoops, neither."[33]

Southern daughters were at the center of the movement to adopt home-spun cloth and saw it as a symbol of their patriotic support. The cost of clothing coupled with the demands to provide uniforms for soldiers sent southerners searching for an alternative cloth for their wardrobes. More-over, the South's insufficient industrial development and dependency on the North for finished goods, created shortages after the states left the Union. Many southerners supported domestic production as a means to encourage the self-sufficiency of the region. Homespun cloth became the popular option, especially among young women whose parents encouraged them to accept the coarse and often plain material into their wardrobes as a way to do their part for the Confederacy. They responded positively to the homespun campaigns launched by the adults in their community, viewing it as a symbol of patriotism within the youth culture. At their social occasions and patriotic meetings, young women wore the dresses and chastised those who refused to follow the trend. Local newspapers also did their part to encourage young women to add homespun to their wardrobes by emphasizing its popularity among their peers. The *Charleston Mercury* reported that at an upcoming ball in Raleigh, North Carolina, the young women of the town planed "to be dressed in homespun." The same paper also periodically printed other occasions when young women donned the new fashions, hoping to inspire a trend within the culture of youthful females. One article included a description of a sighting of well-known young women: "Two of Portsmouth's [Virginia] fair daughters appeared in its streets Tuesday in homespun, and the general verdict was they looked charming." A Mississippi newspaper described "a Calico Ball" attended by a number of young men and women, who proudly displayed their homespun ware. "What we took especial notes of," the author added, "was the improved appearance of the ladies in the 'calico,' far outviening [*sic*] the more costly and extravagant toilet of silk and satin. Never to our eyes did the fair creatures present so lovely an appearance."[34]

Young women also adorned their homes and personal items with Confederate symbols and collected war mementoes as a sign of patriotism. Martha Moore bought composition books printed with Confederate emblems and throughout her journal drew the Confederate flag. Clara Solomon hung a flag in her home. "I placed it there with my own hands," she defiantly wrote, "and . . . dare any Federalist to lay his polluted hand upon it." Fannie Lewis Gwathmey of Virginia boldly approached General Thomas J. (Stonewall) Jackson to ask for a lock of his hair, which he willingly cut off and gave her. When General Robert E. Lee passed through Leesburg, Virginia, in 1862, Alice Janney Harrison made rings from hair taken from the mane of Traveller, Lee's horse. The rings became a coveted symbol of southern patriotism among the young women of the neighborhood.[35]

Such ardent support for the Confederacy often led to strained relationships among female friends. In East Tennessee, where strong Union sentiment existed, Myra Inman experienced conflicting emotions when asked if she wanted to participate, along with her female peers, in making a United States flag. Ultimately, her mother interceded and refused to allow her to join in the venture. Even as Inman's schoolmates participated in a flag presentation to a Union company in Cleveland, Tennessee, she chose to remain at home. Some young women also found their friendships with northern peers disrupted. When the war began, Louise Wigfall, living in Boston, Massachusetts, with relatives, admitted having a hard time maintaining her temper

Fig. 4. Myra Inman. Private collection, *Southern Tennessee Digital Archive*, Cleveland State Community College.

amid her northern classmates. News of Fort Sumter tested her friendship with her close friend Emma, and the two concluded to refrain from political discussions. Nevertheless, Wigfall eventually broke the agreement when she felt compelled to give Emma a copy of a public statement delivered by Jefferson Davis. Wigfall's breach of the agreement could have stemmed from her family ties. As the daughter of a southern politician, the young woman supported the Confederacy and felt compelled to voice her patriotism even at the expense of a friendship.[36]

Young women's notions of duty to the Confederate cause also influenced their relationship with southern men who remained on the home front. While many men of the slaveholding class joined the army early in the conflict, some avoided serving by hiring a substitute or by utilizing exemption laws, such as that for owners of twenty slaves or more. Some young women whose brothers or fathers served in the army viewed these men as shirkers and cowards. Annie Jeter, for example, criticized the "stay at homes" in New Orleans and refused to socialize with them unless they had "a mighty good reason for so doing." Louise Wigfall also expressed contempt for those "who had never 'smelt powder.'" Amanda Worthington, of Washington County, Mississippi, called one resident of her hometown a "cowardly sluggard" for avoiding enlistment and exclaimed, "he ought to be thrashed and made to leave." Kate Foster of Natchez, Mississippi, remarked that the young men in her community who used the exemption laws "ought to be drummed out of society." While staying in the Confederate capital of Richmond, Virginia Hankins noted that she preferred the company of soldiers to the young men who had avoided military service. "Several young men were here," she wrote, "the first I've seen since the Marylanders left. But I don't like substituted young men!"[37]

Fears of reproach from their female peers proved a useful tool in shaming young men into service. In a letter to the editor of the *Charleston Mercury*, signed "A Warning Voice," the anonymous author warned "the young men of the city" to enlist in the army or run the risk of receiving on Valentine's Day "a doll baby, or a hoop skirt, or something of the kind" from a young woman. Another article in that same paper wryly reported, "the girls in Columbus, Ga., have organized a 'Home Guard' for the special protection of the young men who have concluded to remain home during the existence of the war." The implication was that men who invoked the exemption laws failed to live up to the masculine ideals of the Confederacy and it was up to the female population, bearing a shortage of "true" men, to protect the city. A group of women in Charleston issued a general letter to the "Soldiers of the Confederate Army" praising the soldiers for fulfilling their duty to the cause of independence. The letter, which was published in a local paper, also chastised those men who refused to join the army. "Men guilty of such infamy," the women warned, "sell *your blood* and *our honor*, and give up the Confederacy to its wicked invaders. In after years, from generation to generation, the black title of tory and deserter will cling to *them*, disgracing their children's children." The men who served in the Confederate effort, however, "will be honored in peace as the saviours of your country, and the pride and glory of your countrywomen."[38]

The realization that their loved ones would remain on the front longer than expected challenged some young women's patriotism. After her brother reenlisted, Amanda Worthington exclaimed "how I do long for peace to be declared!" The reality of war shocked Worthington. "I never thought in times of peace what an awful thing war was," she wrote, "but now that I have two brothers and four cousins in the army I can realize it." Nevertheless, while the seventeen-year-old wished for peace so her family could reunite, she believed that "the South must be victorious, her cause is the right." Sallie Independence Foster secretly wished the war to end after hearing news about family friends wounded or killed in battle. "My God do let this horrible war end," she remarked, "and let sweet, sweet 'Peace' reign over our beloved country once more."[39]

Most daughters, however, viewed the separation of family as part of the necessary sacrifice for independence. Pauline DeCaradeuc, of Aiken, South Carolina, knew firsthand the worst effects of war on a family, for two of her brothers died in battle. Nevertheless, the young woman refused to accept Lee's surrender. "[M]any think the war is over, and we are subjugated entirely, I won't believe that," she wrote. "Subjugation! Never." The loss of family members in fact often strengthened young women's support for the cause. Kate Foster's disdain for the Union grew after her two brothers died in battle. "God grant that I may some day feel they were taken for some good," she wrote, "how can I ever love the Yankees as brothers when they made these deep and everlasting wounds in my heart?" Elizabeth Collier declared that she would never accept defeat at the hands of an enemy who had killed so many southern men: "Reconstruction! how the very word galls—can we ever live in peace with the desecrators of our homes and the murderers of our Fathers, Brothers, and Sons—Never—We are bound to rise again."[40]

As the Union army occupied areas of the southern home front, daughters found new reason to demonstrate their loyalism openly. The thought of Yankee soldiers in their towns appalled and frightened young women, but actual contact with the enemy nurtured their animosity toward the Union and upheld their dedication to the cause of Confederate independence. When soldiers occupied Murfreesboro, Tennessee, Alice Ready wrote that the "only relief from them will be death, and then I pray for it." Amanda Worthington swore that she would "rather die than submit to the Yankees." Sarah Wadley likewise vowed that she "would rather die than see our armies humiliated by flight, our country ruined by submission. . . . [W]orse than death would be our conquest by the Yankees." When federal soldiers occupied her community in April 1864, Virginia Hankins grew to resent her occupiers. Her first experience with them came when cavalry came to her home looking for supplies. The invasion of Union soldiers into the domestic circle heightened her anger toward the enemy; she expressed this by calling into question the honor of northern soldiers. "Ah! These were brave men," she wrote to her brother, "charging so valorously on women and little children, how proud and undaunted they looked." Union soldiers approached the Hankins home asking for brandy, but eventually departed with the family's mules. The subsequent arrest of her male neighbors, who supported the Confederacy, left Virginia with nothing but hatred toward the occupiers. She intimated to her brother that if she were in possession of a pistol "I should not hesitate to use it."[41]

For those living away from home, news of Union occupation from family members fueled their rancor for the enemy. In 1864, as the state of Virginia experienced shortages of supplies and rising inflation, the Hankins family faced the prospect of poverty. The daughter of a once wealthy planter and member of the southern gentry, Virginia Hankins had spent portions of the war visiting relatives and friends in Richmond. When she received word of the sudden downturn in her family's economic fortunes, Virginia grew concerned about their fate. Her mother had warned that "if the affairs in this portion of the Confederacy [Surry County] don't change . . . very soon every person will be ruined." Virginia's father also sent word that bands of deserters threatened to take what remaining sup-plies they had saved from the Union troops. "I wish we had 50 or 100 scouts," he wrote, "it would certainly break up all these marauding par-ties from the river." Jane Sivley also received word that federal soldiers had visited her community, leaving several homes burned in their wake. The daughter of a wealthy planter in Hinds County, Mississippi, Sivley spent the war away at boarding school in Marion, Alabama. Throughout the course of their separation, Sivley's mother kept her informed of the family's well-being through regular correspondence. The letters, however, increasingly contained stories of the contentious interaction between the family and the Union soldiers who had begun to occupy their region by 1863. William Sivley, Jane's brother, expressed to his sister his own fears of the emotional and financial toll on the family resulting from federal occupation: "I am fearfull [*sic*] they [Union troops] have been there and burned out every body." "I would give anything," he added, "if Pa was out of there with all his affects."[42]

Reports concerning the horrors of battle heightened their bitterness toward the Union army. While some male kin were reluctant to disclose gruesome details of the dead and wounded, others willingly described scenes of suffering. Such stories stirred the anger of young women toward Union soldiers as they came to view their occupiers as responsible for the dangers their male kin faced in battle. James Hankins depicted a gory landscape to his sister after a battle in Virginia. "The carnage is awful," he wrote, "the dead bodies of Yankees strewed the field in every direction and the wounded were crying out for assistance or praying to be killed to end their suffering. . . . Thousands of our dead been buried [but] no one can tell where they lie." Mary Wills received numerous letters from her brother while he served in the Confederate army. Buried within his correspondence were snapshots of the emotional toll that military service exacted from soldiers. In one letter, he described an incident in which a soldier "had gone suddenly deranged . . . [and] took up a gun and took de-liberate aim at one of our men." The shooting that left one man wounded and another dead revealed to Mary the dangers her brother encountered not only from the enemy but also within his own ranks.[43]

Constant reports from home and battlefront along with the increased occupation of southern communities inspired many young women to demonstrate their loyalism openly in the face of the enemy. Such defiance of Union troops was nothing new on the home front. Women of the older generation often refused to concede to the enemy in very public ways. For example, after New Orleans fell to Union troops in April 1862, women, believing their gender exempted them from punishment, openly defied the authority of their occupiers. In their daily interaction with troops they insulted soldiers, refused to sit in the presence of officers, and avoided walking under the U.S. flag. Some women even went so far as to spit on soldiers in the streets or dump the contents of chamber pots on them. After several such incidents Union major general Benjamin Butler, the commanding officer overseeing the occupation of New Orleans, passed General Order No. 28. Any woman caught insulting Union soldiers would be categorized as a "woman of the town" and treated as such. To be branded a prostitute threatened the public reputation of women from the middling and elite classes and thus was enough to quell their behavior. While the example of New Orleans demonstrates older women's willingness to lash out at the occupiers, most women were aware of the potential dangers that such actions entailed. Gender did offer a modicum of protection for all southern women, as most Union men remained within the boundaries of middle-class respectability when interacting with women. Moreover, they held cultural perceptions of southern women as docile and demure creatures.[44]

However, southern daughters discovered that, in addition to gender ideals, their youth and claims of naivite afforded them a greater degree of freedom in their resistance. Thus, they became more blatant and assertive in their criticisms of Union troops and in defense of the Confederacy. By invoking conventional notions of female behavior and claiming inexperience as adolescents, young women avoided forced oaths of allegiance to the U.S. and punishment for defiance. They recognized the leniency of Union officers and took full advantage of it, taking any opportunity to express their patriotism. Mary Conway Shields of Natchez, Mississippi, for example, played tricks on Union soldiers who visited the plantation to forage. On one occasion in 1863, when a soldier asked her how to eat a pomegranate, she told him to bite right into it, knowing the fruit would yield a bitter taste if one ate more than the seeds. Although the soldier became enraged as the seventeen-year-old began to laugh at him, he eventually left without punishing her. Shields's mother, however, had a much different experience when she refused to walk under a Union flag: a federal officer ordered her to leave the city and confiscated her house. Southern daughters perceived their loyalism within Union lines as a duty, first to their fathers and brothers off fighting the war and second to the Confederate cause. Moreover, their daily interactions with northern soldiers gave them a way to vent their frustrations over the war while remaining devoted to southern independence.[45]

Emma Cassandra Riely took full advantage of the freedom her age allowed her. Born in 1847 in Winchester, Virginia, Riely had just entered adolescence when the war began. After Union troops occupied Winchester, Riely's parents sent her to live with relatives in nearby Luray. The youth soon tired of life away from home and decided to go back. Because she would be passing through Union lines, she viewed the trip as a way to help the Confederacy. Confederate soldiers gave her letters to carry to Winchester, which she hid in her shoes. As she approached the town, Union soldiers stopped her and demanded that she take an oath of allegiance. Riely refused and asked to speak with the general who issued the orders. That officer immediately noted her age and exempted her from the order, stating that it applied only to those over twenty-one. Riely then brought the letters into Winchester undetected. Riely also used her ability to move unhindered about Winchester to help Confederate prisoners of war in the local federal hospital and at the same time secretly defy the occupiers. On several occasions, she stole food and brandy from two Union soldiers quartered in her home and smuggled the goods to Confederate soldiers in the hospital.[46]

A popular way to defy Union authority was through young women's fashion. In New Orleans, where Union commanders cracked down hard on manifestations of southern nationalism, women risked punishment for wearing Confederate emblems. After General Butler's order, many women refrained from public displays of patriotism or tempered their activities. Yet teenage girls in the cities continued to flaunt their Confederate sentiments by using their dress. For example, Annie Jeter and several female peers wore red and white roses in their bonnets as a show of southern defiance. In occupied Iberia Parish, Louisiana, Martha Moore and her classmates wore black crepe on their shoulders as a sign of mourning on the anniversary of the Union navy's passage of Forts Jackson and St. Phillips.[47]

Even when soldiers threatened to punish young women for their defiance, they typically relented. During the occupation of Iberia Parish, federal soldiers visited Martha Moore's school and demanded that all "secession emblems, flags or anything treasonable be handed over," Moore and her classmates hid their composition books bearing Confederate flags before the soldiers could confiscate them. One classmate, Lizzie Davis, was quite open in her refusal to relinquish the contraband. As Moore reported, Davis "sat on her desk hugging a book, as tho' it were her dearest friend, and, declaring she would not give it up . . . for it had a flag in it, and she would not resign the emblem of her country." The soldiers left without forcing her to give up the book.[48]

Cordelia Lewis Scales of Holly Springs, Mississippi, refused to keep quiet when Union officers commandeered her home in December of 1863. One evening an officer's wife asked Scales to play something on the piano. She complied, but only after warning the woman that she played only "rebel songs." The next day, Captain Flynn of the 90th Illinois visited Scales. Hearing of her talent on the piano, he asked her to play "My Maryland." At first she refused, but when her father reminded her that Flynn had provided food for the family, Scales relented. After she finished playing, she wrote out the words of the song at the officer's request, but also took the opportunity to send him a message: she drew a Confederate flag above the lyrics and wrote "no northern hand shall rule this land." Although most soldiers she met viewed Scales as harmless, some did not. One officer warned her that her rebel defiance might provoke the federals to shoot her. Scales replied that she "did not expect anything better from Yankees, but he must remember that two could play at that game." Before the matter went any further, however, Confederate major general Earl Van Dorn and his troops drove the Union army from Holly Springs.[49]

Social activities provided a means of political expression in the midst of Union occupation. Many Union officers and their wives hosted social events while stationed in a town, often extending invitations to the younger female citizens. Officers who boarded in citizens' homes also expected to visit with the young women there. Some young women enjoyed the attention of Union soldiers, attended their social events, and welcomed their courtship. Many others, however, used such occasions to assert their Confederate patriotism and rebuff the enemy. Ellen Renshaw House recorded her disgust with her female peers who willingly attended Union officers' parties and dances, while Myra Inman turned away Yankees seeking to court her. Inman wrote that a lieutenant stopped by to visit but she refused to see him because "he is a yank."[50]

Fig. 5. Officers and ladies on the porch of a garrison house. Fort Monroe, Virginia. Library of Congress, Prints and Photographs Division [LC-DIG-cwpb-03816]

Union occupation also brought with it romantic temptations. The increase in the number of eligible young men seemed attractive, given the fluctuations of the southern male population. But however willing local belles were to socialize with the invaders on occasion, the peer pressure to maintain their patriotic allegiance kept them from going any further. To engage in a romantic relationship with the enemy would symbolize a disrespect of the cause. Thus, their notion of patriotic duty also included sacrificing potential relationships with the opposite sex. This was no easy task for some. Emma Riely contemplated an evening out with a Union officer but was unwilling to risk being marked as unpatriotic by other young women. "[I]t was oftentimes hard to resist," she recalled, "and required all the loyalty I could bring to bear to do so." One evening a Union colonel asked her to go on a sleigh ride, suggesting she wear a veil if she wanted to go unrecognized. Riely responded that her "conscience would be behind that veil" and turned the colonel down. The decision was difficult for her, however: "what a severe test it was to my loyalty and devotion to my country to be able to resist my enemies when I might have enjoyed so many privileges dear to a young girl's heart." Although Riely's recollection of her sacrifice was exaggerated in her attempts to construct a positive image of teenage girls in the Confederacy, the story still reveals the internal struggle she faced when opportunities for courtship arose. Kate Foster also experienced some difficulty resisting the company of Union officers stationed around her home near Natchez, Mississippi. With few potential suitors in Natchez, many of Foster's friends socialized with the Union soldiers. Foster disliked the idea of mingling with men she regarded as "our enemy." Yet she made a point to learn the names of the lieutenants and described them as "gentlemen" in her diary. She admitted that she welcomed the attention from the officers but refused to pursue a serious courtship out of respect for the "relatives, friends or lovers in our army." Foster worried that if her friends and family in the military knew that Union soldiers courted the women in her community "it might weaken a strong arm in time of battle and sicken a stout and loving heart."[51]

Mingling with soldiers from the same socioeconomic class often created conflicted feelings about the enemy. Living in Richmond after its occupation by Union troops in May of 1865, Maria Smith Peek expressed disgust at the idea of living in "Yankeetown." Yet, she felt a sense of comfort with the officers boarding at her home who, in her view, displayed the mannerisms of gentility. Seemingly surprised by their refinement, Maria admitted that she feared "they will succeed by their leniency and kindness in winning over the Southern people and healing their wounds." In 1862, Maria's family had lost their home in Hampton, Virginia, to a fire after federal troops occupied the community. Forced into a refugee household in Richmond, the young woman's resentment toward the enemy grew. Even with the occupation of Richmond and the subsequent end to the war, she hoped "to fan and keep alive the spirit of revenge." One evening, however, as she stewed over the Confederacy's defeat, she heard soldiers playing music that "wafted on the summer breeze" and realized an internal struggle taking place inside her as the music "was almost melting my soul into forgiveness." As her interaction with her boarders continued, she intimated to her beau the difficulty in reconciling her feelings toward the men she had learned for four years to both fear and despise. "As far as we have had to deal with them," she revealed, "we have found them polite and obliging guarding our premises strictly and thereby saving us much trouble." Maria, nonetheless, admitted that "no matter how polite, how courteous, how handsome they may be" it was not enough to overcome her feelings of anger toward the enemy that "have been fighting for the last four years in deadly conflict against my brothers and my friends."[52]

Young women who did engage in romantic relationships with federal soldiers faced rejection by their peers. Nannie Haskins, for example, became enraged at an acquaintance who continually discussed her engagement to a "Yankee beau." She observed that the young woman "carried on shamefully and . . . any girl that had one particle of modesty would not have talked as she did." After she left, Haskins resolved not to allow her back in her home and promised never to visit her again. When Ellen Renshaw House heard that one of her friends had become engaged to a Yankee soldier, she expressed her disappointment: "how a southern girl can marry a Yankee I cannot see." Maria Peek felt a sense of shame when she learned that her cousin Ann had married a minister from Vermont. Her concerns stemmed from the fear that her cousin's association with the Union would dishonor her aunt and uncle. Maria had reason to be concerned, as some community members had ostracized Maria's extended kin. In a letter to her beau, Maria offered reassurance of the family's faithfulness to the cause by noting that Ann's sister "is as true to the South and to her sacred memory of her precious dead as ever."[53]

The instability of slavery along with the presence of African American troops in union-occupied areas also fueled young women's devotion to the Confederate cause. Reports of individual acts of rebellion against masters signified to young women that the traditional racial order of their society was falling apart. Pauline DeCaradeuc heard stories that she regarded as proof that without slavery African Americans would abuse their former masters and mistresses:

> The ladies whom circumstances unhappily compelled to take the oath of allegiance to Lincoln, had to sign it before a Negro man, one lady's hand trembled whilst she was writing, and the impudent demon—perhaps fresh from a cotton plantation,—had the audacity to take her hand and hold it down, while talking most insolently and abominably the while.

Attending church in 1863, Kate Foster angrily witnessed a former slave attempting to take a seat among the white members of the congregation. She blamed his boldness on the influence of Union soldiers: "I should not be surprised if some one of our enemies had sent him the church as an insult to us." Foster, however, could not escape the weakening of control of slaves in her home, and grew to resent them. "Ned and May are still with us but they do no work," she wrote, "Ned goes to town every day after something connected with the Devil no doubt. Matilda left last night. We think all will go whensoever it pleases their majesties." Other slaves who had found refuge in the Union camps attempted to return to their former plantations to claim other family members. Slaves living near the Hankins home in Virginia had seized the opportunity to run away as Union troops moved into the community. Several of the Hankins' own slaves were among those living as refugees. Some had returned to the plantation hoping to collect other slaves who had stayed behind. However, the Hankins family sought protection from federal soldiers, hoping that their presence would scare the slaves away.[54]

Sixteen-year-old Alice Williamson also expressed disgust with the newly freed slaves in her hometown. After Union troops occupied Gallatin, Tennessee, in 1864, northern humanitarians established a school there for freed men and women. As the daughter of a slaveholding family, Williams had absorbed the paternalistic lessons her parents taught her about slavery. But, after the Yankees came, Williamson renounced her familial approach to race relations. When a regiment of East Tennessee Unionist soldiers garrisoning the post clashed violently with local African Americans, Williamson lauded their treatment of the freed people, remarking that "the soldiers are behaving very well I do not suppose the negroes think so." Williamson also saw the presence of freedmen schools in the community as appalling, and her disdain for blacks in freedom festered. When a federal officer brought the head of the freedmen school to Williamson's classroom, the young woman found the notion repellent, and with sarcasm confided in her diary "what a learned city—or rather yankee nest—this will be. I suppose some of us citizens will get a situation as assistant teacher in the 'Freedmen's University.'" The educator returned to Williamson's school seeking supplies for his own classroom and encountered a hostile room of young women. He took all the benches in the classroom but one, noting that it was too dirty for his pupils to sit on. Williamson and her classmates reacted by indignantly hurling the bench outside in protest. The implication that freedmen and women deserved the same opportunities to learn as whites seemed to turn Williamson's world upside down.[55]

The presence of black soldiers in their communities also signified to young women a disruption of the traditional social order. Some feared that seeing African American troops armed and in uniform would entice their slaves to revolt. Susan Bradford grew uneasy when a black unit marched through her community, believing that seeing armed African Americans would provoke her slaves to leave, or even attack her family. Judith Ann Robertson recalled that the presence of black soldiers during a Union raid on her community frightened her so much that she hid her valuables and refused to leave her home when they asked to search it. Cloe Tyler Whittle felt resentment, which she directed toward the Union government, over seeing African American soldiers in her hometown of Norfolk, Virginia. "Yankees in their insolence and wickedness," she wrote, "have armed the negroes. A regiment of them have come to pollute Norfolk with their detested presence."[56]

The same notions of gender that eroded older women's support for the war sustained their daughters' patriotism even as the war came to an end. Using traditional ideals of masculinity, young women criticized political and military leaders for the South's surrender. While they were happy to see their fathers and brothers return from the battlefront and begin rebuilding their family circle, they separated this from the loss of

Fig. 6. Company E, 4th U.S. Colored Infantry at Fort Lincoln. Library of Congress, Prints and Photographs Division [LC-DIG-cwpb-04294]

Confederate independence. To most young women, the blame rested squarely on the shoulders of the leaders; southern men were merely following orders. Thus, southern daughters welcomed back their male kin while criticizing Confederate officials and the army as a whole. They envisioned the Confederacy as metaphorical family and its leaders as the patriarchs. When the South surrendered, young women accused southern leaders of shirking their masculine duty and handing them over to what many regarded as "northern despotism." This critique of Confederate patriarchs did not lead, however, to a fundamental shift in their view of gender convention. Their desire for cultural continuity did much to sustain their belief in the division of power between the sexes. Even as they questioned the decision to surrender, they avoided any evaluation of patriarchal power. Rather by envisioning Confederate leaders as the father figures of the South, they validated the traditional gender hierarchy.

Anna Green used traditional notions of gender to criticize Georgia's political leaders. As Sherman's troops neared the state capital in November 1864, she attended a meeting of the legislature both to show support for the Confederacy and to see how the legislators would respond to the crisis. The scene she encountered was "truly ridiculous," she wrote. Instead of a "display of cool, wise, legislation and undaunted courage and exalted patriotism," she saw weakness and cowardice. Rather than stand and fight, the legislators voted to evacuate Milledgeville if Sherman came near, thus, in Green's view, abandoning their masculine duty to protect the community. "[T]hey could not stand for the defense of their own capital," she wrote in disgust.[57]

When news of Appomattox made its way through the South, young women continued their gendered criticism of southern leaders. Elizabeth Collier, for example, declared that the masculine honor of Confederate soldiers was tarnished by surrender. "You are a disgraced and ruined people," she proclaimed in her diary, "and yet men of the South you are content—content to be slaves—content to be ruled by the vile in blood . . . shame on you forever—Think of the great heart of Jefferson Davis as it breaks hour by hour. Janet Weaver of Warrenton, Virginia, also thought that the South's decision to surrender betrayed the sacrifices soldiers had made. "The thought is sickening," she wrote, "that after all the hardships, and suffering our noble men have endured, and the many precious lives, that have [been] sacrificed . . . that at last we should have to submit."[58]

Some young women, such as Pauline DeCaradeuc, had a harder time separating the decisions of Confederate leaders from the actions of individual soldiers. DeCaradeuc also expected southern leaders to remain faithful to the Confederate cause and found a glimmer of hope in Jefferson Davis. When she heard of Davis's plan to regroup and continue the war in Texas, she insisted that all soldiers had a responsibility to follow him: "every man is a traitor and coward who doesn't go with him and fight to the death to keep us from this disgraceful union." DeCaradeuc, who spent many of her days involved in social activities, also refused to attend a picnic marking the end of the war, saying "I . . . never thought of going, now, that the country for which I have worked, suffered, and prayed for . . . has met with the greatest of all trials." DeCaradeuc underscored her protest when she rejected the invitation of some returned Confederate soldiers to attend the picnic. She believed that the soldiers had shirked their masculine duty to protect the nation by not "rallying on the trans Mississippi," and was appalled at their intention to "dance and be merry over the death of their country, shame! shame!" Rather than decline their invitation through a message, however, DeCaradeuc used a symbolic gesture to protest their actions. When the soldiers sent a buggy to carry her to the picnic, DeCaradeuc sent it back empty.[59]

Southern daughters stood to lose everything in the event of the Confederacy's defeat. The expectations of southern womanhood inculcated to them by educators, clergy, and parents seemed at stake as the South engaged in a war to preserve slavery. The war also threatened the safety and security of their family especially as male kin enlisted to fight in the Confederate army. The only way to ensure the survival of their family and the future that they had come accept was to throw all their support behind the Confederacy. Such demonstrations of loyalty allowed them to create their own political culture on the home front using the characteristic activities of their youth. Although some of their patriotic expressions mirrored that of the older female generations—joining in war work, volunteering in hospitals, and defying the enemy in occupied regions—they placed the stamp of youth on their actions. They expanded the meaning of female self-sacrifice to include not only male kin but also potential suitors. They transformed traditional pastimes for female adolescence into acts of patriotism for the Confederate cause. Their public performances, social activities, and dress now allowed them to voice their support. In doing so, southern daughters believed that they were providing the necessary support to sustain the Confederacy through the war and into victory. Their allegiance made it difficult to concede to the enemy when defeat seemed inevitable. While the war transformed young women's community activities into acts of loyalty, it also changed the nature of their work in the home. They viewed their contributions to the household economy either through their labor or through paid work as necessary to sustain the family throughout the war.

3

The Self-Sufficient Daughter

ON THE EVE OF THE CIVIL WAR, Isabella ("Belle") and Anna Mason Smith had little notion that the impending conflict would turn their once comfortable world upside down. The two young women were the daughters of the well-known planter William Mason Smith and his wife Eliza Middleton Huger Smith of South Carolina. Belle, born in 1847, and Anna who came along two years later, were the older daughters of the Smith's six children. As members of a wealthy slaveholding family, the young women enjoyed all the luxuries bestowed upon children of the elite social class, including a formal education, fashionable clothes, and numerous invitations to social engagements. Their father's death in 1851 had disrupted their family circle and left their mother a widow with six children. The Smith sisters, however, were too young to remember the event and spent the remainder of their childhood surrounded by their mother, siblings, and extended kin. Yet the young women would soon exchange the carefree days of winters at "Smithfield," the family's plantation in the Beaufort District, and summers at the family home in Charleston, for a life of uncertainty, fear, and isolation. Federal occupation of Port Royal in November of 1861 forced the family to abandon their South Carolina domiciles for a refugee home in Greenville. At first, the move hardly disrupted the lives of the two young daughters. Despite bouts of home sickness, they mostly enjoyed visits with family and were invited to a number of social engagements in the community. Their lives soon took a dramatic turn in June of 1864 when news that William, their oldest brother, had been wounded during the Battle of Cold Harbor reached the refugee household. Eliza Smith left to nurse William, leaving her two teenage daughters to assume the responsibilities of the home and family. Gradually, they learned to manage domestic affairs, taking care of the household finances and caring for the younger children. Both Anna and Belle experienced some resistance from their mother, who was unable or unwilling to recognize her daughters' ability to handle adult responsibilities. Nevertheless, despite her opposition, Eliza had little choice but to entrust the young women with caring for the home in her absence. The daughters likewise were left no alternatives but to do their part in sustaining the family through the remainder of the war.[1]

The transition of the Smith sisters from dependent daughters to autonomous managers of the home and family exemplified the transition of the generation of women coming of age in the Confederacy. Before the war, age and class allowed young women of the middling and elite slaveholding classes to avoid wage-earning work and the household responsibilities reserved for older kin and slaves. But the war transformed their roles within the home, and economic necessity propelled them into the southern workforce. They acquiesced, sometimes reluctantly, to their new responsibilities out of a sense of duty. As their fathers and brothers sacrificed on the battlefront, and their mothers struggled to manage the household in their absence, southern daughters came to accept that they too must make sacrifices. They believed that their contributions to the household economy in the form of labor would help the family survive the war intact and preserve the security of their home. The sense of self reliance that came from their work in and, sometimes, out of the home did lead to tensions in households on occasion, as parental authority seemed distant or removed from the home. The demise of slavery, moreover, disrupted their dependence upon household servants and brought them to question the loyalty and necessity of slavery. Young women's sense of autonomy gained through the reorientation of familial roles in Confederate households, however, failed to produce any fundamental change in their perceptions of patriarchal power. Contrarily, they took on new responsibilities in an effort to preserve their racial and class privilege, believing that when the war ended they would return to their prewar roles and relationships in the home. The irony of young women's situation was evident by the end of the Civil War. Southern daughters had gained a sense of autonomy from patriarchal dependency through their efforts to sustain the domestic economy.

The absence of fathers and brothers in slaveholding families forced a redistribution of power and labor in the household. Mothers both on the plantations and in the cities found themselves thrust into traditionally masculine duties of managing the family business. In the rural South, women had the option of leaving such tasks to a male overseer or experienced slave; others, however, proved capable of managing the cycle of planting and harvesting, sending crops to be warehoused and marketed, and instructing their slave labor force. With much of the Civil War fought in their communities, southern women also assumed the role of protector of the home and family in the face of Union occupation. Some attempted to defend against the confiscation of food and supplies while others sought shelter as refugees with friends and family. As the Confederacy endured rampant inflation and shortages of supplies, they also turned to paid labor to sustain the household economy. With their men away from the home, therefore, women learned to live without the reciprocal relationship between husbands and wives. Material hardships and relocation, moreover, forced slaveholding families into a state of self-sufficiency and weakened the patriarchal grip on dependents. Daughters, who witnessed this transformation in the power relations between parents, believed that they too must assume roles outside those traditionally prescribed to women of their age and class.[2]

Separation of family members played a factor in young women's wartime autonomy. The war took many fathers and brothers away from home and to army or government service. Sallie Walker's father, for example, was colonel of the 2nd Tennessee Infantry and was away from home for long stretches. Sallie Independence Foster watched her father and uncle leave home after Union officials arrested them for aiding the Confederate army. Mothers also left the family for extended periods during the war. Some traveled to hospitals to serve as nurses while others went to care for sick or wounded relatives. Moreover, for at least the first year of the war, women of the upper and middle class continued the tradition of extended visits to faraway friends and relatives. Isabella Middleton Smith's mother, for example, lived away from her family for a time to nurse her oldest son in a Confederate hospital, but she also spent time traveling to visit relatives. Sarah Wadley experienced periods during which both of her parents were absent from the home. Her father took a position with the Confederate government as superintendent of railroads, which often required him to spend as much as a month away from his family. Sarah's mother also continued her prewar ritual of extended visits to relatives.[3]

Those in single-parent homes experienced a different shift in the distribution of roles. Some young women were already familiar with the loss of a parent long before the war commenced, and while many fathers and mothers remarried, some continued to run the home without a partner. When the war began, daughters of single-parent homes remaining in the household often relied on the assistance of slaves or older siblings. Sallie Walker, for example, whose mother had died before the war, stayed at home with only her brothers, sisters, and several slaves while her father served in the Confederate army. Lucy Blackwell Malone, of Franklin County, Alabama, lived with her father and siblings after her mother passed away in 1857. When the war commenced, Lucy's father feared leaving his daughter alone during his trips away to tend to the family plantation and sent her to the Salem Academy in North Carolina.[4]

Out of concern for their daughters, many parents sent their daughters to live at a boarding school to shield them from the dangers of war. Schools in the South remained open in those years and, in some cases, even saw an increase in enrollment. Parents thought schools provided a safe haven for daughters from the dangers of war, especially in areas under Union occupation. Eliza Sivley, of Raymond, Mississippi, believed that her daughter Jane was out of harm's way at her boarding school in Marion, Alabama. After the fall of Vicksburg, Sivley worried that the journey home would place her daughter in danger and instructed Jane "to remain as long as they will take confederate money" if she were cut off from the family. Despite economic downturns on the Confederate home front, parents willingly made financial sacrifices in order to keep their daughters at school and out of harm's way. Ellen Cooper of Conway County, South Carolina, recalled that after she and her sister, Adie, finished the tenth grade they wanted to attend the Spartanburg Female College, but the family could not afford it. Her father decided to borrow the money from Cooper's older sister and brother-in-law, and the daughters agreed to pay it back after graduation. Jane Sivley also relied on outside sources for money for school. In 1864, her family experienced financial hardships that threatened to keep Sivley from attending school. In desperation, Sivley's mother turned to her eldest brother for tuition fees and asked the headmaster to provide for her daughter's living expenses.[5]

Teenage daughters also faced the possibility of living as refugees away from the familiarity and comfort of home. News of approaching Union troops prompted many families to uproot their families and relocate to other locales in the South and away from military engagements. Those from middling and elite slaveholding families often had the financial means to travel and reestablish their residency with relatives. Some daughters made the trip to stay with friends or relatives alone. Louisa Sheppard had to leave her family behind when military engagements threatened her home in Missouri. Anxious about her safety, Sheppard's parents sent her to live with relatives in Mississippi until they thought it was safe for her to return. Anna Cagdell Howell of Nashville faced living without her parents after the governor recommended that all women and children leave the city following the surrender of Fort Donelson. Howell and her sister packed their clothes and a few valuables and went to live with relatives while their parents stayed behind. In 1865, Sue Montgomery of Columbia, South Carolina, had to leave her home and parents behind when the news came that Sherman's troops were approaching the city.[6]

Other young women experienced refugee life with their family intact. As Union invasions threatened southern communities, many families of the slaveholding class left for a safer location. The possibility that slaves would leave for Union lines also prompted many slaveholders to move their families farther into the southern interior. With access to transportation and the financial means to relocate, parents packed up their families "black and white" and headed for what they saw as safer ground. Emma Cassandra Riely, for example, recalled that when her hometown of Winchester, Virginia, was threatened, the family gathered as many clothes and valuables as possible and moved in with friends in Luray. After Union troops occupied Atlanta, Mary Rawson's family evacuated the city and reestablished their home in Iowa until the war ended. Sarah Wadley's father helped his family make the move from Monroe, Louisiana, to Georgia after hearing that Union troops were approaching.[7]

Initially, the refugee experience seemed exciting to a youthful, teenage daughter. When Sarah Wadley's family prepared to leave for their new home in Georgia, where they would reside after the war, she feared leaving her home behind. Once embarked on her journey, however, she was enchanted by the different landscape she encountered and noted various unfamiliar plants and animals in her diary. Mary Rawson of Atlanta took the opportunity to document the attractions and people she saw on her journey. Even as Rawson's parents struggled to maintain a household while

Fig. 7. Secesh women leaving Washington for Richmond. *Harper's Weekly*, January 24, 1863, volume 7, no. 317

traveling as refugees, the young woman enjoyed herself. Maria Peek found that living in Richmond, Virginia after the evacuation of their home in 1862 gave her opportunities to develop close bonds with distant relatives living nearby. After one visit with kin, she wrote, "it seems almost impossible to get away. I believe they would have me to live with them if I would do so. . . . They are certainly dear friends to me." The refugee experience also provided new opportunities for socializing with other members of their generation. While their parents labored to provide food, shelter, and transportation for the family, daughters often saw their travels as a way to make new friends and run within different social circles. Louisa McCord recalled living in a refugee household with several female peers who often spent their evenings laughing and gossiping about potential beaux. When McCord's mother decided to take the family on an extended visit to Charleston, South Carolina, to be near her sons, McCord and her sisters were excited about the prospect of seeing soldiers and attending social events in a new city. Mary Rawson's journey as a refugee required an extended boat ride during which she and the other young women aboard organized a dance. After Union officers ordered Emma Cassandra Riely's family to leave Luray, Virginia, her parents worried about where they would stay. Nevertheless, Riely, along with the other female relatives her age, viewed the opportunity to travel with excitement. "We were rather elated at the prospect of seeing all our friends," she wrote.[8]

Living apart from family members or relocating from their childhood homes created emotional stress for young women. The irregularity of mail service in the Confederacy forced daughters to endure long periods without receiving a letter from family members, leading them to speculate about the safety of their loved ones. Anna Cagdell Howell, of Forsythe County, Tennessee, went to live with an uncle after the Confederates surrendered Fort Donelson in 1862. Although Howell lived comfortably with her relatives, she confided to her diary that the idea of leaving her father and mother frightened her, especially as Union troops came within miles of their community. Sue Montgomery lived in Sumter County, South Carolina with her mother, father, and sister. By early 1865, word had reached the family that Sherman's troops would soon be approaching their community. Fearing that rumors of federal troops pillaging the countryside and taking food and supplies from Confederate homes would prove true, Sue's parents decided to send her and her younger sister away to a "secure place." Sue, however, expressed reservations about leaving her parents behind to face Sherman's men alone. Homesickness added to young women's anxieties. After some time at her boarding school in Alabama, Jane Sivley believed she could no longer be apart from her family and requested to come home. Mrs. Sivley, however, wanted her daughter to remain at school, especially after Union troops had occupied their community in Raymond, Mississippi. She perceived the influences of federal soldiers would be "very injurious to the mind and morals" of her young daughter and asked her to "do for your Mothers sake try and be contented and learn to make yourself happy in any circumstance and condition of life." Emma Cassandra Riely also grew homesick after living as a refugee and away from her childhood home. When Riely and her sister first set out to move in with family, they saw it as a great opportunity to socialize with relatives their own age. But the longer she lived in the refugee household the more she longed to return to the comforts of home. In desperation, Riely organized a traveling party, acquired a wagon, and returned to her hometown without help from her parents or older sister.[9]

Parents viewed separation from their daughters with a degree of fear as war raged in southern communities. A large concern was the conditions of their young women in the boarding schools. Mothers and fathers entrusted educators as well as family members living close by to protect their female children. But when federal troops neared a school, parents grew increasingly anxious for the safety of their offspring. As a result, some parents pulled their daughters from school. Mary Rawson, who attended Pine Hill Seminary in Atlanta, recorded that the boarders left the school as news that Sherman's men were approaching spread throughout the city. Some schools had little choice but to close and send their young charges home as the fighting made its way into their community. Sally Clayton recalled that by 1863 the enrollment in her school had dropped considerably. With too few students to keep the school open, administrators decided to allow the building to be used as a Confederate army hospital. Those parents who left their daughters at home worried constantly. Mothers away caring for family members in the hospitals or on extended visitations with kin also expressed concern and sometimes guilt for leaving their daughters behind without their guidance. They grew concerned that in having to fend for themselves, and in many cases for their younger siblings too, they forced their daughters to forgo their youth for more adult responsibilities.[10]

To ease the sadness associated with their absences, mothers and fathers urged their daughters to view their hardship as a duty to the Confederate cause. Mothers serving in the hospitals or fathers volunteering for the army couched their participation in terms of sacrifice. Such sacrifices would help ensure the safe return of male kin from the battlefield. Equally important, their service to the Confederacy would contribute to the success of southern independence and, thus, the survival of the family's status. Southern daughters believed that they too must do their part by enduring the emotional trials of separation. By 1864, Jane Sivley had spent most of the war away from home and had grown homesick. After asking if she could return home, her mother encouraged her to remain out of a sense of responsibility to the family. "When your Parents are willing to make such sacrifices for the good of their children," she wrote, "you ought to be willing to do all in your power for your own good." She reminded Jane that her brother William was making a similar sacrifice for the family's honor by serving in the Confederate Army and that she should count herself lucky that she could avoid "the miserable life your poor Brother chose."[11]

Many adolescent daughters dealt with the separation from loved ones by attempting to recreate the family structure. Those who attended school often turned to their classmates to fill the void left by absent siblings. Expressions of deep devotion and love for another female student were common in the diaries and letters of schoolgirls. While in some cases bonds between young women were substitutes for romantic relationships, many viewed their friends as sisters or part of a larger family. Lucy Blackwell Malone recognized the "spirit of home" that the students helped to create with their friendships. Jealously and rivalry between young women at school also illustrate the familial ties they attempted to create as a way to overcome their homesickness. In extreme cases of emergency, students looked to their headmaster or teachers to offer the same protection they would find from parents. If a military engagement occurred near the school, educators moved their students to a safer area. Taking on another type of parental role, teachers guarded their female students from impropriety, especially in occupied areas. The teachers of Ellen Cooper, for example, restricted her guests to family members. If she left school, she had to go about under a teacher's watchful eye.[12]

The experiences of young women at school, in the home, or as refugees challenged traditional standards of female behavior. The absence of parents from the home forced a restructuring of domestic responsibilities that weakened the patriarchal structure of the household. Even during periods in which one or both of their parents were present in the home, young women witnessed a dramatic redistribution of labor. Daughters were ill-prepared for the changes in their home life. While their education in the antebellum era emphasized the ideals of domesticity, most of the skills they learned at school focused on the ornamental subjects of music, needlework, and art. Their training in household tasks was also limited. They typically took care of minor household chores, such as cleaning their rooms and helping with preserves, while their mothers oversaw major responsibilities such as planning meals, caring for children, and cleaning. Their parents, furthermore, took primary responsibility for the slaves so that daughters learned very little about their overall care or management. Moreover, their socioeconomic status had shielded young women from paid labor. From their earliest childhood, southern daughters had come to accept the reciprocal nature of the patriarchal household that upheld women's economic dependence on the male head of the home. The war, however, altered the traditional expectations of domestic responsibilities, including the support of the household economy. As mothers took over the management of the plantation or business, they expected their young daughters to assume the household chores. A restructuring of domestic tasks also occurred as many slaves sought opportunities for freedom during the war. Moreover, as the instability of the southern economy threatened to undermine the economic security of households, southern daughters found themselves in the world of paid work.[13]

With fathers and brothers off at war, many families found it difficult to maintain a household without the help of their adolescent daughters. Some parents who sent their daughters to boarding school soon called them back home to help the family. When Cordelia Lewis Scales's brothers joined the army, her parents were emotionally devastated and the young woman decided to leave school. "Duty prompts me to stay at home and do all in my power to cheer my parents," she wrote; "I have never seen two people break as fast as they have done since the boys left home." Although her parents insisted that she return to school, Scales believed that her proper place was at home and that, in any event, "with anxiety for my brothers and parents . . . there would not be very much studying done." Judith Robertson's mother refused to let her daughter return to school after her older brother enlisted in the army. Her father had died when she was thirteen and the family relied on the eldest son to support the family. After her brother left, her mother's health declined and Judith felt obliged to stay home to care for her as well as manage the household.[14]

Young women demonstrated an ability to adapt to their new domestic roles despite their lack of household training. After her father, a widower, became colonel of the 2nd Tennessee, Sallie Walker was left at home with only her sister, brother, and a number of house and field slaves. In adjusting to the absence of their father, the children redistributed duties within the home but without disrupting traditional gender roles. Her older sister, Maria, ran the household while Sallie helped with daily chores in the home and her brother oversaw financial matters and plantation business. The Walkers, however, once again reassigned household duties when their brother turned seventeen and enlisted in the Confederate army. The restructuring of domestic duties also placed some in the role of caretaker to younger siblings. At the age of eighteen, Louise Wigfall took care of her sister during her parents' absence from the home. While she was in charge of her sister's welfare, news of Sherman's army approaching Macon, Georgia, sent a wave of fear throughout the town. Gathering a few personal items, the young woman left with her young charge and sought temporary refuge with strangers.[15]

Fig. 8. Contrabands coming into camp. *Harper's Weekly*, January 31, 1863. Library of Congress, Prints and Photographs Division [LC-USZ62–88812]

Southern households experienced another transition as the war began to break apart the system of slavery. The war disrupted the normal routines of the plantation and, in some cases, took away the master, creating a void in the power structure. Slaves saw such situations as the ideal time to run away. Others saw the presence of Union troops as a means to leave the plantation and sought work in the camps. Throughout the course of the war, southern slaveholding daughters witnessed this migration of their former servants. Lucy Blackwell Malone, for example, watched more than one hundred slaves on her father's plantation leave with Union soldiers who passed through her neighborhood. Sarah Wadley found that the longer Yankee soldiers remained in her community of Monroe, Louisiana, the more slaves attempted to escape.[16]

Many young women stood in disbelief that so many of the slaves whom they saw as trusted and loyal would choose freedom over remaining with the family. They prescribed to the notion that the clothing, shelter, food, and medical care provided to their slaves and the genuine sense of familial bond on their part was enough to keep them on the plantation. But, when the numbers of runaway slaves grew, slaveholding daughters, along with many of white society, explained their slaves' leaving as a demonstration of disloyalty stemming from racial character flaws rather than a repudiation of the slave system itself. Most rationales emphasized the inability of slaves to resist the temptations of Union soldiers. Sarah Wadley explained away her household slaves' departure by blaming what she saw as the naiveté of slaves and the persistence of Union soldiers in offering "the false idea of freedom." Amanda Worthington articulated a similar argument when she attributed the loss of slaves to the Union presence in her town. In her view, federal troops "demoralized" her family's slaves by tempting them to leave the plantation. Sally Independence Foster pointed to an inherent weakness in her slaves who became victims of coercion rather than willing seekers of freedom. She also blamed the immorality of Union soldiers whom she believed resorted to "taking" or "stealing" the slaves from her home. When Union soldiers failed as an excuse for the loss of slaves, Foster turned to other rationales. When one of her family's slaves left to "go fishing" and was still gone after several days, she dismissed reports that he had run off and instead assured herself that he had drowned. Louisiana Hankins wrote her daughter Virginia that during her absence, occupying troops had forced three of their field slaves to leave with them. She described the incident as a terrible scene during which she "never saw a servant so disturbed in my life." Such details of Union soldiers taking the slaves instilled in Virginia the belief that her slaves had gone against their will.[17]

The flight of their household servants and field slaves stunned young women. Young Bettie Alexander could scarcely believe that her slaves ran away when Union troops occupied her community. Her shock and sense of betrayal turned to anger when she learned that one of her favorite household slaves was among those who escaped. She saw the fugitives as traitors, insisting that "the country is very well rid of some of them." Sarah Wadley was likewise surprised that many of her family's slaves left when Union soldiers occupied Monroe. After hearing rumors of poor conditions in the contraband camp, she told herself smugly that the blacks would soon see that they were better off as slaves. "The negroes say that they have to eat in the ditch," she wrote, "when they are sick the Yankees . . . do not give them any medicine . . . they have a guard over every twenty four negroes." Alice Ready's shock quickly turned to dismay as the loss of her household slaves brought her to feel "as if the family was broken up."[18]

Young women viewed slaves who remained on the plantation as faithful members of the family. Emma Florence LeConte lauded the behavior of the slave Henry as Union troops in Columbia brought the opportunity for freedom. She recorded that although Henry's wife and children were preparing to leave with Union soldiers, he assured the family that he would remain unless the soldiers threatened his life. Pauline DeCaradeuc praised the loyalty of her house slaves as Union soldiers looted her home. One slave, Solomon, chose to face a soldier's gun rather than disclose the whereabouts of the DeCaradeuc gold and silver. "Solomon is as true to us as steel," she wrote gratefully, "so are they all, all faithful and friends to us." Elizabeth Waties Allston believed that her slaves chose to remain on the plantation because they shared her distaste for the North:

> You want to know what the negroes think of the war. I think the generality of negroes in the neighborhood are nearly scared to death they think now that the North are trying to take them and sell them. Some of ours say they would rather stay with the master they have as to be taken to some other man they did not know anything about.[19]

The slaves' decision to remain often had little to do with loyalty, however. In the case of the Inman family slaves, their uncertainty of life beyond the plantation was a consideration in their decision to stay. The Inman household consisted of nine slaves during the war, including two elderly servants, Ned and Phoebe. The couple had come to the Inman household through Anna's inheritance of property from a relative. Ned and Phoebe were married before arriving to the Inman household and remained together throughout the course of the war. Although the family regarded all their slaves as an extension of the immediate familial circle, they considered Ned and Phoebe among their most trusted servants. In anticipation of Union occupation, for example, the family went about concealing their valuables. Although they waited until the slaves had gone to bed, unwilling to disclose their hiding place, they recruited Ned and

Phoebe to help believing that that they would prove trustworthy under scrutiny from federal soldiers.[20]

Ned and Phoebe remained with the Inman family during the conflict. The Inman daughters viewed their decision to stay rather than flee to the occupying Union troops as a testament to their familial loyalty. However, Ned and Phoebe more than likely considered their age in making the choice of whether to stay or go. Ned was in his sixties at the outset of the war, and Phoebe, over fifty, was in bad health throughout the conflict. In 1864 Phoebe died and Ned soon fell ill. The couple's decision to stay with the family also stemmed from their fears of federal troops and eventual experiences with occupying soldiers. Historian Jacqueline Glass Campbell, in her study of Sherman's march through the Carolina's, illustrates the complex reactions of slaves to Union soldiers. Slaves often found themselves the target of federal soldiers pillaging the countryside for supplies. This interaction with soldiers led to feelings of uncertainty and distrust toward those whom they had regarded as their liberators and, in some cases, compelled slaves to remain with their mistress. As General Ulysses S. Grant's forces swept through East Tennessee following the battles for Chattanooga in late November 1863, Union troops moved into Cleveland, setting up camp near the Inman home. In search of food and provisions, federal soldiers visited the homes of both citizens and slaves, taking what they could. One evening, soldiers encamped nearby entered Ned's home and took food and supplies, including Phoebe's quilt from her bed. Such experiences would have seemed frightening to the elderly couple, who had limited interaction with Union soldiers up to the occupation of Cleveland.[21]

Acts of kindness performed by slaves reinforced young women's belief in slave loyalty. Some slaves showed compassion toward their mistresses as food became scarce and as Union invasion threatened to dislocate families. When the sacking of Columbia left Emma LeConte and her family with barely enough provisions to survive, their slaves willingly gave food. "The negroes are very kind and faithful," LeConte wrote, "they have supplied us with meat and Jane brought Mother some rice and crushed sugar for Carrie. . . . How times change! Those whom we have so long fed and cared for now help us." Isabella Richardson's family likewise ran short of food after soldiers destroyed their crops, and thus they turned to their slaves for help. Anna Green noted her slaves' loyalty not only to her family but to the Confederate cause as well. When one slave gave her own shoes to a Confederate soldier, Green proclaimed with satisfaction that "if the Yankees knew of . . . one of our negroes doing that act of kindness to a soldier and because he was a Confederate soldier they might feel a little less kindly to our servants than they pretend."[22]

As the war progressed, some young women questioned the desirability of slavery. While their mothers and fathers continued to rely on the labor of slaves, young women saw their presence as the source of their family's anxieties. Alice Ready noted her father's worries about keeping his slaves away from Union troops. Seeing her home broken up and her family subjected to hardships, she came to see slavery as the cause. "I should be very willing to do without the slaves," she declared in her diary, "I am not willing to have them taken from me, but would gladly see them all free, if this war ended with it." Lucy Breckinridge also saw slavery as a "troublesome institution" and secretly wished that "for the sake of the masters . . . it could be abolished in Virginia." Kate Foster believed that without the responsibilities of maintaining slaves, southerners could concentrate more on the war. "Let the foe take all our negroes," she argued, "they are welcome to them and the sooner we are rid of them the quicker we will whip our enemy."[23]

Material deprivation and the devaluation of currency stripped some slave owners of the means to provide for slaves and forced them to let some of their slaves leave or to hire them out. As Sarah Wadley's family prepared to seek refuge in Georgia, her father gave the slaves the choice of going with her brother or with the Union soldiers. Jane Sivley's father hired out his remaining slaves to the Confederate army because he could not afford to support both them and his family. The increased economic burdens of maintaining their slaves also caused Isabella Richardson's family to contemplate sending their slaves away. When several slaves returned from working on another plantation, the family had little food to give them. To help ease the financial strains, Richardson's mother chose to lend the slaves to another plantation.[24]

Young women's domestic labor took on greater significance as southern households experienced a loss of slaves during the war. After Union troops entered Columbia, South Carolina, on February 17, 1865, the LeConte family slaves seized the opportunity to escape to freedom. To avoid over-burdening the only remaining household slave, the family redistributed the domestic duties, some of which fell to Emma, the LeConte's daughter. "[I]f Jane offers to clean up our room, all very well," she wrote, "if not, we do it ourselves." Emma Cassandra Riely recalled that after an exodus of slaves from her plantation, only one house servant remained, placing the responsibilities of dusting, washing, and cooking on Riely and her sister. Isabella Richardson's family moved their house slaves to the fields after several field hands left, forcing the young woman, her older sister, and mother to take over the housework. Louisa McCord also took on dusting and washing after several of her family slaves left for the Union lines.[25]

Young women eventually adapted to their new responsibilities in housekeeping, cooking, and caring for younger siblings after coming to terms with the unaccustomed physical demands. When Louisa McCord and her sister, for example, took over the dusting and laundry after their slaves left, they complained about blisters and made many mistakes in cleaning the bedrooms. After a period of adjustment, the young women proved adept at household chores and created a routine to make their chores seem less cumbersome. The daughter of a wealthy slaveholding family, Caroline Ravenel had grown used to depending on her mother and servants to perform the chores essential to running a household. Young Caroline lived with her mother and father, a merchant in Charleston, South Carolina, where the family resided. Throughout the war, however, Caroline's mother was frequently absent from the home, requiring the young woman to manage the household and its servants. In addition to her daily chores of overseeing meals and cleaning, Caroline provided childcare to her two younger siblings. She woke the children each morning, fed and clothed them, and listened to them recite their school lessons. In a letter to her friend Isabella Smith, who was also learning new domestic chores, Caroline admitted that the burdens of caring for the home left little happiness for a youth. "I do not suppose either of us ever feels joyous," she wrote, "indeed I do not think anyone does, unless children." Yet, Caroline boasted to her young friend that she felt capable of running the house and that caring for the children left her feeling "motherly."[26]

Anna Inman, a widow, called on her three daughters to take on additional chores as the family opened their home to boarders. Throughout the war, Anna relied on boarders for financial support. Business had been steady, but by the end of 1863, they experienced a sharp increase in boarders when federal troops overran the town of Cleveland, Tennessee, during the Union advance into the eastern portion of the state. Scrambling to accommodate the overflow of patrons, the Inman family underwent a redistribution of domestic roles. The three Inman daughters, Mary, Myra, and Rhoda, each performed specific duties that helped maintain the family business. Myra listed the order of the labor division noting that "We do our own work. Rhoda is the main cook; I am the chambermaid; Mother acts as housekeeper; whilst Sister [Mary] performs sundry duties." The young women also assisted the two household servants in the washing as well as serving the many guests in their homes. Although Myra adjusted to the change in household responsibilities, understanding their necessity in providing economic support for the family, she found that such work "fatigues us a great deal as we are not accustomed to it."[27]

Sarah Wadley struggled to maintain her new role as mistress of the household in her mother's absence. Wadley's father spent several weeks away from their Louisiana home attending to his duties with the Confederate government. Rebecca Wadley, Sarah's mother, also left her young daughter at home as she went on extended visits to relatives and friends. Sarah spent her days consumed with assisting the servant with cleaning and cooking and took charge of her five younger siblings, including an infant. The Wadley home also had a constant flow of visitors, some of whom stayed for several days. In her mother's absence, Sarah assumed the role of hostess for her guests, providing entertainment and overseeing meals. Although she adjusted to her domestic role, Sarah found the responsibilities overwhelming at times. On one occasion, their servant, who usually performed most of the daily drudgery of cleaning and cooking, fell ill and Sarah had little choice but to manage the home without assistance. The experience left Sarah questioning her own capabilities as a housekeeper. "I have not borne it very well," she confided in her diary, "have several times been very much fretted, our house is so large, and there is so much sweeping and dusting to do." Despite her misgivings, however, Sarah continued to fill in for her mother, eventually becoming at ease with household management and caretaking.[28]

Without the presence of fathers and other male kin in the home, daughters living in areas under Union occupation also took on the role of protector. Rumors of Union atrocities contributed to their apprehensions about being a household of women. Fear of molestation or rape added to their anxieties about living among their occupiers. Many young women responded to these perceived dangers by learning to use a pistol. Fathers and other male kin in many cases entrusted daughters with a pistol and taught them how to use it. Very few young women who carried a gun expressed reservations about using it to protect the home. Alarmed by rumors of soldiers threatening and robbing women, Cordelia Lewis Scales of Holly Springs, Mississippi, armed herself with a pistol while Yankee troops occupied her community. Alice Ready became apprehensive about her family's safety after Union soldiers imprisoned her father. He had left his pistol with her and had taught her to use it. Ready felt a sense of empowerment carrying the pistol, and fantasized about using it. "I could do as David Crockett," she boasted, "pile their dead bodies at the door as they attempted to enter." Ellen Cooper of Conway County, South Carolina, actually used her gun in defense of her family against a band of Union army deserters attempting to break into her home. When one deserter began shooting at the house, Cooper grabbed her gun and fired back. After engaging in a brief exchange of fire, Cooper crawled into another room and hid from the men until they left.[29]

Daughters also used other means of guarding the home from theft. With little, if any, male protection around, they helped protect their family's possessions when soldiers entered the home. Rumors of soldiers stealing gold, silver, and other valuable possessions prompted families to secure everything they could before soldiers entered their homes, and daughters helped devise ingenious methods to hide their valuables. With her father gone on government duty, Emmeline Allmand Crump's family scrambled to save their valuables from soldiers. Crump helped move their silver to a relative's home before Union troops occupied Richmond in April 1865. Her mother placed her in charge of hiding the family gold, which she tucked beneath her clothing. When officers used Louisa McCord's home as a headquarters, she hid her jewelry and clothing in a bag she could easily conceal. Myra Inman sewed pockets in her chemise to save her jewelry and other items in anticipation of Union soldiers occupying her hometown. Some young women even found themselves defending the family home from destruction. Ellen Cooper exemplified the determination of young women to save their homes from fire and looting. When Union soldiers came looking for food and valuables, Cooper realized that they intended to destroy her family's property as well. After they set fire to the turpentine still, Cooper attempted to put it out. With the help of a male slave, she threw water on the fire and moved burning barrels away from the house to keep it from spreading.[30]

Parents were sometimes reluctant to accept their daughter's newfound sense of self-reliance in domestic matters. Daughters learned to manage the home and children yet parents often refused to grant them complete independence in making decisions concerning the household and family. Mothers especially worried that their daughters were unable to shoulder the burden of caring for younger siblings and managing finances. Isabella and Anna Smith, for example, had taken over their mother's domestic duties in her absence. Although she admitted that her daughters would have to attend to their own needs, she refused to hand over complete control of certain decisions. In several letters, she set out detailed instructions on how to manage the household finances, what clothes to wear, which items to purchase for the home, and how to manage the slaves. While the two daughters welcomed the advice, they frequently wrote their mother assuring her that they were managing the home with little difficulty. After living without parental supervision for over a month, they had gained a sense of autonomy that their mother found difficult to accept.[31]

Parents were also unwilling to concede a degree of autonomy to their daughters who attended school away from home. Although under the care of school officials, many young women received detailed letters instructing them on how to care for themselves. Jane Sivley had taken care of budgeting her allowance and purchasing supplies for school. Her mother, however, continued to write letters with instructions on how to manage her money as well as what items to buy. The bulk of Jane's money she left with a family friend in Marion, Alabama to distribute as needed. When in early 1864, the friend was preparing to leave the country, Mrs. Sivley arranged for a professor at the school to take charge of Jane's money and expenses. Samuel Sanders used his letters to his daughter to exert parental control while serving in the Confederate army. During his daughter's stay at the Columbia Female College, Sanders entrusted an aunt and uncle, who taught at the institution, to act as surrogate parents to Mary Jane. Sanders asked Mary Jane to "submit cheerfully to their judgment" and request their permission to attend social engagements. Sanders continued to advise his daughter from a distance, emphasizing issues ranging from her schoolwork to social graces. In one letter, he gave Mary Jane instructions on how to care for her health. "You must not allow yourself to stoop over your books," he wrote, "or to set long in the same position without moving." He also directed her to take care of her teeth and "take plenty of exercise everyday."[32]

Older brothers also continued to assert authority in their relationship with young sisters. While Jane Sivley attended school, her brother wrote frequently offering advice on how she should attend to her studies. One of his greatest concerns was the distractions of war and Confederate soldiers who would divert Jane's attention away from her schoolwork. "I am so glad you have go off to . . . school," he advised, "There you will have no Yankees to disturb you . . . now take my advice apply yourself to your studies and not think about home and the Texas scouts you will have plenty of time to think about the boys when you complete your education." Mary Wills's oldest brother Richard also expressed concerns over her studies and encouraged her to put all her effort into learning. "Remember these opportunities will not last always and they may be taken away sooner than you think," he wrote. He advised Mary to call on traditional notions of southern femininity in her conduct, asking that "above all things be a good girl and try to do right." In a fatherly tone, Richard added that she must remember to nurture her religious conviction, to "think about and feel what you say" when delivering a prayer, as well as avoid conflict and "cultivate a sweet temper." Mary's younger brother, George, also was unable to acknowledge his sister's autonomy at school and offered guidance on how she should approach her studies. George reprimanded Mary on one occasion after learning that she had quit her music lessons. "I think it a wrong step," he wrote, "and if you will begin now and take them the balance of the session, I will pay the cost." A brother's attempts to offer guidance could lead to tensions in the sibling relationship. While Isabella Smith managed the household during her mother's absence, her brother attempted to offer direction regarding household chores, which she resented in light of her new sense of self-reliance. After several instances in which her brother instructed her on how to handle the slaves, the tension came to a head. Isabella vented her frustrations to her mother: "he presumes to advise me about keeping the servants in order, assuring me that good temper is of the greatest importance." Eventually she retaliated: after witnessing her brother scold a slave, she decided to give him the same "lecture."[33]

Financial hardships beginning in the second year of the war threatened to undermine the day-to-day functioning of southern households. The devaluing of Confederate currency made it harder for families to purchase crucial items for the household. The Union blockade kept merchants from adequately supplying their stores. Scarcity and currency devaluation led to enormous inflation despite government efforts to curtail rising costs. These economic problems affected primarily the poorer classes. Yet slaveholding families whose wealth was in land and slaves began to feel the pressure, too, particularly if their slaves ran off. Between 1860 and 1870, southern wealth declined 60 percent. Likewise, southerners reported rampant shortages of goods in the stores and inflated prices for the few available items, making it difficult to purchase even the most common household necessity. By late 1863, Pauline DeCaradeuc noted that in Charleston, South Carolina, "a *cheap* calico or homespun dress costs $100.00 now, and one bushel of corn $4.50 and $5.00, a pair of turkey $35.00 and $40.00." Pauline's financial troubles continued the following year. During a trip to Augusta, Georgia, she recorded the economic problems plaguing southerners. "All the talk is about the unfortunate currency, and thousands and one taxes," she wrote. Young DeCaradeuc, although from a once affluent family, recognized that inflation coupled with shortages of goods made it difficult for southerners to purchase foodstuffs. She observed that "Butter is $10.00 a pound in Augusta. Flour $200.00 a barrel. Currency, currency, nothing but that. $50.00 to have one tooth filled." In war torn areas of the South, rising prices compounded the economic woes of those on the home front. In early 1865, after fire ravaged the city of Columbia, South Carolina, Emma LeConte observed that the destruction of the city combined with the rising cost of food forced her family to depend on "rations from the town" to supplement their diet. In Natchez, Mississippi, Kate Foster believed that inflated prices in the stores bordered on extortion and had become "the bane of one's existence."[34]

In response to the economic situation, southern families relied more on domestic production and recruited their teenage daughters to assist in the process. Mothers took to spinning and weaving their own cloth as a means to curtail household expenses, and they passed this skill on to their daughters. Young women embraced the use of homespun not only as a form of age-appropriate political expression, as discussed in the previous chapter, but also as a means to sustain their interests in fashion during a time of material deprivation. Ellen Cooper recalled that young women had little choice but to learn "to weave, spin, and knit . . . for there was no way to get anything—it had to be made." Young women, under the direction of their mothers or older female kin, learned the process of cloth production. Sarah Wadley, for example, congratulated herself on producing cloth for the first time. Louisa Sheppard and her family likewise turned to weaving when the scarcity of clothing in her hometown made it hard to replenish her wardrobe. When Margaret Ridley's trunk of clothes was stolen, she had to rely on weaving in order to replace the items. Parents often encouraged their daughters to produce their own clothing and took pride in the self-sufficiency of the household. George Whitaker Wills, who was serving in the Confederate army, expressed his pleasure that Lucy, his sister, had taken up the charge to produce cloth for the family. In a letter to a family member, he communicated great satisfaction with his sister's efforts and asked to see a sample of her cloth when she finished.[35]

A young woman's willingness to forgo store-bought clothes and rely on her own skills in wartime was another means of contributing to the household economy. Shortages of clothing in the stores and the exorbitant prices of finished dresses and accessories made it difficult for them to purchase their clothing. However, rather than put aside their concerns for dress, teenage daughters utilized their newfound domestic abilities to stay on top of the trends. Excited about beginning school in Spartanburg, South Carolina, Ellen and Adie Cooper insisted on arriving with a new wardrobe. Prewar economic conditions would have permitted their parents to fulfill such a request; but financial downturns during the war strained the family budget, and they had little money to purchase cloth from a store. Refusing to give up their quest for new clothes, the two sisters used the weaving and sewing skills their mother had taught them to provide new dresses. The homespun garments that young women such as the Cooper sisters produced were common among many of their generation. Susan Olivia Fleming, of Baker County, Georgia, was the daughter of a well-to-do planter. Before the war, her wealth had allowed her to purchase the latest popular clothing. However, the family struggled to weather the financial hardships wrought by war, which left little extra income for store-bought luxuries. As a result, Susan resorted to making her own clothes to keep up with fashion trends. Chief among her worries was how to supply hoops for her skirts when the family had little money to purchase them. Hoopskirts were common among young women even during the war. Rather than ask her parents to buy the devices, Fleming decided to rely on her own resourcefulness, cutting and scraping oak strips to make her own. Emma Cassandra Riely found that by altering a particular dress, she could supply an outfit for any social event:

> My ingenuity was sorely taxed . . . as I had only one good dress . . . I would appear one night with a choking collar and basque, with the basque tails put inside, and a belt. Third I would make a "V" neck by ripping off the collar; fourth, out would come the sleeves and then I would repeat each style in succession.[36]

The changing economic landscape of the Confederacy also propelled women into new roles outside the home. Most women of the upper and middle class resisted working for wages in the first year of the war. Laboring beyond the confines of the domestic arena conflicted with the ideal image of the elite southern woman. Yet scarcity and inflation forced many to find jobs in order for their families to survive. Moreover, the dearth of men on the home front created a void in a number of positions in the southern workforce. Thus, a need for female employees arose during the war and southern society accommodated their entrance into paid employment. Middling and elite southern women found jobs in areas such as teaching, nursing, and clerking that seemed an extension of their domestic and maternal training and therefore appeared less challenging to traditional gender expectations.[37]

Daughters followed their mothers into the world of paid employment, but with greater ease. Because those coming of age during the war were free from marital and maternal constraints, they could more readily take jobs to help the family. In many cases government work helped supplement the family income as well as provide money for tuition. The Confederate government offered a number of positions for young women willing to work. With few men available, officials turned to women to fill positions. The *Richmond Examiner* reported that the Confederate Military Telegraph was in such demand for operators that they opened a school to train young women. Although women held a number of jobs in the Post Office, Quartermaster Department, office of the Commissary General, and elsewhere, their main source of government employment was the Treasury Department, where they signed bank notes and cut sheets of currency. Working in a government department posed little threat to their "proper" role as women of the upper and middle classes. Government officials enforced traditional female subservience, and most women found themselves in low-level clerking positions and usually under the supervision of a male with little, if any, opportunity for advancement. Young women, furthermore, received considerably lower wages than their male counterparts. The inequalities in pay and promotion grew out of the officials' attitude that women's presence in the government workforce was only temporary, as well as their belief in female inferiority. Moreover, the elevation of men to supervisory roles while women filled the ranks of service-oriented positions mirrored the patriarchal structure of the southern household.[38]

There was one attempt to increase the pay of clerks in the Confederate Treasury Department. By 1864, inflation and supply shortages created an economic crisis in Richmond. Many women employed at the Treasury depended on their wages to keep their families financially stable during the war. But the cost of living had become so high that many were living close to poverty. In January of that same year, a plea went out to the Confederate Congress asking for a pay increase for female clerks in the Department. Notions of female dependence rather than the value of female labor or gender pay equity formed the basis of their argument. Women, the author posited, depended on the financial support of men. Since the war called husbands and fathers away from the home, women needed some way to add to the family income and high prices kept them from providing even the necessities for their families. Thus, the Confederate government, the article stated, had an obligation to step in as the financial provider and pay women enough to survive the economic conditions.[39]

The majority of daughters from the South's middle and upper classes found teaching more suitable to their cultural expectations. Their entrance into the work force, however, did little to challenge the antebellum gender and class ideals that they had learned from parents and educators. They understood their labor was essential in helping the family avoid destitution and in preserving their childhood homes, and, as a result, accepted their new roles out of a sense of duty to their family, expecting to leave the workforce at the war's end. Teaching seemed a natural route for those seeking wages outside the home. It allowed them to preserve their class identity by taking positions that appeared an extension of women's maternal duties in the home.

As men left for the battlefield, school administrators faced a shortage of teachers and thus called on women to fill teaching posts. The *Richmond Daily Enquirer*, for example, ran ads continually throughout the war of private households as well as formal schools seeking female teachers. The growing demand for female teachers from the South led to a movement to restructure female education in the South. Female seminaries and institutes that had previously served as "finishing schools" became training grounds for future teachers. Wartime curricula in the schools focused more on reading, math, grammar, history, and philosophy. Since many young women of the middle and upper class continued their education during the war, they took full advantage of the changes in the curriculum. The great demand for teachers along with the continuity of female education during the war allowed southern daughters to move into teaching positions with greater ease than those of the preceding generation.[40]

With the decline of the southern economy, many families encouraged their daughters' education as preparation for teaching. Jane Sivley received letters from relatives urging her to take advantage of her schooling, as it would prove helpful in her intellectual development as well as employment opportunities. Her cousin wrote that her education was now crucial since "their future *husbands* are all in the army and will be to a great extent deprived of the great advantage of thorough education." By 1864, Jane's education took on greater significance as her family faced destitution. The cost of Confederate taxes and constant flow of soldiers in the Sivley home had depleted the family's resources, leaving them destitute. Yet, her parents were willing to continue the financial sacrifices to keep their daughter at school and prepare her "for resourcefulness." Samuel Sanders had sent his daughter to school so that she could develop her ability for "usefulness and close thinking in after life." Nevertheless, having witnessed economic hardships on the home front, Sanders also encouraged Mary Jane to pursue her education as a source of financial security. He implored his daughter to study hard and "understand every text book" in preparation for becoming a teacher, adding, "if fortune should fail, as it often does, you will be able to be independent."[41]

Young women taught in a number of informal and formal schools throughout the South. As regular schools struggled to remain open, parents increasingly relied on their older daughters to teach younger children at home or called on other young women in the neighborhood. Caroline Ravenel, for example, taught her two siblings in the morning before heading off for school. At her father's request, Susan Bradford taught her neighbor's young sons two hours each morning before attending to her own studies. Such home and community teaching served as training for many young women who later took jobs in regular schools or began schools of their own. While Louisa Sheppard was home from school, she taught her aunt's two children. After word spread throughout her neighborhood, Sheppard's class increased to more than twenty students. Jobs in established schools offered more benefits for a young teacher, including a better salary with more job security, and the income and board provided allowed young women to ease the financial burdens their families experienced during the war. When Ellen and Addie Cooper finished their education, they found jobs teaching in order to help their parents pay back the debt they had incurred for tuition. Those young women who married during the war found that teaching offered a regular salary to supplement the expenses of a new household.[42]

Although young women of the Civil War entered the teaching labor force with greater ease than their mother's generation had, they experienced problems stemming from class and gender prejudices. Especially in situations where they taught a large number of boys, young women had difficulty asserting their authority. Sarah Wadley struggled to teach her younger male relatives, who often resisted doing their lessons. On one occasion, a young scholar refused to acknowledge her as the teacher and began questioning her intelligence and teaching ability. Wadley, who had been afraid to assert any authority over the boy, now began to punish him. He eventually submitted to her and took her instructions. Louisa Sheppard likewise confronted problems teaching male students, especially those close to her age. She recalled one such student who refused to remove his hat in class and kept the students "in an uproar with his pranks." When he refused to obey Sheppard's requests to remove his hat, the young teacher reprimanded him in front of the class and noted that "it completely quelled young Joe to be laughed at instead of with."[43]

The war transformed southern households, redistributing domestic responsibilities and altering familial relationships. Absent parents from the home created new roles for daughters who were expected to take on the adult responsibilities of financial manager and caregiver. Moreover, the weakening of slavery forced them to rely less on the assistance of slaves and more on their own domestic abilities. The panic stirred by wartime inflation and supply shortages encouraged southern daughters to step into a new world of wage-earning work. These contributions to the household economy eventually brought daughters to rely less on the hierarchical relations of the slaveholding family and assert instead a sense of independence. Southern daughters however accepted these new responsibilities as a duty to help their family survive the war. Although they expected to return to their prewar roles in the home at the end of the conflict, young women soon discovered that four long years of war had taken a toll on the South's economy, and the abolition of slavery had wiped away any hope of returning to a world of dependence.

4

The Perfect Woman

IN 1862, fourteen-year-old Janet Weaver of Warrenton, Virginia, penned a description of the qualities she believed characterized the ideal woman. "A perfect woman," she wrote, "must be amiable, kind, and affectionate" and must manifest "all the love of a mother" in raising her children. "When her husband comes home from a hard days work," Weaver added, "she does not go to meet him with a troubled brow but tries to look cheerful and bright and make him feel that he is always welcome at home." An ideal wife and mother also ran her household "like clock work" and kept peace among family members. The young woman concluded her essay by observing that a model of femininity "fears God and loves to walk in his Holy ways." Weaver's composition illustrated her acceptance of antebellum gender norms, and her interaction with her male peers demonstrated the force of those ideals in shaping her feminine identity. Throughout the war, young Janet maintained correspondences with Confederate soldiers hoping that at least one among them would emerge as a potential suitor. Weaver's willingness to engage in courtship activities also garnered jealous observations from one of her correspondents who feared that the dearth of men on the home front would force her to find an "old beaux" among the "Yanks" who had visited her home. Although the war brought them into new worlds of civic and domestic responsibility, young women such as Weaver continued to view marriage and motherhood as the final stages in their maturation.[1]

From their earliest education, southern daughters viewed marriage as the realization of feminine duty. Romantic affection played an important part in ensuring the blossoming of a relationship between two young people. However, gender and class ideals did much to dictate the choices of eligible men for young women of the slaveholding society. From their parents and educators, southern daughters had absorbed the idea that they should seek a mate who could fulfill his prescribed masculine responsibilities as the patriarch of the household, including providing for the material and physical comfort of his dependents. Whether conscious that these ideals guided their choices or not, few young women of the middling and elite classes ventured outside of their socioeconomic group for suitors. Mothers and fathers, moreover, guarded their daughters' courtship activities closely to shield them from sexual impropriety or an inappropriate choice in a beau. Notions of romantic love, however, did allow young women a measure of freedom in their decisions. They were free to enjoy a period of social activity and to pursue as many courtships as they wanted before marrying. They attended parties, dances, and balls, and hosted visits from young men in their community.[2]

The Civil War, however, called into question traditional courtship practices and attitudes toward marriage for this generation of southern daughters. Despite the departure of their potential beaux for military service, most young women clung to the notion of one day marrying. The typical courtship and social activities associated with a young belle became a significant source of continuity for teenage daughters in a world disrupted by war. Conditions on the home front, however, complicated traditional romantic rituals, undermining the process of finding a mate. Yet rather than succumb to a life devoid of romantic pursuits, they adjusted their courtship practices and expectations to suit wartime conditions. They created new rituals and found opportunities for clandestine relationships that allowed them a greater degree of freedom over their choices and conduct, a development that often made parents uncomfortable. Parents attempted to regulate their daughters' behavior and choice in suitors but found that the new freedom offered to their daughters in their wartime romances often frustrated these attempts. This willingness to adjust romantic practices, along with the young age of those in the period of adolescence, placated any sense of urgency to marry that those born before 1843 experienced. Yet while the war challenged antebellum social conventions, it did not change southern daughters' worldview. They continued to uphold marriage and eventually motherhood as the crowning achievements of a southern woman. Even though economic and social conditions in the years after Appomattox caused hardships in their marriages, young women accepted a return to the domestic ideal. Such a reliance on traditional notions of southern femininity provided a sense of stability and normality for them in the aftermath of war.[3]

Engaging in the rituals of courtship, even if they had to create new ones, provided the normality they craved amid the confusion and horrors of war. Southern norms driving expectations of marriage served as a cultural link between their former world of the antebellum South and the constant shifting and changing nature of the Confederate home front. Moreover, romantic pursuits ensured the preservation of timeworn notions that marriage and motherhood were the means to fulfilling their feminine duty. The ideals of companionship marriage remained important considerations for couples in wartime. Their letters and diaries are evidence that reciprocity, mutual respect, and balance were always explored in weighing the possibility of a serious relationship. But roles were clearly demarcated along gender lines in the relationship. Women's responsibilities stemmed from domestic and familial concerns while men were providers and protectors of the home and its dependents. Elizabeth Collier identified such a separation of roles between men and women. "A man may be self sufficing," she wrote, "he may, independent of the other sex, devote himself to fame or the pursuits of intellect . . . while women learn the necessity of dependence on Him by the necessary resting of their nature on men." Janet Weaver emphasized the reciprocal nature of marital roles when conceptualizing her perfect woman. "Without a responsible partner," Weaver argued, "a woman would be hard-pressed to fulfill her role as mother and wife."[4]

Opportunities for courtship continued during the war. The stationing of Confederate soldiers in southern towns and cities increased a young woman's chances of meeting a potential suitor. The Confederate capital of Richmond offered a constant flow of young soldiers throughout the course of the war. Margaretta Ellen Wise and her peers attended several parties and dances in hopes of meeting a young soldier. At the very least, such encounters presented opportunities to exchange information and begin correspondence after the soldier was restationed. When Pauline DeCaradeuc visited family in Augusta, Georgia, she received more social invitations than while living on her parents' plantation. "I really didn't recognize Pauline DeCaradeuc in the character of a belle," she wrote, "she has been so long in quiet and retirement, that I had almost forgotten her in society." DeCaradeuc became infatuated with several soldiers who came through Aiken and Charleston, South Carolina, where she also visited kin. She promised to correspond with many young men she met. For those in areas less populated by eligible soldiers, teenage daughters often took it upon themselves to organize social events when troops passed through, however short the visit. Alice Ready realized that any opportunity to mingle with those of the opposite sex was a rarity: "I think the girls here must appreciate their visits more than almost any others, because beaux are a very scarce article." Mary Fries of Salem, North Carolina, went with a group of friends to toss bouquets at a regiment when it arrived. Some of the soldiers returned the gesture by serenading the young women one evening. Sarah Wadley and other young women in her town held events such as dances and parties for the officers and soldiers when they came through Monroe, Louisiana.[5]

Despite the dearth of soldiers at times, young women continued to adhere to class strictures concerning their choice in a potential suitor. They rarely extended or accepted social invitations to young men outside of their socioeconomic group. Sarah Lowe, who joined several of her classmates in passing out bouquets to soldiers as they arrived in Hunts-ville, Alabama, made this distinction when she observed that "some of them were very rough looking . . . others were very nice looking men"; she ignored those who she presumed did not meet the standards of her class. The temptation to meet a soldier, however, did bring some young women to ignore the parameters of their class when mingling with the opposite sex. Amanda Worthington, for example, enjoyed socializing with all the soldiers in her Mississippi town. Like many of her peers, she viewed Confederate soldiers as heroes and was awestruck by their stories of the battlefield. Although many she met were clearly not of her own social class, she confessed that "I love all Confederate soldiers." Nevertheless Worthington and others of her class group were not likely to challenge the conventions of their class seriously. Interactions with soldiers who did not demonstrate the qualities of middle class respectability, as dis-tinguished by their military ranking or familial ties, were merely novelty and produced no long-term relationships.[6]

The war often intruded on the rituals of bellehood and forced young women to refrain from social activities, at least temporarily. When a close family member died in the war, most parents expected their daughters to dress in mourning and decline social invitations. After Susan Bradford's brother died from wounds, she concluded that "it is not suitable that we should be seen in gay places" and refused offers to socialize until several months had passed. Sarah Wadley also stayed away from social events in her community after her brother died in battle. Even those who accepted social invitations expressed a sense of guilt about it. After attending a party with dancing, Virginia Hankins confessed to her diary that "I can not fully enjoy myself in such scenes now, it looks like recklessness or carelessness in respect to the sorrow and terrors around us."[7]

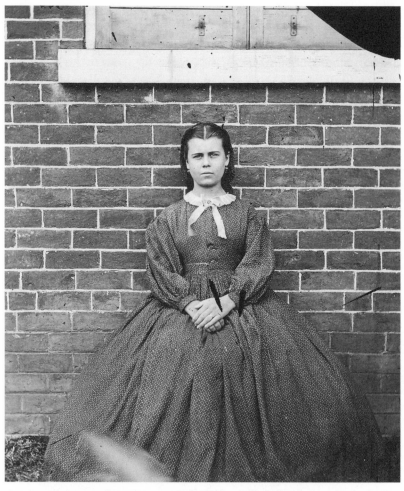

Fig. 9. Young girl at Aiken House, Aiken's Landing, Virginia. Library of Congress, Prints and Photographs Division [LC-DIG-cwpb-01916]

The scarcity of eligible men in some areas created obstacles for young women, forcing them to ponder a life without romance. Social opportunities were scarcer for young women isolated from the military presence. While attending school in Monroe County, Virginia, Bettie Alexander saw her social life diminish with the departure of young men her age. Attending a friend's wedding, she found it boring because only a few members of the family showed up. When troops eventually left a community, they created a void in the population, leaving young women to question their future as wives and mothers. Myra Inman, for example, bemoaned the absence of potential beaux after volunteers in her community left for the front, and she and several female friends thus resolved "to live by ourselves and never marry." Pauline DeCaradeuc noted that a friend of hers thought spinsterhood likely because of the absence or death of so many men. "I don't doubt it," was DeCaradeuc's comment, "neither do I care very much." The absence of suitors prompted Nannie Haskins to ask "if I will ever marry or if I will always be simple Nannie Haskins."[8]

For this generation of southern daughters, age played a large role in their decision whether to marry. Most daughters of elite and middle-class families waited until their early twenties to marry, and the war did very little to change this custom. Most young women coming of age, those who were between twelve and eighteen when the war began, saw themselves as too young to marry. Sally Independence Foster, who turned twelve when the war commenced, turned down many courtship opportunities throughout her teenage years until she married in 1870. During the course of the war, Anna Cagdell Howell confided to her diary that she also felt too young to marry: "I don't think I ever would feel old enough to be married unless I were an old maid of course." Clara Solomon saw little benefit in marrying at a younger age. After hearing of a friend's short engagement and subsequent marriage, Solomon criticized her decision: "She is foolish to get married, while a girl she was the admired of admirers—but a married belle is detestable." In the subject group, only about 26 percent married between 1861 and 1865 (appendix, table 6). This group included the older members of the age group who had reached their early twenties during the war. The largest number, close to 74 percent, married between 1866 and 1877, when most had reached their early twenties.[9]

Romantic affection, in addition to age, guided a young woman's choice to continue a relationship. This was not always the case for women who had passed through the adolescent stage of development before the war began. For older single or widowed women, their sense of urgency, aggravated by a lack of suitors during the war led them often to choose a mate hastily and forego a long courtship process that encouraged the development of romantic affection. The luxury of youth, however, allowed younger women to postpone marriage until they found a suitor who met their ideal. Elizabeth Collier, for example, wanted to find a beau who fulfilled her romantic desires: "I long more intensely if possible for human love, which it would seem that I am fated never to have." Rather than rush to the altar out of fear of never finding a mate, Collier, like many of her female peers, contemplated living without marriage altogether. "I feel that I am growing strong in self-confidence," she wrote, "that I can live without love." Cordelia Lewis Scales broke off several engagements when she found her romantic expectations unfulfilled. "I do not love nor never have loved a man well enough to marry him," she confessed, "I think I shall be an old made [*sic*]." Anna Green turned down a proposal from a man several years her senior. She believed that her suitor, a widower and father of four, was searching for "a mistress in his home." "In courting me," she told him, "the argument that shall win must be I love you."[10]

The conditions of a wartime marriage also played a factor in a young woman's willingness to postpone or prolong engagements. Although southern daughters viewed courtships with soldiers as alluring, they understood that such relations involved risks. Chief among their concerns was the potential for becoming a widow. Others disliked the idea of beginning a marriage separated from their husbands. Youth, in these cases worked to their advantage. These southern daughters felt very little urgency to marry and thus could put off marriage until after their beaux returned from battle or the war's end. Annie Jeter, for example, found that many of her peers refused to marry "for fear of being left widows." Witnessing several older women of her community rush to marry soldiers, Catherine McLaurin resolved to put off marriage until after the war: "I do not believe in the fashion of marrying and then your husband leaving right off for the wars."[11]

Close, platonic bonds between young women were common in the antebellum era, and the war often strengthened them. Young women turned to the affections of sisters and female friends in the absence of male suitors. Notions of female friendships as a means to fill an emotional void left by the absence of family were common in the antebellum era. Such was true for southern daughters living in areas with a diminished male population. Historian Drew Gilpin Faust illustrates that "young girls deprived of the distractions and excitements of heterosexual courtship and romance turned increasingly to one another for a surrogate interior life." Female friendships provided an emotional substitute that enabled them to put off marriage until the war's end. Most young women developed these close friendships with peers from school or with visiting family and friends. Pauline DeCaradeuc had a young friend join her at her home for the duration of the war. DeCaradeuc's family invited her friend, Carrie Griswold, to stay with her to help ease Pauline's anxieties and loneliness. Sally Independence Foster developed close relationships with several young family members who stayed with her for extended periods during the war. In some cases, the affections between young women had romantic undertones, but few admitted in their letters or diaries that their relationships were sexual. Lucy Breckinridge had long visits with female friends whom she felt closer to than to her suitors. She confided to her diary one evening that she had "fallen in love" with one of her friends and wondered if "there was a mistake made about me by Mother Nature. . . . I fall desperately in love with girls and do not care a straw for gentlemen."[12]

Although their aspirations for marriage seemed rooted in the past, southern daughters realized that the war had altered the rituals of courtship. In response, they created new methods of pursuing romantic relationships that fit wartime conditions. Correspondence between young men and women replaced traditional visitations between courting couples. The use of letters as a means to pursue relationships was common among women and men from both regions. Despite the geographic distance of northern soldiers from the home front, many Union men pursued relationships through correspondence. Their dependence on letters from home stemmed from their refusal to engage in relationships with women they viewed as "improper," such as prostitutes, matronly nurses, and southern women. Some Union soldiers went so far as to place ads in newspapers and periodicals in their communities seeking young women who would correspond with them. These relationships provided a source of comfort for soldiers as well as a means to finding a woman who fit within the Victorian standard of proper femininity. Similarly, southern men and women used letters to engage in wartime romances. The presence of Confederate troops on the home front allowed young women to meet potential suitors with whom they could correspond. Myra Inman, for example, found a wartime correspondent when she met a soldier as he passed with his unit through Cleveland, Tennessee. Sally Independence Foster's first courtship was through letter-writing with a young soldier, John Martin, who had passed through Florence, Alabama. Cordelia Lewis Scales bought cards to send on Valentine's Day to soldiers whom she had met and promised to write.[13]

The issue of war pervaded the contents of their letters. Worried for the safety and survival of their soldier-beau, southern daughters often expressed a deep sense of relief when they received a letter. Men on the battlefront too often wrote that constant dispatches from home were a source of comfort. But for courting couples, their letters also provided a sense of reassurance both of the safety of their romantic interest and of the security of their relationship. Robert Mitchell saw letters from his fiancée as "visits from home" that helped to ease his homesickness. "My heart was filled with sadness dark dismal and gloomy were my thoughts," he wrote, "but your letter like a sweet messenger of love dispelled all the dark and dismal thoughts." In much of their writings, young women offered encouragement to their suitors to lift their spirits. Writing from a refugee home in Richmond, Virginia, Maria Peek offered spiritual support to Daniel Marrow, her future husband, during his service in the 3rd Virginia Cavalry. As the Confederacy began to suffer defeat after defeat Maria tried to boost his confidence in the southern cause. "Our cause is just and God is with us," she wrote in June 1864, "To what other source can we attribute our success, amid so many fearful odds!"[14]

Courtship letters also provided comfort to young couples as they endured the emotional strains of war. Those who lost brothers and fathers to the battlefield often relied upon their beaux for comfort. Nettie Fondren turned to her fiancé Robert Mitchell after her brother died in battle. Her letters became therapeutic as she described to him the emotional scene when the news reached her family. Letters also became a means to vent frustrations for those living in Union-occupied areas. Virginia Hankins used her courtship letters with John Vaughn Willcox to express her anger after federal soldiers ransacked her home, taking valuables and supplies. And he responded with words of encouragement during her period of "troubles and afflictions," expressing his disappointment that he could not be with her "to alleviate them." The private nature of letters also gave men an outlet for emotions usually kept hidden from fellow soldiers. They rarely mentioned feelings of fear, as such feelings were antithetical to the heroic image they hoped to portray to their loved ones. Their letters did, however, sometimes describe dismal scenes of wounded after a battle in details that allowed the writer to disclose his fear of meeting a similar fate. Letters also permitted a young man to intimate the discomforts of camp life in private without fear of seeming weak to his fellow soldiers.[15]

The letters exchanged between George Washington Nelson Jr. while a prisoner of war and his fiancée, Mary ("Mollie") Scollay, demonstrate the importance of letters for young men and women. Nelson served in the Gettysburg Campaign after which he received a furlough. The young man took the opportunity to visit Scollay in the Union-occupied area of Middleway, whereupon he was seized by federal officers and spent the remainder of the war in various prison camps. For Nelson, his correspondence with Scollay provided a much-needed connection to the life he had left behind before the war commenced:

It is not a happy time with me at present . . . with what delight I look at the one bright place in my heart, which even in this sad time consoles me beyond all description. You, my darling, have for the last few days been more in my thoughts than ever. And thought made happier the more, I think, from the conviction of possessing your constant love.

Scollay likewise turned to Nelson for emotional support while living under federal occupation. He urged his betrothed in one letter to "tell me your sorrows, let me at least share with you the knowledge of them. . . . Grant me the privilege of comforting you with words of love."[16]

With the infrequency of visits between young women and their soldier-beaux, letters became ways for couples to explore their expectations for a future spouse. Southern daughters often tested their beaux by discussing the duties expected of men and women in marriage in their letters; and, their letters mimicked the roles within a marriage, revealing to each other an acceptance of traditional gender norms. Some young women, for example, envisioned their role in the courtship as one of a helpmate, providing comfort and support to their beaux away at war. Nettie Fondren believed it was her duty to keep her fiancé, Robert Mitchell, cheerful and his mind off the dangers around him. Throughout her letters to Mitchell, Nettie illustrated to him her willingness to assume traditional domestic tasks for women in a marriage. In his letters to Nettie, Mitchell likewise demonstrated his adherence to the ideals of masculine behavior. He expressed a belief that in serving in the Confederate army he was fulfilling his role in defending not only his political cause but also his family and future wife. "I will freely sacrifice my very life," he wrote, "to defend and protect you . . . be cheerful and bear it bravely for it is the will of God." Fondren was grateful to Mitchell for living up to his masculine duty. "You with the other noble men," she wrote, "have behaved nobly . . . and we, the weak perhaps timid ones at home thank you . . . how much for your bravery, gallantry, and heroic conduct never shall we forget."[17]

Because of their emphasis on finding a man who fit their marital ideal, young women worried about the moral fortitude of their beaux. They feared that camp life would corrupt their suitors, leading them down a path of dishonor and thus threaten their reputation in the community. In their letters, young women offered encouragement for soldiers to resist the evils of camp life, demonstrating an acceptance of the antebellum notion of female piety. Nettie Fondren, for example, discussed the possibility of immoral behavior, such as drinking and illicit sex, that faced soldiers serving on the front and encouraged her fiancé to "overcome all the temptations." In one letter, she scolded Mitchell for reading romantic novels. "It is much more interesting," she wrote, "to read of the deeds of some noble warrior, than a love sick Italian." Maria Peek urged her fiancé to shirk offers of liquor and criticized soldiers for their drinking. "I too frequently hear of the beastly and disgraceful conduct of our generals," she wrote, "I mean the worship at the shrine of that enticing god—Liquor!" She argued that unless they shirked the bottle and "devote their lives to a nobler purpose" that "God's wrath will fall yet more heavily upon this afflicted people and the innocent suffer with the guilty." She pleaded with Daniel to rely on his moral conviction in hopes of protecting his reputation. "Do these words fall upon your ear without any effect?" she asked. She hoped that he would turn to the "influence of the Holy Spirit" and "fall upon the mercy of God." In her letters, she encouraged him to recognize the Sabbath "by holy meditation and making your words and works pleasing in the sight of God." Maria beseeched him to cultivate his spirituality, arguing that all men and women have a duty of "improving our talent, of strengthening our weak faith, of cultivating our love to God; of devoting our mind and heart to the service of God in this life." Despite her continued pleas for him to avoid the temptations in his camp, Maria's anxieties continued to creep into her letters, and she reminded him of his promise that he "would try to be good" even if it required his "whole strength."[18]

Courtship letters also afforded couples greater freedom to communicate their romantic feelings. With little parental supervision over their letter writing, daughters openly professed their love to suitors. Robert Mitchell wrote frequently to Nettie Fondren expressing his love and received similar letters from her. In one letter, he described a dream in which he returned from the battlefield to greet Fondren and "exchange tears of joy at the happy meeting of two of the warmest hearts on earth." Nelson and Scollay also conveyed their romantic feelings in their letters while he was in a Union prison. Scollay described her letters to George as "a few lines of love," while he often addressed her as "my beloved" or "my love."[19]

The correspondence between Virginia Hankins and John Vaughn Willcox exemplifies the freedom of expression of many young couples in their courtship letters. Willcox was deeply infatuated with Virginia and pursued a courtship with her even after he left to serve in the Confederate Signal Corps. While serving with Jubal Early's division, Willcox wrote several letters to Hankins asking her to marry him. Virginia turned down his proposals, but Willcox, determined to marry Virginia, pursued her by sending romantic letters conveying his deep affection toward her. "Although truly unhappy and grieved that you cannot return the affection that I feel for you," he wrote in 1864, ". . . I feel not entirely without consolation being convinced as I am by your letter that though you cannot love me as I wish, I nevertheless occupy a place in your affections as a friend." Willcox, however, refused to give up the pursuit, asking, "is there no course of conduct that I may pursue, that will have a tendency to make you feel a deeper interest in me than you do now." Despite Virginia's rejections, Willcox revealed that he would continue to write in hopes that he could "persuade you to love me."[20]

John saw the source of Virginia's rejections in his reputation. In a letter after the war, Willcox admitted that the weakness in his character stemmed from his immaturity and lack of monetary success, and that those qualities had caused Virginia to turn him away. "I know that I am not what the world calls a very sturdy man," he admitted, "I know that I am imprudent sometimes." But, John argued with Virginia that if she would only love him and "exert the proper influence over me" that his "habits would entirely change." He pleaded with her to reconsider his proposal, promising that if she consented to marriage, he would "eventually become a good man . . . worthy even of you." John was also determined to demonstrate to Virginia the sincerity of his romantic affections: "Oh! Miss Jeannie [Virginia] if you can return my love, I assure you that the chief aim of my life will be to make you happy, alas!" Despite Willcox's proclamations of love and promises to become a respectable man, Virginia continued to turn him down and the couple never married.[21]

Separation caused a new set of concerns for courting couples. Young soldiers worried that their fiancées would find another suitor in their absence. Robert Mitchell, for example, believed that his sweetheart was losing interest after several weeks passed without a letter from her. He confessed his fear that the distance between them would cause her to break their engagement. Richard Mortimer Williams worried that his fiancée, Rose Anderson, was still in love with her previous suitor, who had given her a ring before he left for the army. Nelson's insecurities over his relationship with Scollay grew as opportunities for his exchange diminished. He feared that Scollay had grown impatient waiting for his exchange and found another beau. His betrothed attempted to alleviate his anxieties, writing that she had "not thought of bestowing my youth and beauty upon any other soldier."[22]

Young women sometimes did little to allay their suitors' insecurities. By making a beau jealous, a young woman could sometimes force him to make a proclamation of love that might lead to engagement. Educators and parents often discouraged daughters from engaging in coquetry. But their letters, kept private from the watchful eyes of parents, permitted young women to engage in coquetry—usually in hopes of receiving a proposal. Although Scollay offered reassurances to her fiancé that she would remain faithful during his imprisonment, which lasted from October 1863 until the end of the war, she began to show signs of impatience with his extended absence. The couple had gone over a year without seeing each other, and Scollay's uncertainties about the relationship emerged in her letters. "I don't know what might happen," she warned, "if you don't get out of prison before the Summer is over." Her concern over the status of

Fig. 10. Richmond ladies going to receive government rations. Sketched by A.R. Waud. "Don't you think that Yankee must feel like shrinking in his boots before such high-toned Southern ladies as we?" *Harper's Weekly*, June 3, 1865. Library of Congress, Prints and Photographs Division [LC-USZ62–116427]

their courtship, however, was more than likely an opportunity for her to test his resolve to marry her. Judith Ann Robertson told Eldridge Foster, her future husband, that she had many suitors when their relationship began. Her efforts to arouse his jealousy stemmed from the hope that if he thought she had many suitors, he would deem her a worthy prospect for marriage. Foster grew concerned when Judith went several weeks without writing to him, prompting him to propose marriage. Richard Mortimer Williams became jealous after his fiancée refused to give back the ring from a previous suitor. When he learned that she still spoke with the man, he declared his intention to ask her parents for permission to marry her.[23]

Parents grew increasingly concerned with the freedom their daughters had in their relationships. The frequent absence of parents from the home and the mobility of southern families weakened control over women's behavior. Many daughters traveled with groups of women rather than the traditional male escort and gained more privacy in their relationships. Younger women, however, found that despite changes in their courtship practices, their parents attempted to guide their social interaction. The concern that worried mothers and fathers the most was their daughter's conduct with Confederate soldiers. Hearing about instances of women rushing to marry soldiers, parents grew concerned that their daughters would place themselves in danger of impropriety. Those separated from their daughters worried even more about inappropriate behavior. Jane Sivley who spent the war away at the Judson Institute in Marion, Alabama, received several letters from her mother imploring her to avoid any unsuitable associations. Rumors of young women marrying soldiers only to be abandoned by their husbands, never to be seen again, exacerbated Mrs. Sivley's anxieties about her daughter's conduct. In 1864, she warned Jane that "some of the Raymond [Mississippi] girls are causing a good deal of talk . . . some of the Shurbuta [Mississippi] girls are going to have *babies*, the girls are acting disgracefully the men will soon have no respect for them." Away from her watchful eyes, Mrs. Sivley worried that her daughter would follow down the same path and urged Jane to avoid hasty courtships with a soldier. "It really looks like the girls will marry anybody these days," she wrote, "my dear daughter keep a strict watch over your affections and don't be deceived, men are very deceiving." She implored Jane to stay clear of "strange soldiers."[24]

Even as wartime demands increasingly separated parents from their daughters, they insisted that their young women follow traditional standards of female behavior with their suitors. Fear of impropriety and the loosening of social restrictions heightened parents' sensitivity to their daughters' actions. Clara Solomon's mother intercepted a letter from a soldier to Clara's sister that she believed was too familiar and sentimental by elite standards. Jane Sivley's mother grew concerned that her daughter remained too sheltered at her boarding school and advised her to "go into society as much as possible and try and improve your manners." Fearing that her daughter's unsociable habits would discourage any suitable marriage prospect, she warned Jane that "without good manners you will never show off to a good advantage" and told her to act "more dignified and graceful" at social events.[25]

Samuel Sanders chose to send his daughter to boarding school at the Columbia Female College in South Carolina to protect her during his absence. But Sanders continued to worry about the effects of Mary Jane's freedom from home and the guardianship of her parents. Sanders's chief concern was that his daughter live up to the ideal of female morality in her personal relationships. One source of concern was in the friends Mary Jane chose and he asked her to avoid "bad girls" who encouraged improper behavior. "You know how anxious I have been [that] you shall have a good, honest, and pure soul," he warned, "It will break my heart if you are not a very good girl, even the very best." When a college friend became angry with Mary Jane, Sanders advised his young daughter to take a moralistic approach and turn the other cheek. He was angered that "any one in the college should so far forget what is expected of a lady as to quarrel and fight." Sanders informed his daughter that it was "indecent for a young lady to quarrel under any circumstances."[26]

Wartime conditions, however, created ways for daughters to circumvent their parents' guardianship. The reliance on correspondence and the privacy it granted encouraged clandestine relationships. Many courting couples waited to tell their parents about their intentions to marry until they were sure to gain their approval. Such a practice was common in the antebellum era—and continued during the war. Lucy Breckinridge, of Grove Hill plantation in the Shenandoah Valley, was briefly engaged in 1862 to David Gardiner Houston, a captain in a local company, but the couple chose to keep their relationship a secret for several months. The reason for the secrecy was that Breckinridge feared her parents would disapprove of the union. At one point she was "gallantly determined to break off that engagement" because her parents "would never like it." There was cause for Breckinridge's concern. Houston, although an officer in the Confederate army, was seen as an inappropriate match for the young woman of a prominent slaveholding family. He lacked the community reputation and economic ambition required of a proper spouse. But Breckinridge had faith in his abilities and believed that once the war was over, he would be "a great man." She eventually told her mother, who advised her to keep the engagement hidden from her father until the couple was sure that they would marry. Lucy lost interest in Houston, however, and ended the engagement by the close of the year. Sometime after that, Lucy's father intercepted a letter from one of her friends discussing her relationship with Houston. In response, her father grew distrustful of his young daughter and attempted to reassert parental supervision of her relationships by opening her mail. Richard Mortimer Williams and Rose Anderson kept their relationship hidden from their families because of their conflicting loyalties. Williams served in the Union army while Anderson and her family were ardent Confederates. After their engagement, the couple continued to keep their relationship secret out of fear that Anderson's father would disapprove.[27]

Some couples engaged during the war grew impatient waiting for the conflict to end. Despite concerns about absentee husbands, death, and financial hardships, over a quarter of the young women in this study who left records of their marital status went to the altar during the war. Nettie Fondren, for example, informed her betrothed in 1862 that she could no longer wait for the war to end and wanted to marry despite his absence. Annie Jeter also chose to marry during the last year of the war. Immediately after her wedding, her husband, Emile Carmouche, returned to the front, leaving Jeter with her family until he returned. Mary Fries's uncle advised her to marry her fiancé in May 1864, arguing that no one knew when the war would end. Some young women married their fiancés following their medical discharge from the army. Alice Bailey's fiancé, Simon Boozer, lost his leg at Gettysburg. After his release from the army hospital, he married Alice, whom he had been courting through correspondence. Sarah Wadley attended a wedding of a friend who married a soldier whom she met while nursing in a hospital. At the wedding, Wadley noted that the soldier was still weak from injuries and could barely stand up at the altar to say his vows.[28]

Although some young women resolved to marry during the war, they continued to express conflicted emotions over their pending matrimony and the loss of freedom gained during courtships. Lucy Breckinridge saw marriage as fraught with hardships and misery for women. After her engagement to Houston, Breckinridge confided to her diary that she was willing to put off marriage for a time, even considering life as a "sweet old maid." Later, however, she abandoned any determination to remain single and became engaged to Thomas Jefferson Bassett in 1864. Yet she continued to question the desirability of marriage and pondered her future with skepticism. "Let people talk as much as they choose about engagements being happy," she wrote, "my late experience does not increase my faith in the idea. Engagements lead too certainly to matrimony." The source of Breckinridge's consternation came from the loss of freedom she had gained during the courtships of her teenage years, noting that "I envy girls who are free—they cannot realize the blessedness of it." Although she posited adamantly that she disliked "the idea of marriage," she admitted that she continued to uphold matrimony as the feminine ideal and would "dream of connubial bliss." Determined to resolve her fate as a soon-to-be married woman, Breckinridge came to the conclusion that her romantic affection for her betrothed was enough to overcome the burdens placed on wives:

> I do not look forward to that time with much pleasure though I do love him a great deal more than he loves me—more than any selfish, wicked man can love. . . . [I]t is woman's nature to love in a submissive, trusting way, but it is better and safer to rely altogether upon themselves—poor creatures!

Having come to the realization that her marriage would entail difficulty along with the happiness that came with a companionate marriage, Breckinridge and Bassett married in 1865.[29]

Wartime financial hardship affected many elite and middle-class weddings. Antebellum slaveholding families typically had enjoyed elaborate weddings that displayed their wealth and status, but the war imposed constraints. The blockade, scarcity of supplies, and inflation constricted the availability of gifts, clothing, and food. Moreover, elaborate ceremonies struck some as frivolous amid the financial and emotional devastation of war. Mary Washington Cabell noted that she attended a wedding in which the attendees "made a far less showy appearance." Mollie Brumby, the daughter of a farmer in Holmes County, Mississippi, decided to proceed with her ceremony despite financial strains placed on her family during the war. At the age of eighteen Mollie married Gus Vaughn at a small ceremony at her home. She described her own ceremony as a "calico wedding" in which the bridal party wore homemade dresses. Despite the limited wedding finery, she believed that she "looked very nice" and had a "very nice table." Louisa McCord recalled the difficulties she encountered in preparing for her wedding to Augustine Smythe in the last year of the war. With little money to spend, she borrowed a veil, gloves, and ring from a family member, while her mother bargained with a shopkeeper for a white dress and sold household items to pay for it. Most weddings of elite and middling daughters during the war were attended only by relatives and friends who lived close. Problems of moving about the occupied, South in addition to the financial strains of traveling a long distance, made it impossible for family members to attend distant weddings. Mollie Brumby had hoped that her older siblings, Robert and Sarah, would attend her wedding. But, distance kept Sarah from making the trek from Louisiana to Mississippi and Robert was unable to secure a furlough from the army. As a result, Brumby had only a few friends and family in attendance. Alice Bailey also had a small wedding with the presence only of a few family members who lived in her community. Bailey's sister, whose husband was away at war, refused to travel without a chaperone; and, unable to secure an escort, she remained at home.[30]

When the Civil War ended, young men and women faced an uncertain economic and emotional future. Material loses drove many to the brink of poverty and despair. Elizabeth Waties Allston and her mother, for example, were forced to open a school to provide an income after Union troops destroyed their rice plantation. Rising costs forced Myra Inman's family to close their Cleveland, Tennessee, home to boarders in December of 1865, leaving the family to seek help from relatives. The emotional and physical scars of returning soldiers also took a toll on southern communities. Historians have recently examined post-traumatic stress in Civil War veterans and its effects on employment, family life, and mental health. Many Civil War veterans experienced symptoms such as depression, alcoholism, and anger in the postwar years. Moreover, those wounded in combat bore physical scars.[31]

Many southerners responded to the problems of returning soldiers by focusing inward on the family. They found that the home and family offered the best means by which to reestablish a social and racial hierarchy. Because the war had eroded traditional validations of elite, white, male power, they attempted to reconstruct a masculine identity by reaffirming the patriarchy and relegating women to the home and family. This domestic model excluded African Americans and poor whites, who depended on the work of women outside the home, and gave credence to the authority of elite, white males. Although women had gained entrance into civic and political life through a variety of activities during the war, they supported the postwar domestic ideology.[32]

Young women attempted to uphold the new social creed that lauded women's maternal and domestic roles, but social and economic conditions often hindered them. The consequences of four years of bloody and destructive war presented obstacles to courtship and marriage. One was the decline in the male population, which forced many daughters again to reconsider their futures as wives and mothers. Economic difficulties, furthermore, prohibited many from marrying after the war. As a result, young women in the postwar period faced a dilemma. On the one hand, they reaffirmed traditional gender norms by seeking marriage and motherhood. On the other, they confronted the increased likelihood of a spinster's life. Most, however, eventually managed to resolve, or at least adjust to, this dilemma.

Demographic changes forced many young women to alter their courtship expectations in the postwar period. With the severe loss of life on the battlefield and in the hospital, southern society experienced an unbalanced sex ratio. At the end of the war, 260,000 Confederate soldiers were dead and another 190,000 were left wounded, leaving fewer eligible young men. Among those in this study whose marital records were available, their average age at marriage was 22.7, which is comparable to prewar marital patterns. Changes in postwar marital patterns tended to deal more with cultural expectations as the decline of the male population forced young women to reconsider courtship standards. While social class continued to influence strongly a woman's choice in suitors, age became less important. Before and during the war, younger women chose men close to their own age. But, after the war, some young women relaxed this standard. While living in Columbia, South Carolina, William Huger, for example, wrote to Isabella Smith, a family friend, that he had noticed a drastic change in young women's interactions with the opposite sex. Namely, he recognized that several belles were willing to socialize with younger men, a practice uncommon in the antebellum era. Huger recounted one such event at his social club during which the women in attendance socialized and danced with younger men, noting that only a handful of the males were near twenty years old.[33]

The psychological and physical scars of war also affected postwar courtships. Alcoholism and depression afflicted many returned soldiers. Some young women seeking courtship found their potential suitors wracked with emotional problems. As a result, they adjusted their expectations of the ideal marriage partner. Instead of rejecting men who suffered from depression and alcoholism, they accepted their emotional problems as part of the female burdens of war. Anna Green met her future husband while he was in the Milledgeville, Georgia, asylum, where her father worked as a doctor. Samuel Austin Cook had gone to the asylum seeking treatment for alcoholism after he returned from the war. His treatment completed, Cook approached Green's father to ask for her hand. Although Green expressed concerns about Cook's alcoholism, she agreed to marry him. Young women also confronted a generation of men physically scarred and maimed by war. They had to revise their expectations of a suitable beau to accommodate the bodily damage to southern manhood. Here too, rather than reject these men they accepted their scars and disabilities as a necessary burden. Ellen Cooper, for example, married Charles L. Johnson, who had lost a leg in the battle of the Wilderness in 1864. The couple met a few years after the war and pursued a short courtship before Cooper agreed to marry him in 1869.[34]

Despite the emotional and physical obstacles facing young couples, courtships provided a source of continuity with the antebellum past. By continuing to seek relationships in hopes of one day marrying, southern daughters upheld the postwar domestic ideal so closely tied to rebuilding southern masculinity. Courtships also demonstrated young women's commitment to the Old South value of marriage. A sign of young men and women's desire to continue the courting rituals was in their willingness to carry on social activities despite economic hardships in the postwar era. Susan Bradford, for example, witnessed the return of social activities after the war. Young men and women, she observed, attempted to bring some stability to their tumultuous environment by holding dances and parties at which they could seek courtship opportunities. Sally Independence Foster enjoyed the return of soldiers because it afforded chances to attend dances and parties.[35]

Even with the continuation of social activities, some young women continued to face the probability of life without a husband. The dearth of men and economic hardships in the postwar period made it difficult to find a mate. Young women's fears, however, reveal their support for the postwar domestic ideology. In expressing concerns about marital opportunities, they upheld the belief that a woman's primary goals were marriage and motherhood. Anna Green was one who worried about spinsterhood: "I almost feel that death were preferable to remaining alone in the world." Kate Foster was similarly troubled: "An old maid's life is one of struggle," she wrote, which "presents no allurements to a woman who feels that a woman's life is incomplete without Man's sustaining influence . . . a woman alone, in this cold world, how sad it is."[36]

Ideals of romantic affection and companionate marriage that characterized antebellum and wartime courtships continued in the postwar era despite the obstacles to marriage. The courtship of Mary Walker Gibson and John Chamberlayne of Virginia exemplify the strength of romantic ideals. Gibson was born in 1849 the daughter of Churchill Jones Gibson, a notable Episcopal minister, and Lucy (Atchison) Gibson. Her father's reputation as a minister and slave owner afforded her membership into the southern gentry before the war. By the early 1870s, she had begun a romance with John Hampden Chamberlayne, son of a prominent slaveholding family in Hanover County, Virginia. Chamberlayne, a graduate of the University of Virginia in 1858, had enlisted and served in the artillery of the Army of Northern Virginia. When he began a courtship with Gibson, Chamberlayne was searching for viable employment. Geographic separation in the early stages of their courtship forced the couple to rely primarily on correspondence to sustain their relationship. Throughout their letters, Chamberlayne and Gibson expressed a commitment to seeking a marriage based on the ideals of love and companionship. Gibson explained her desire to do more than assume the role of housekeeper; she wanted her beau to regard her as a partner and companion. After a visit from Chamberlayne, she penned a letter proclaiming her affections, noting "I could not let another day go by without telling you I think of you all the time and love you more." She encouraged her betrothed to reciprocate her affections in his letters. "You may tell me just as often as you please," she wrote, "that you love me and admire me and even tell me in what respects I command your admiration and I believe it will do me nothing but good." Gibson, however, expressed some fears that the responsibilities of marriage would diminish their hopes of true companionship: "My fear is that you will influence me more than I do you for I greatly prefer my notions as a general thing, to yours." Yet she held out hope that if "we love each other as I believe we do" they would attain their goal of a partnership in marriage.[37]

The postwar period also did little to ease parental control over courtship activities. Although Gibson and Chamberlayne expressed a deep commitment to each other, promising one day to marry, gaining approval from Mary's parents proved a formidable obstacle. Churchill, like many fathers of middling and elite families in the region, expected his daughter to marry a man of good standing in the community and with the financial capability to support a wife and household. Chamberlayne, however, appeared a less than acceptable prospect for a husband. The young Virginian had struggled to come to terms with the Confederacy's defeat and assert an identity in the postwar South. Following the surrender at Appomattox, he attempted to join Joseph E. Johnston's troops in North Carolina, until news of Johnston's April 18 surrender reached him. The young man, refusing to concede defeat, decided to join the remaining troops in Mississippi. Nevertheless, en route to his destination, Chamberlayne resolved that the Confederacy was lost and took the oath of allegiance the following month. Like so many southern men in the postwar years, Chamberlayne struggled to find financial success. Up until 1867 he worked on his mother's estate, but then suffered an emotional breakdown. His illness was but a temporary setback, and he began again to seek an economic livelihood, this time by becoming a telegraph operator and eventually a journalist. In all probability, the Gibsons knew about Chamberlayne's emotional and financial difficulties after his service in the military and deemed the young man unfit to provide for their daughter. In making plans for a visit from John, Mary warned her suitor that given her family's opinion of him he would "not receive a very cordial welcome."[38]

Efforts to circumvent parental interference likewise remained an option for young women. Gaining the blessing of parents for marriage proved a difficult task for courting couples. The economic situation of the postwar South made it difficult for southern men to attain the economic stability that played a factor in parental approval. Thus, as in wartime, southern daughters found it necessary to hide their engagements until their suitors could demonstrate an ability to support a family. Gibson and Chamberlayne made the decision to conceal their engagement until he could prove himself worthy of providing for his wife and their household. Their efforts to keep the relationship a secret proved daunting. "How I wish we could be married without any of the necessary preliminaries of having to gain the consent of anyone," Gibson admitted. "However," she added, "we have as much to be thankful for and we ought to try to be content with our present lot. The way will be opened for us on our Father's own good time." The couple failed to keep the relationship hidden from Gibson's friends and family, and eventually her parents learned of their engagement. The revelation caused tensions within the Gibson family, as Mary pointed out in a letter to John:

> When I left home I was under the impression and told you as I believe, that cousin Mary was the only member of the family that knew of anything of our affairs but I have since learned that all of them know everything. . . . As cousin Mary told me just now, they will be glad to see you as a friend but as long as my parents oppose our marriage they cannot welcome you as if you were already one of the family.

The couple's tenacity in remaining together combined with John's gradual ability to gain a degree of financial security eventually won over Mary's parents, and the couple married in 1873.[39]

Financial stability concerned courting couples as well as their parents. Although young women and men supported the return to a traditional division of gender roles, they discovered that the economic effects of war made it difficult to reestablish them. If a man was to assume the role of family provider, he needed an income; yet many returning soldiers had a hard time securing employment. Many returned home to find slaves and other property gone and little capital with which to rebuild their wealth. Thus, courting couples were willing to postpone marriage until they secured an income. Eldridge Foster wanted to establish himself as a merchant before marrying his fiancé. Susan Bradford and Nicholas Eppes also put off marriage due to financial concerns; only after Eppes got a job working on the plantation of Bradford's father did the couple marry. Ellen Cooper encouraged her betrothed, Charles Johnson, to find a job before they settled on marriage, a search complicated by the loss of his leg. He finally got the position of auditor for Horry County, South Carolina, in 1868, and married Cooper the following year. Sarah Chaffin urged her cousin to postpone his marriage until he accumulated some savings. "I rather think Willy contemplates an early consummation of his engagement," she wrote "I am sorry for it, as he has nothing to support a wife and the expense must fall heavily upon his father."[40]

In some cases, young women postponed marriage after the war out of reluctance to give up the freedom that courtship allowed them rather than for financial reasons. Views of the courtship period as a time of freedom for young women persisted after the war. Those young women born between 1846 and 1849 were at the height of their courtship opportunities and thus were willing to wait to marry. With the return of soldiers, young women saw more opportunities for social interaction, and often were loath to abandon those opportunities. Sallie Independence Foster, for example, welcomed the return of the beaux with whom she had corresponded during the war. She received three proposals over two years, but turned them down, arguing that "girls must have some fun."[41]

The marriage ideal, however, drew more young women to the altar in the postwar period. About 74 percent of the young women in this study married between 1866 and 1877 despite the financial constraints placed on young couples. Many southern daughters had come to accept it as a common condition early in a union and were willing to go forward with marriage. Susan Bradford accepted her fiancé's poverty as a consequence of his military service and confided to her diary that she would willingly make the material sacrifices needed until he could earn an income. Sarah Chaffin noted that the young women in her community paid little attention to financial issues when deciding to marry. "It seems poverty doesn't restrain people from getting married," she wrote, "judging from the frequency of such occurrences."[42]

The degree of extravagance of weddings in the postwar period kept pace with the southern economy. The ravages of war, couples with the demise of the slave system, made it difficult for the region to regain its economic footing immediately after the war. Such conditions forced brides to forego large weddings, and the destruction of railroads and bridges during the conflict often posed an obstacle for family members wanting to travel to attend a ceremony. With little money to spare, Sarah Chaffin was unable to purchase gifts for her friend's wedding and bemoaned traveling a long distance to attend the service. She criticized the couple for marrying when "everyone is so hard pressed." Judith Ann Robertson settled on a small wedding and relied on her mother to supply food and clothing for the service. Susan Bradford asked her guests to refrain from bringing gifts, knowing that many were destitute. When the southern economy began to improve, however, the scale and expense of weddings increased. Toward the end of the Reconstruction era, elaborate displays of wealth and prestige like those of the antebellum times returned. Mary

Washington Cabell, for example, described her 1876 wedding as a grand affair with family, friends, and neighbors present. She purchased a wedding dress and received numerous gifts from guests.[43]

Newly married couples who returned to plantation life found it difficult to establish a home and support a household economy in the postwar years. The instability of the agricultural market coupled with the lack of capital available in the economically depressed South brought few financial rewards for those just starting out. For young couples with little money to invest in land and labor, establishing a plantation or even small farm proved a Herculean task. Judith Ann Robertson Foster's husband tried to make the transition from merchant to planter, but could not muster sufficient capital and thus had minimal success. Louisa McCord Smythe and her husband invested all their money in a farm and found themselves thereafter financially strapped. To alleviate economic burdens, some couples sought financial assistance from their families. The financial hardships of the Smythe family remained a constant burden for Louisa. Yet, she sought comfort with her family who lived near her plantation and turned to them on numerous occasions for economic help. Susan Bradford Eppes and her new husband settled on her family's estate and relied on her father for financial support. Nicholas wanted to establish a plantation but was unable to save enough money to purchase the land. And, he continued to work on the Bradford estate until he found employment elsewhere.[44]

Some young couples who endured the financial hardships of starting up a farm found the experience rewarding. Lucy Wills Ball, for example, lauded plantation life despite the early struggles she and her husband faced as they commenced farming. Lucy was the daughter of William Henry Wills, a Methodist minister and cotton planter, and Anna Wills, of Halifax County, North Carolina. Throughout the war, Lucy continued her education; she eventually took a teaching position after the conflict to contribute to the domestic economy of the Wills's household. She married James Ball, also a Methodist preacher, in the late 1860s and the two moved to a farm in French Broad, North Carolina. Lucy appeared pleased with her husband's efforts to farm. She wrote to a family friend about her husband's success, noting that "we seem to be prospering." By 1870 she could write, "Our little farm is quite productive...we expect to make nearly 200 bushels of wheat and plenty of corn, potatoes. . . . We have plenty of milk and butter." She also seemed pleased that the farm had yielded enough profit for her husband to purchase "six nice little mules." Work on the farm also allowed James to remain close to the home to assist in "educating the little ones." "He [James Ball] wants to educate them properly and start them out early in the service of the church," she wrote. When confronted with the prospect of James becoming an itinerate preacher, Lucy had reservations about the move and what effect his absence would have on the farm and family. She told her friend that if James was "convinced it was his Master's will for him to lay all these things aside and itinerant and trust the support of his family and the chances of educating his little ones to Him he would cheerfully and at once do so." But, James seemed reluctant to separate himself from the farm and his children and chose rather to rely on divine providence to "direct and control the matter."[45]

While some wives willingly backed their husbands' efforts to farm, others encouraged a move away from the countryside. The economic instability of the postwar South, along with the changing social landscape caused by emancipation, made the prospect of farming a less than attractive venture for many. As a result, a movement from plantation to town began during Reconstruction and accelerated in the 1880s and 1890s. As historian Jane Turner Censer found, white women in the South supported this trend. Foremost among their concerns was the fear of debt as the South struggled to endure a declining commodity market. The cost of farm supplies and labor were high, and the new political and economic rights granted to African Americans in the Reconstruction era, according to Censer, "made rural whites uneasy about the state of the social order and prone to fears of possible uprisings or black disorder."[46]

Those who viewed plantation life with hostility encouraged their husbands to seek careers outside of agriculture. Maria Peek urged Daniel Marrow, her future husband, to find his fortune beyond the confines of the countryside. Daniel hoped to start a career as a clerk but lacked the capital with which to start a firm. Maria encouraged Marrow to borrow money from friends, hoping that his venture would eventually become profitable enough for him to repay his debts. "I can't see why your want of money," she wrote, "can't be supplied by some of your more fortunate friends who remained at home during the war." As Daniel searched for a viable means of financial support, his fiancée continued to push him to find an alternative to farming. When a clerkship in Hampton seemed impossible, he turned to medicine as an alternative. Maria appeared supportive of his decision, writing, "it is worth your exertion."[47]

The struggle to gain an economic footing in the early years of their marriage strained the relationships of some couples. Sarah Chaffin's husband decided to become a merchant and invested most of his money in the business, leaving the couple on the edge financially. She disliked the idea of her husband becoming a merchant, worrying that the new business would thrust them into debt and poverty. Yet in the end she decided that she "must acquiesce cheerfully in his plans and shall aid him in every way I can." The pursuit of employment or starting up a business often called men away from the home for lengthy periods, causing emotional stress for young women who found themselves either alone or forced to stay with relatives. Couples also had to face the fact that financial investment in a new business drained the family's resources, often forcing them to postpone plans to establish their own household. After marrying her fiancé in 1862, Mary Vaughn waited until the end of the war for her husband Gus to purchase a home. Gus, however, found his economic prospects diminished following Appomattox and his discharge from the Confederate army. Like many men in the South, Vaughn wanted to try his hand at business rather than rely on farming. Yet Mary hoped that Vaughn would stay in their hometown of Goodman, Mississippi, and purchase a farm. The conflict over the couple's residency and Gus's decision to shun plantation life created tensions in the marriage. Eventually, the young man found a potential career in "the Importation of Ales and Porter" and immediately invested in the business. He wrote Mary of his decision, noting, "of course now I cannot purchase a home yet, all my money must go into the business." He added that his decision was not self-serving but rather a move that he saw as "best for both of us." Relocation to New Orleans, however, meant that Mary had to postpone her ambitions of owning a home until the business could turn a profit. Moreover, his investment ensured that Mary would leave her hometown, a move she viewed with great sadness. Recognizing that his decision would create difficulties in the marriage, Gus urged Mary not to "scold me or cry about this disappointment," and promised his young bride that "next year if I am successful I will buy a nice cottage in this city."[48]

Economic and social conditions during and after the Civil War altered courtship and marriage practices but did little to undermine young women's acceptance of the domestic and maternal ideals closely tied to notions of familial duty. At an early age they began their preparation for marriage and motherhood, and as the war began they continued to view these roles as the last phases of their growth into womanhood. The war temporarily called into question the likelihood of finding a husband and forced many young women to postpone marriage. The absence of male suitors also altered traditional courtship practices, allowing young women greater freedom in their choices and conduct. Although parents tried to regulate their daughters' choice in beaux, they found that conditions on the home front frustrated their attempts. And yet, while the war altered courtship practices, it did not change young women's worldview. As the South entered the postwar period, society turned to the home and family as a source of stability. In the face of economic and social upheavals, young women found comfort in the new-yet-traditional domestic ideology.

5

The Confederate Belle Ideal

SOME NINETEEN YEARS AFTER the end of the war, Caroline Joachimson, a South Carolina native living in New York City, penned her reminiscence of life behind the Confederate lines. Her story begins with a household of young women sitting quietly at home sewing and knitting items for soldiers while awaiting news of whether their male kin, including Joachimson's brother, had enlisted in the Confederate army. Suddenly Cecil, her eldest sister, is surprised to see her sweetheart enter the room. The young man, according to Joachimson, was "grand in his magnificence of figure, showing symmetry and repressed strength in every limb, over the general height by several portions" and a "specimen of physical health and beauty" much like, in her words, the Greek god Apollo. Yet, her sister refuses to greet the young man because he had yet to join the Confederate army and vows to have nothing more to do with him until that time. Cecil's beau then whispers to his betrothed that he, in fact, had enlisted with the local company. The news filled the room with excitement as the younger sisters shouted with joy while Cecil kissed her now soldier-beau. Joachimson then shifts the focus of her story to several months into the war where the reader finds the sisters engaged in every effort to support the Confederate cause. Scenes of young women spending countless hours hovering around a circle stitching clothing for the "gallant soldiers" were common, according to Joachimson, as were southern daughters sacrificing their material comforts for the good of the cause. "One by one," she recalled, "they gave up their expensive ornaments, their jewelry, their silk dresses—nothing was held back or bestowed grudgingly—and proud of doing all they could." Joachimson also brought attention to another crucial role for her peers during the conflict, the social and romantic relations between young women and Confederate soldiers. Such "distractions" for soldiers—from extravagant parties to short rides in the countryside—in her estimation boosted the morale of soldiers and allowed them to carry on the fight. Joachimson ends her narrative with the loss of Cecil's beau and her brother toward the end of the war. These sacrifices, she concludes, were a source of enormous grief for her and her family but necessary to sustain a cause she truly believed was just.[1]

Examining young women's recollections, like those of Joachimson, reveals how those who came of age in the war contributed to the Lost Cause culture of the South. Contained in the pages of the stories written by members of Joachimson's age group, whether for private or public use, are the memories of a generation of southern daughters who hoped to place their unique mark on how history would judge the Confederacy. How they attempted to come to terms with the consequences of war, namely defeat, emancipation, and financial ruin, reflected their stage of development during the Confederacy's short-lived existence. Youth became the central theme and the means of reconciling loss and understanding just what all of the turmoil meant in their lives. Age also became a way for this generation to articulate to the next one their place within this saga of southern history. While regional literary figures carefully constructed what historians describe as the metanarrative of the Lost Cause, young women of the war generation worked to create an image of themselves in wartime that fit within the growing cultural battle to venerate the Confederacy.[2]

Young women's literary contribution likewise put forth a cultural vision for the New South. The war precipitated changes to the southern social, economic, and political order. The destruction of slavery and the transformation of thousands of slaves into freedmen and women created a sense of anxiety among white southerners, who saw this period as nothing short of social chaos. Moreover, the disfranchisement of former Confederate supporters, along with the election of Republican governments in the South, replaced the hegemonic rule of white, slaveholding elites of the Old South. In response, whites turned to a variety of legal and extralegal means for resurrecting the racial order. Southern daughters, who had now reached adulthood, saw that they too had a responsibility in promoting this return to white supremacy, and their postwar reminiscences became the vehicle for articulating their vision of the New South's racial order.

In the aftermath of Appomattox, and the subsequent surrender of the remaining Confederate armies, southern whites began to construct a caricature of the Confederate cause that by the turn of the century reached mythological proportions. As early as 1866, Edward A. Pollard, editor of the *Richmond Examiner*, produced a narrative that offered a validation of the war and rationalized Confederate defeat, while the *Southern Historical Society Papers* in the 1880s began a series of articles that promoted what its authors termed a true representation of the past events. Other works soon followed in an effort to create an acceptable defense of the Confederate cause that would trump northern literature on the Civil War that, at first, emphasized southern defeat as the triumph of free labor over slavery, and eventually embraced reconciliation. The Lost Cause mythology posited a set of ideas that served to shape a provincial and eventually national understanding of why southerners went to war and why they lost. Defenders of the Confederate cause tended to downplay the centrality of slavery. Rather, it was the antagonism of northern abolitionists and the cultural differences of the two regions that created sectional disagreement. They argued that secession was a constitutional means of reacting to Federal attempts to undermine southern culture and its sacred institutions. In addition, authors tended to present southern culture as idyllic, emphasizing the honorable, chivalrous nature of the planter class and portraying slaves as contented and cared for in their servitude. The language of the Lost Cause also idealized Confederate soldiers as gallant men fighting in defense of their homeland and stressed the unanimity of non-combatants in supporting the war. Popular histories of the conflict stressed the greatness of military leaders such as Thomas "Stonewall" Jackson and Robert E. Lee, elevating them in the process to near sainthood. The purpose of such portrayals was to demonstrate that the war was not lost because of a flaw in the South's cause or for a lack of heroism on the battlefield, but rather resulted from the overwhelming resources and military force of the North.[3]

Southern women of all ages played an essential role in promoting Lost Cause mythology as the dominant cultural narrative of the war. Their reminiscences, along with public memorials and fictional works, served as cultural tools in defending the southern cause in the historical record. Hoping to claim a victory in the battle over public memory, many women took pen to paper, writing their own histories of the war that upheld the Lost Cause dictates. They scripted a defense of the Confederacy that trumpeted the constitutionality of secession and touted the war's purpose as the defense of states' rights while eschewing slavery as the cause of war. They, like other Lost Cause authors, constructed romantic epitaphs to the South's plantation lifestyle and portrayed relations between slave owners and slaves as familial and harmonious. Southern white men emerge in this narrative as heroic protectors who went to war in defense of their homes and families, while women are portrayed as figures of unrelenting sacrifice, maternal duty, and loyalism.[4]

The fictional works of southern female authors played a prominent role in the cultural battle between the North and South to lay claim to the memory of the war. Historians have concentrated much of their energies on these fictional works, illuminating their significance in creating and sustaining the Lost Cause defense of the war and romanticization of the Old South. Augusta Jane Evans's famous domestic novel *Macaria, or Altars of Sacrifice* (1864) offered a portrait of a household of women left to provide for themselves and protect their home from enemy forces to demonstrate the validity of the southern cause and the transformative nature of the home front experience. The efforts to venerate the Confederate cause accelerated, however, after the end of the war and it is in this period that the Lost Cause narrative begins to take shape in women's fictional works. One example of this comes from southern women writers countering the romantic reunification stories published out of the North after 1865. At first, northern authors took an anti-reunion approach to their critique of the war and its implications for the nation. But, by the Reconstruction period, some writers had shifted their focus to embrace reunification. They cultivated the motif of marriages between northern men and southern women to exemplify the union between two once divided regions. These stories typically involved some northern soldier in the Civil War who found himself in an inhospitable South. The soldier meets a young belle who falls in love with him, and the two overcome insurmountable odds, including anti-union sentiments, to marry eventually. Such imagery, as historian Nina Silber posits, "justified the northern view of the power relations in the reunified nation." It provided an example of how a conquered region could return to the Union. Southern women, attempting to offer their own interpretation of the war and its implications for the two regions, created a defense against the romantic reunification stories. They refuted reunion by using the motif of doomed love affairs between northern men and southern women, signifying the inability of the two regions to reconcile. The fictional works of southern female writers continued to play a significant role in gaining a wider acceptance of the Lost Cause metanarrative. These literary constructions, ranging from Mary Ann Cruse's *Cameron Hall*, published in 1867, to the publication of Margaret Mitchell's *Gone With the Wind* (1937) demonstrated the popularity of women's efforts to defend the Confederate mission and offer an idyllic portrait of the Old South.[5]

Fig. 11. Raleigh Confederate Monument, Raleigh, North Carolina. Library of Congress, Prints and Photographs Division [LC-DIG-ggbain-15279]

By the late nineteenth century, southern women formed a more cohesive approach to shaping the public memory of war through the creation of the United Daughters of the Confederacy (UDC). Members of the UDC constructed a dominant narrative that encouraged a provincial explanation of the causes for war and southern defeat. As a result of what the organization saw as a "divine imperative" to construct such a memory, they set forth guidelines for members in writing accounts of the war that supported the Lost Cause narrative. Moreover, the organizations committee on textbooks reviewed history books used in the classrooms and public libraries and pressured public schools and libraries to ban any that took issue with the antebellum South or the Confederate mission. The UDC also took their agenda to public venues in the campaign to memorialize the Confederacy by commissioning memorials in honor of the military and home front effort. They dedicated statues honoring key figures such as Lee, Jackson, and Jefferson Davis and remembered the Confederate dead through gravesite dedications to fallen soldiers. The UDC included statues in honor of the home front, many of which emphasized the supportive or maternal role of women. These memorials along with their efforts to control the histories written about the war were intended to exonerate southerners and claim a cultural victory for the region in the national struggle to create a cohesive memory of the war.[6]

A generalized female imagery has emerged in these efforts to promote the Lost Cause narrative and hence overshadowed the significance of age in distinguishing wartime memories of women. Southern daughters, like the generation before and after them, endorsed the maternal female figure as the dominant public image of women. They supported public memorials and published histories, both fiction and nonfiction, that touted women as the "mothers" of the Confederacy. In Louisa Wigfall's account of the war, she lauded the motherly portrayal of southern women as an example of female strength during the conflict. "I have in my mind, as I write," she offered, "a picture that comes before me whenever I hear of the suffering of the women of the South." In 1865, while on a train, Wigfall sat across from a mother and her son. The mother, who "had journeyed from her far-away home in Alabama to the hospital in Richmond to find her boy and bring him back with her," was determined to endure the trip despite the "weariness and painfulness" of nursing a wounded son. What awaited the mother and son, Wigfall recalled, was a destroyed community and ravaged home, but "in the heart of the poor old mother there was still room for great joy . . . he was alive!" Wigfall believed that it was the "spirit of her mother love" that would allow the young soldier to survive his wounds. This homage to the strength of a mother's care demonstrates the acceptance of the maternal figure, as the embodiment of unrelenting sacrifice, among women of all ages. Images of married or widowed women nursing ill or wounded soldiers proved a powerful motif in fictional works. The stories of women caring for their homes and families while enduring supply shortages, enemy attacks, and other hardships on the home front also served as a potent metaphor for the supportive female role.[7]

Young women's reflections on their own wartime experiences, however, offered a much different female image. As the previous chapters have demonstrated, this generation was devoted to the Confederate cause as a means of fulfilling their expectations of southern womanhood. As the losers in the battle for independence, however, young women went searching for ways to venerate the Confederacy and the cause that they had devoutly supported. Moreover, Confederate defeat and the demise of the slave system forced them to break from the past and reassess their future lives as southern women. To help reconcile themselves to defeat and the cultural changes that followed, young women created a defense of the Confederate cause in their personal and published recollections using imagery that reflected their age and position in the family during the war. In addition, they found continuity with the antebellum past by endorsing traditional gender ideals and racial hierarchy in their memoirs. They interpreted female support and sacrifice using imagery that, collectively, I distinguish as the Confederate belle. Young women themselves avoided such labels when penning their recollections. However, an examination of their writings reveals common themes used repeatedly to express their defense of secession and war that form the structure of the belle image. The motif of the Confederate belle was that of the self-sacrificing daughter who exchanged the frivolities associated with teenage girls for a life of war work and material hardships in the name of southern independence. She transformed the flirtations and courtships typically associated with her belledom into public acts of support for the Confederate cause. Young women's descriptions of their war work, material and familial sacrifices, and social interactions with soldiers contributed to the Lost Cause narrative by constructing a defense of the struggle for southern independence as a politically and morally just purpose. Depictions of wartime courtships promoted an idealization of the Confederate soldier that contributed to the reconstitution of southern white masculinity. A more complex issue, however, was that of race. Like women of the older generation, southern daughters downplayed the centrality of slavery in the causation of the war. But, for daughters, the issue of race permeated their memoirs. They hoped to convey to readers the reasons why southerners had come to replace paternalism with a harsher, less familial relationship with African Americans in freedom. For this, they turned to the antebellum beliefs in the intellectual and moral inferiority of the black race as a way to explain why this transformation took place.

The audience for whom these southern daughters constructed their memoirs illuminates the cultural purpose of the Confederate belle imagery. Some of the young women wrote about their experiences with the intention that only family members would read them, never hoping to publish them. These recollections, according to their authors, were for the purpose of leaving an "accurate record" for the next generation. In essence, the narratives that they constructed for their daughters and grand daughters were intended to ensure the continued acceptance of the Lost Cause mythology and their distinctive place within it. The notion that the next generation, through their disconnect with the Civil War era, would lose sight of or begin to question the validity of the Confederate mission certainly lingered above them as these women of the war generation approached their elderly years. Ellen Cooper Johnson, for example, penned her reminiscences for her family members in 1924 at the age of eighty. Judith Ann Robertson Foster likewise felt that as a woman in her seventies, she needed to provide her children and grand children with some record of her wartime experiences. But the message conveyed within their narratives was clearly one that promoted a veneration of the Confederate cause as well as offering a commentary on the political, economic, and social environment in which they were writing. Thus, these memoirs, although never published, served as a form of indoctrination of the next generation into the Lost Cause mythology as well as the championing of racial hierarchy and conventional gender ideals.[8]

Southern daughters reached a wide audience with their published memoirs. Between the 1880s and 1920s, they offered up their recollections to a number of publishing houses located both in and outside the South.

The Charleston, South Carolina, *Weekly News and Courier*, for example, published a series of articles in the early 1880s by southern women detailing their experiences in the war. Eventually the newspaper had the articles bound and published as a collection in 1885. The intention of the series, according to the *Weekly* editors, was to "give the public . . . some faint idea of what they saw and what they did, what they hoped and what they feared, in those exciting times which are gone forever." The female authors concurred that their experiences warranted publication, given their sacrifices and trials on the home front, and the noble ideals of the Confederate cause. Other young women of the war who published their works were also aware that their memoirs served a useful purpose in providing a record of the Confederacy, one that trumpeted the cause of independence and upheld a return to prewar societal norms. In the opening of Louise Wigfall's narrative, published in 1905 by the Doubleday press in New York, she offered an explanation for her recollections, arguing that "I am conscious that the days are passing, and that if done at all, the chronicle had best be written ere the eye that has seen these things grows dim and the memory faulty." Wigfall, however, also argued that she had a duty to provide a memory of the war for the next generation not only for her private family but also for the consciousness of the general public, an audience that garnered significantly more attention from advocates of the Lost Cause. "I would fain live in the thoughts of the children," she wrote, "who shall come after me, and have their hearts, as they read this record, beat in unison with mine." Through her record of the Civil War, Wigfall hoped the next generation would accept her defense of the southern cause, and, in doing so, they would "be linked together in these memories."[9]

Young women's wartime memoirs emphasized foremost the supportive nature of their war experiences. Recalling their participation in organizations such as soldiers' aid societies and other more informal groups was intended to help substantiate the erroneous notion of southern unanimity on the home front. Louisa McCord Smythe described how she and her female kin gave clothing and food to soldiers staying in their home. Mary Washington Cabell Early likewise boasted of women's willingness to work long hours sewing clothes and cooking food. Oranie Virginia Snead wrote proudly that everyone in her community struggled ardently to "secure [the South's] independence." Caroline Joachimson described women's war work as a family affair in which all female members used their skills to produce needed items for soldiers. She explains that in the opening days of the war, each of her sisters engaged in some type of production. "Cecil, the eldest daughter, was busy making a 'minute man's' badge, of a sky blue ribbon with a silver star, and the letters M.M. on the corner. Lizzie was knitting a stocking, and brown-eyed Katie was shredding palmetto to make up into cockades." The most difficult items to produce were those for family members going off to fight in the war. But, for Joachimson, this type of production was a way to ease the hardship of watching their male kin leave for war. In the case of her brother, her mother's tearful sacrifice was eased as her sisters "made him up a solder's [*sic*] wardrobe and filled his needle book as if for a woman's use; then they crocheted him a cap of gray chinchilla worsted with a crimson border for his comfort in the camp." Such descriptions of young women's war work demonstrated their peer group's acceptance of the Confederate cause of independence. As Florida Saxon of South Carolina explained, "The brave and loyal daughters of the South, though their hearts were bleeding at every pore, sat not down in idleness. There was work to be done, and they did it." [10]

Although women of all ages included discussions of war work in their recollections, those who came of age during the conflict often saw this effort in terms of age differences. One young woman writing anonymously for the *Weekly News and Courier* discussed how her peer's support for the cause encouraged them to sacrifice their traditional antebellum education for one that served a more pragmatic purpose. "The pressure of the time," she wrote, "caused the Southern girl to lay aside her books and learn to knit socks for the soldiers, pickling, roll bandages, make cartridge-bags and various other things that women found to do at that time." But, those of similar age, she argued, were willing to make such changes "for so dear was 'the cause' to the heart to every Southerner that the women vied with each other, each doing her utmost to help the men." She recalled that all women willingly provided homemade supplies for the army, noting that none could resist for "such a holy cause." The young woman also emphasized the generational connections between older women reared in the American Revolution and those of her own peer group in the Civil War. She claimed that while on sewing clothes for the Confederate troops, she listened to her grandmother tell stories of "the days of '76 when she was a 'wee one'" doing her own part to help the cause of independence. Another woman who came of age during the war described how her peers despite their limited sewing skills rose to the challenge of providing for soldiers. She depicted a scene of young women running "the little spinning wheel" with such enjoyment that they often broke into songs of patriotism. "Listen and you'll catch the words as with flashing eyes and cheeks aglow," she wrote, giving little indication of the problems young women experienced in learning to sew or knit. The songs that she mentioned likewise stressed the uniformity of female support for the war: "Our wagon's plenty big enough, the running gear is good. 'Tis stuffed with cotton round the sides and made of South wood; Carolina was the driver, with Georgia by her side, Virginia'll hold the flag up and we'll all take a ride."[11]

Lelia C. Morris of La Grange, Georgia, chose to focus on public displays of loyalty by young women that identified with the heritage of the American Revolution. In 1902, Morris presented a history of the "Nancy Harts," a troop of young women organized to provide protection for their community in the absence of their male kin. Since its inception, the UDC encouraged members to construct histories of the Civil War that fit within the Lost Cause narrative. Members presented an analysis of events that emphasized the constitutionality of secession as a justification for independence and claimed that all southerners supported the cause. The Nancy Harts proved a valuable tool in constructing an age-specific interpretation of the Lost Cause mythology. First, the home guard had taken its name from a female figure during the American Revolution who had defended her Georgia frontier home from invading loyalists. Using the name invoked the image of the woman on the home front who bravely faced the enemy to protect of her home. Imbued with a sense of patriotism and the youthful energy of teenagers, the Harts home guard, according to Morris, illustrated the importance of young women in sustaining the southern cause. The second purpose of connecting the guard to the Revolutionary era was the desire to justify the Confederate mission by arguing that, just as colonists had fought to shake off the tyranny of the British monarchy, so too had southerners engaged in war to fight northern infringement upon their rights. Although the Nancy Harts never confronted Union soldiers, the organization found a unique place in the young woman's memory of the war. Morris compared the members of the company to Spartan women, emphasizing their bravery and loyalty to a noble cause: "But my friends, modern history has awarded to Southern women, not

Fig. 12. Emma Samson Monument. This monument, one of few depicting female youths, is in honor of Samson who, after Union soldiers had burned the bridge across Black Creek in Gadsden, Alabama, allegedly led General Nathan Bedford Forrest to a ford so that his troops could cross. Erected by the Gadsden, Alabama chapter of the United Daughters of the Confederacy in 1906. Photograph courtesy of John Vanover.

only the honor of sacrificing their brave men, sires, and young boys, but given them the proud distinction of having the courage of defending their homes and firesides by armed resistance."[12]

Young women also included the theme of self-sacrifice in constructing their defense of the Confederacy. Material sacrifices proved especially popular in demonstrating the validity of the southern cause. Teenage girls, as female authors stressed, willingly traded in their fashionable clothing and comfortable lifestyle for simple living and plain dress to help keep the war going. Implicit in these depictions was that they would have avoided such sacrifices for a less noble cause. Ellen Cooper Johnson proudly detailed the ingenious methods she devised to feed and clothe herself as shortages and high prices afflicted the home front. Mary Early wrote a series of articles describing the obstacles southern families faced in purchasing cloth and the various forms of household production used to alleviate their privation. Another young woman used her discussion of wartime hardships to demonize the North, noting that "'Uncle Sam's' treasury was not accessible to 'Rebels.' Our government was young, and Confederate bonds and money yet in their infancy." But, such difficulties, she proclaimed, were met with the ingenuity of southern women who willingly took up spinning and weaving as a means of supporting the region through the war. A common theme in her description was the willingness of her generation to endure supply shortages "cheerfully and gladly." Rather than attempt to maintain the fashions common among young women her age, she explained that they "replaced our worn dresses with homespuns, planning and devising checks and plaids, and intermingling colors with the skill of professional 'designers.'" Such homespun originals she viewed as a "true Confederate style" that rivaled any fashionable trends from their antebellum days.[13]

The most prominent theme in young women's narratives was their romantic interactions with soldiers. Descriptions of their flirtations and courtships with soldiers helped southern daughters to cultivate their own interpretation of women's supportive roles on the home front, one that was unique to their age group. To do so, they frequently placed their social engagements with soldiers in the context of their patriotic activities. The young women who wrote about their romantic interplays with soldiers described these as necessary in maintaining troop morale and thus in sustaining the Confederate cause. Their romantic interest in soldiers, in other words, served as a metaphor for their own engagement with the Confederate mission. In addition, as single youths in wartime, southern daughters were exempt from the motif of separated spouses that their mothers and older female kin used to illuminate the ideal of female self-sacrifice. Instead, they stressed the personal sacrifice entailed in the separation from their beaux.

The idealization of Confederate soldiers within the romance narrative likewise provided the cultural link with the antebellum past that southern daughters had sought to maintain during the war. During the Reconstruction era, southern white men searched for ways to reassert the political and economic power that they had lost after the war, a result of the disfranchisement of Confederate supporters, demise of slavery, and devastation of the region's postwar economy. Young women contributed to the resurrection of southern white patriarchy in the postwar era by offering descriptions of the heroism of Confederate men who valiantly defended their homes from northern invasion. Embracing traditional gender rhetoric, however, offered a dual reward for young women. It justified their husbands' and fathers' efforts to reclaim their positions of power and, at the same time, endorsed gender expectations of masculine honor and duty associated with the Old South.

The politicization of wartime romantic relationships stemmed from young women envisioning such interactions as an extension of their supportive role. As Lost Cause advocates touted the maternal female figure, young women cultivated a different representation that reflected their youth. Their freedom from the burdens of motherhood precluded them from writing about maternal duties and extensions of them in their personal experiences. Rather, the courtships and social activities of the Confederate belle gave voice to young women's supportive roles. In the process, they legitimized the continuation of courtship rituals during wartime—an activity some deemed frivolous in such circumstances—by emphasizing the political nature of their relationships with soldiers. They portrayed their relationships with the soldiers as much needed diversions from the severities of war, helping to boost the morale of troops. They were, like their mothers, providing a service to the Confederate army that would sustain their cause of independence. Mary Bell Claytor wrote in her memoirs that "the young soldier boys made a business of going from house to house to say goodbye [*sic*], and not one opportunity was lost to kiss the girls, for no girl was prudish about kissing a soldier good-bye." Emma

Cassandra Riley described sitting at her window watching soldiers march by "with longing eyes at them, and they with equally longing eyes at me." Louisa McCord Smythe remembered seeing a "crowd of handsome men in gay uniforms coming and going, singing, flirting and generally enjoying themselves with some extremely handsome and conspicuous women."

Others made a more direct connection between young women's flirtations and the Confederate effort. Using romantic imagery in her recollections, Joachimson stressed young women's idealization of a southern soldier:

> The privates of the beloved army were as dear to the female hearts as the most gaudily decorated officer, and each all wished to dance, and to make love, and even flirt, never once being appalled by the fear of quick coming danger. The three eldest girls were sometimes in their plantation home, manufacturing by turns needed garments for the soldiers, or mixing superb Magnolia punch to drink with a Virginia regiment quartered on their native soil.

Joachimson, like her peers, believed that entertaining the soldiers helped to sustain the war effort by providing a respite from the weariness of camp life. Even more important were the close, individual relationships with soldiers that created a personal connection to the Confederate effort. Joachmison's older sister Cecil received a letter from her suitor informing her that the portrait of her in his possession "should be his safeguard, and serve as a talisman to bring him back." Such private relationships between soldiers and young women offered more than a diversion, according to Joachimson. The notion that the soldier had a sweetheart who they were fighting to protect and who would be waiting for them at the end of the conflict, served as a source of motivation for soldiers during the most difficult periods of the war.[14]

The sadness conveyed in the stories of separated lovers also proved a powerful imagery in defending the Confederate mission. Rather than giving their husbands to the Confederate cause, these young women offered instead their suitors and in the process willingly risked losing the potential for marriage. Florida Saxon's story of Katie Weston involves a melancholy scene of a young woman conflicted over her beau's decision to enlist in the army. He has offered to marry her and hire a substitute to take his place. However, as Saxon contended, Katie refused to "forget the cause that is so dear to her heart" and insists that he "bravely do your duty." Although it is never clear if Weston was a pseudonym for Saxon, the purpose of offering this account was to demonstrate that the righteousness of southern independence was enough to overcome the heartache of separated lovers. Joachimson, on the other hand, described the ultimate sacrifices that some belles made when their soldier-beau was killed in battle. She recalled the conflicted feelings that her sister, Cecil, experienced after receiving news that her suitor had died from injuries sustained on the battlefield. When a letter came from a woman who nursed his wounds, Cecil soon accepted that her beau had died doing his duty for the Confederacy. Joachimson concluded that the human cost of war exacted an enormous emotional toll on all families on the home front, but in her view, it was "the price they paid for peace." Such claims served to diminish the fears many expressed over the dangers their male friends and family members faced on the battlefield. Nor do they acknowledge the anger felt over the loss of loved ones, as expressed in their wartime writings.[15]

The romance narrative of the Confederate belle image also encouraged the reconstruction of southern white masculinity in the postwar years. Thousands of Confederate soldiers returned from the battlefield to confront a crisis of identity. Their service in the army had informed their sense of self, but defeat led to feelings of emasculation. Adding insult to injury, congressional control over Reconstruction led to the disfranchisement of many returning men, and the transition to free labor coupled with the economic ruin of the postwar South, left many former slaveholders without a source of capital or labor. This change in the political and economic structure of the South sent southern white men searching for new ways to reclaim their authority in the social order. A return to traditional gender expectations became a tool to help white males regain their power. More specifically, the promotion of a domestic ideal that touted men as the patriarchal head of the family and women as the supportive, dependent helpmate, legitimated the reassertion of the prewar status quo. This rhetorical construction, rooted in antebellum gender convention, contributed to a public masculine identity for disfranchised and impoverished southern white men. Overtime, white southerners came to accept that those men who demonstrated patriarchal qualities were among the "best men" to lead the region, so that by the close of Reconstruction the social hierarchy in most southern states resembled the prewar distribution of political and economic authority.[16]

Young women of the war generation, hoping to find a source of continuity with the past to which they had clung so tightly during the war, supported a return to gender convention and used their personal and published recollections to achieve it. Their depictions of Confederate troops as the embodiment of masculinity and their idealization of the soldier-beau created a historic connection between the southern man in the postwar era and the honorable, dutiful man of the Confederacy. This connection, based on traditional notions of masculinity, justified a return to the prewar distribution of power, one that ensured the authority of southern white men and the subordination of white women and African Americans. The story of Mattie Jarnagin of Terrace Landing, Mississippi, exemplifies this reverence for the Confederate soldier. After moving to Memphis to attend school, Mattie reunited with a neighbor from Mississippi with whom she had been "little sweethearts" since their childhood. The war soon tore the couple apart when he left to join the Army of Tennessee. Jarnagin gives a depiction of a tearful good-bye with "promises to be true always." However, she concludes that her pride in his decision to enlist was enough to carry her through his absence, noting that she was "proud of my soldier lover, and thought him handsome, brave and good." Esther Alden, of Plantersville, South Carolina, expressed the same adulation for the Confederate soldiers whom she saw as the epitome of masculinity. While attending a dance at Fort Sumter with several uniformed soldiers, she proclaimed that all of them "seemed to me a hero," adding that her view of the young men changed knowing that they "could be killed to-morrow." Such men, she concluded, were worthy of her attention because they fulfilled their duty to the Confederate cause by enlisting in the army. [17]

The counter-image to the honorable, dutiful male was that of the exempted soldier, who, in avoiding military service, had emasculated himself. These men, described by Florida Saxon as "skulkers," were unworthy of female attention because they shunned the Confederate manhood ideal. Calling on her example of Katie Weston, a former classmate at the female seminary in Tallahassee who fervently supported southern independence, Saxon recalled how young women refused to engage in relationships with men "who shirked their duty." One such man was Henry Jackson who invoked the exemption clause to avoid service. The author recounted that he was a "handsome fellow" who was "captivated by the charms of our fair Katie." But, the young man failed to garner Katie's affections, having "been repeatedly taunted by her with his want of bravery." At a social gathering of youths, the young woman punctuated her disgust with Jackson by humiliating him in front of his peers. During a song, she turned to him to sing the final verse:

> And now, young man, a word to you—If you would win the fair, go to the field, where honor dwells, and win your lady there. Remember that our brightest smiles are for the true and brave, and that our tears shall fall for those who fill a soldier's grave.

Saxon believed that the young man had "learned the lesson" that Katie intended to teach him. Realizing that he had dishonored himself by refusing to enlist, he turned and left the party humiliated and, in the eyes of his female counterparts, less than a man.[18]

The familial sacrifices young women made as daughters and sisters helped complete the rubric of the Confederate belle ideal. Many recalled that the absence of male kin and the potential dangers they would face on the battlefield created much anxiety for those left on the home front. Sallie Walker Boone, for example, reflected on the many women who sat worrying and waiting for information from the front. "Shall I ever forget those sad, sad, days?" she wondered, "the hearts that were broken, the tears that were shed, the homes made desolate." Yet young women in their memoirs were careful to avoid any questioning of the Confederacy's involvement in war. Rather, they emphasized that the Confederacy's purpose for going to war justified the absence of male kin. In recalling the sacrifices of brothers, fathers, and other male kin, young women also found another avenue through which to idealize Confederate manhood and, in the process, reaffirm traditional gender ideals. Although the Confederate service of male kin caused great sadness, according to their personal recollections, they could find solace in knowing that their family members fulfilled their duty to the cause of independence. Florida Saxon once again used the allegorical tool of Katie Weston's wartime experience to explain how the cause outweighed the dangers to family kin. Katie, Saxon described, stood on a bench one day and delivered a speech about the merits of secession, asking "who would be a thrall of the Yankee . . . who in this crowd . . . dares to blame the noble old State of South Carolina for rising in her might and throwing off the oppressor's yoke?" But, Weston's loyalty is soon tested when her brothers enlisted in a Confederate company. "Did she flinch from the trial? Did her heart fail and her patriotism grow cool?" she asked. "No, she was loyal to her heart's core." Weston grieved over the absence of her brothers, but, as Saxon asserts, her pride in their bravery was enough to ease her sadness. Moreover, the Confederate mission to govern their region and families independent of northern encroachment justified the potential dangers her brothers faced.[19]

While young women's recollections served as a formidable tool in promoting the Lost Cause narrative, their writings also reflected the growing racial sentiment of their generation and served as a cultural weapon in the campaign to restore white supremacy. A defeated South had to deal not only with returning to the Union but also with the freedom of African Americans, which meant the loss of the racial caste system that had defined the region's social order for generations. Issues of race and the consequences of emancipation emerged in the recollections of young women and contributed significantly to the transition from a paternalistic outlook toward slaves to harsher, more racist views of African Americans in freedom. Slavery, in their depictions, provided the necessary structure to control the black race and provide an ordered system of labor. In this system emerged familial feelings toward black servants that endured even past the end of the war. Freedom, however, brought the demise of this order as African Americans began to exercise their economic and political freedom. Such demonstrations of autonomy signified chaos to hundreds of former slave owners and prompted a reassertion of white supremacy through a variety of means from economic coercion to white terrorist organizations bent on curtailing the social freedom of blacks. To justify such means, white southerners turned to the imagery of the sexualized African American male who they believed without the constraints of slavery threatened the purity of vulnerable white women. Methods ranging from threats of physical violence to public lynchings were often justified on the grounds of protecting white women from sexual exploitation. While they constructed these rationalizations upon a foundation of false accusations of rape and other forms of sexual assault, their contentions served to validate the subjugation of African Americans in freedom. The gendered arguments in favor of reconstructing racial hierarchy also extended into the world of southern white women who prescribed to the notion that emancipation brought social degeneration.[20]

The women who came of age during the Civil War situated themselves within the struggle to resurrect white supremacy. After the war, the emancipation of slaves, formalized by the ratification of the Thirteenth Amendment, brought southern daughters to confront the reality of a transition to free labor that led them to adopt more racist beliefs. Paradoxically, this generation of women stood to lose the most from the demise of slavery. Within the realm of domesticity, the women of their mother's generation faced a greater struggle in coming to terms with emancipation since the freedom of their household servants added to their domestic labor. And southern daughters' dependence upon slaves before the war never reached the extent of their mothers' because of their age and position in the family. Moreover, the reorientation of household labor during the war encouraged them to become less reliant upon slaves and adjust to added domestic responsibilities before they reached adulthood. Yet the end of slavery posed a greater threat to the class identity of the daughters. Both mothers and daughters confronted the reality that they were no longer members of the slaveowning class. But because southern daughters had yet to realize their position in the southern social hierarchy as adults, the demise of slavery created a different set of anxieties than those experienced by their mothers. How would they position themselves in the post-emancipation South? From where would their authority as maturing adult women come? These questions plagued young women who, after the end of the war, were beginning to reach adulthood. Their answers came from the white supremacist campaigns intended to reestablish the prewar racial order.[21]

Attempts to assert white authority crossed the lines dividing home and community life. Using their only tangible model for dealing with servants in the home, young women strove to establish power over their hired help that reflected prewar relations between mistress and slave. Beyond the confines of the home, young women also demonstrated their commitment to white supremacy by endorsing the racist ideologies that permeated the South during and after Reconstruction. Thus, by the 1890s, we see young women of the war generation positioning themselves at the center of the most brutal periods of southern race relations in an attempt to reestablish the racial hierarchy that had defined their childhood years.

In other words, ensuring divisions between black and white would offer a source of cultural continuity for this generation of young women caught between their commitment to Old South racial ideals and the changing nature of race relations in the postwar South. An examination of their postwar diaries and letters reveals the personal connection of this age group to ensuring white supremacy. Their wartime memoirs written between the 1880s and 1930s, moreover, demonstrate their willingness to articulate a public defense of racial hierarchy. By creating a narrative of the war that upheld the notion that, in freedom, African Americans posed a greater threat to the stability of southern society, this age group situated themselves clearly in the movement to promote Jim Crow laws and racial discrimination.

The emancipation of slaves after the war's end forced young women to face the destruction of traditional race relations. Throughout the South, whites who retained their slaves were forced to tell them that they were free to leave. Many blacks chose to remain with their former masters and sign labor contracts, while others left in search of family members or new opportunities. Southern daughters watched as the slaves they had once considered an extension of their family leave for freedom. Caroline Ravenel stood by as her uncle informed their slaves that they could leave the plantation or stay and work under contract. Susan Bradford's family had a harder time letting their slaves leave. Her father announced that their servants were free to go, but her mother refused to acknowledge her loss of authority, informing one servant that if she left then she would not hire her as a paid domestic. Such scenes forced young women to confront the demise of slavery, and in the process, stirred feelings of animosity, frustration, and confusion toward the new status of their former servants.[22]

Young women varied in their reactions to African Americans in freedom. Like many other southerners, daughters believed that their former slaves could not survive outside the authority of whites. However, they eventually had to accept emancipation as they witnessed freed men and women transition to free labor, seek educational opportunities, change their names, and reunite with family members. Young women responded to the changing status of blacks with both regret and resentment. And, as state and federal Reconstruction policies attempted to ensure the social, political, and economic freedom of the former slaves, they began to see blacks in the community as a threat to white authority.[23]

They scoffed at the idea that their former slaves should enjoy the same freedoms as southern whites. After two freedmen took her family's last name, Caroline Ravenel lamented that her name would no longer be "spotless." She had a difficult time accepting the new status of blacks and saw their prospects in freedom as grim. Like all her peers, she refused to acknowledge former slaves as equals. "Sometimes the idea is so ludicrous that I can't help laughing," she wrote, "and then again it is so dreadful, when I think of our old cook sitting up in the drawing room entertaining company." When Pauline DeCaradeuc confronted a regiment of black soldiers returning from war, she could hardly contain her anger about what she saw as an affront to white society. "I felt every imaginable emotion upon seeing them," she confessed, "they, who two or three months ago were our respectful slaves, were there as impertinent as possible . . . it was all like a pandemonium of black demons, so intense was the noise and confusion. In May of 1865, Maria Peek wrote to her betrothed that the arrest of a white neighbor at the hands of African American soldiers "was exceedingly exasperating" and that she felt outrage that the young man was "subjected to such indignity."[24]

Emma LeConte also believed that the freedom of former slaves in South Carolina signified the demise of social order. LeConte remained in Columbia with her mother and sister after the burning of the city. Without the protection of her father, who was away from the home during the Union occupation, LeConte feared that in an atmosphere of black liberation former slaves would attempt to hurt the whites. What created the most anxiety for LeConte were rumors circulating in the white community that African American troops stationed in Charleston were committing "every barbarity, until at length their outrages reached such a pitch that their officers were obliged to some extent to interfere" and noted (inaccurately) that at least thirty soldiers had been shot for "violating women." She noted that even whites in the countryside faced a population of emancipated slaves "turned loose," whose freedom welcomed "wildest anarchy." It was clear to LeConte that the freedom of slaves had undermined the mechanisms of control that she believed were so essential to the safety of the white community.[25]

Parents added to young women's concerns over the changing status of African Americans and its implications for southern whites. Susan Bradford's mother warned her that their former slaves might seek retribution against the family. Susan believed the threat had materialized when she heard that one evening Frances, a house servant who continued to work in the Bradford home after the war, came into her former mistress's room and allegedly poured chloroform on her pillow as she slept. Soon after, Bradford's mother demanded that Frances leave the plantation. The young woman's parents grew increasingly fearful that their former slaves would attempt to harm members of the family and required her to have a male escort when away from home.[26]

The end of slavery coupled with southern defeat caused some young women to lash out at their former slaves. Seeing African Americans rejoice in the Confederacy's defeat exacerbated young women's resentment. Susan Bradford, for example, never used violence against her family's slaves until after the war. Soon after news of Lee's surrender swept through her community, field hands on the Bradford plantation gathered to celebrate. Eventually the celebration moved toward the Big House, where the freedmen and women openly sang about hanging Jefferson Davis. As they made their way to Bradford's porch, the young woman became frightened. When she heard what they were singing, her fright turned to anger. Grabbing a whip, she emerged from the house screaming at the former servants and threatening to lash them until they dispersed.[27]

While young women begrudged the slaves their freedom, some also felt regret over losing the nurses, nannies, and playmates they had known from childhood. Bradford was happy to see her former house servant, Frances, leave the plantation but lamented the departure of her nannie and maid, Lulu. Even when Lulu boldly approached Susan's mother to tell her she was taking her daughter to live with family members in the Union camp near the plantation, Bradford continued to see her as a member of the larger family. Bradford's mother eventually told Lulu that she would have to leave the plantation herself if she took her daughter away. When the former nanny eventually left the plantation never to return, Bradford was upset at her mother. After Sally Independence Foster's father announced to the slaves that they were free, the family retained a few as hired domestics. Those who remained were among the slaves whom Foster had known during childhood. Three years after the war, Foster recorded her grief over losing Louisiana, their domestic servant and former slave, whom she considered part of the larger plantation family: "A dear, good, faithful servant of ours died . . . she used to watch over me when I was a child, and make all my doll's clothes for me . . . alas! She has gone, but she told me to meet her in that bright home above."[28]

Although young women accepted their new domestic duties, they had difficulty embracing the freedom of African Americans. As freedmen and women asserted their newfound political and economic autonomy with the aid of state and federal government measures led by Radical Republicans, many young women replaced their paternalistic vision of race relations with a more severe approach. Virginia Hankins, for example, found it troubling that a former slave had decided to marry. Denied the right to legal marriages, many African Americans after the war rushed to have their marriages sanctioned by the law. Such was the case for the Hankins's former household slave, who remained with the family as a paid domestic. The servant held a ceremony in which over a hundred members of the African American community attended. Although Virginia demonstrated a grudging acceptance of the marriage, she criticized her servant and the ceremony. "I am afraid she did not marry well," she wrote to her brother, "Some body stole half of the bride's cake. . . . and I had to do every thing."[29]

The efforts of whites to reassert white supremacy politicized the domestic setting as young women attempted to establish power over hired servants in their home. Having black servants to cook, clean, and care for the children not only made slaveholding women's lives easier but also reinforced class and racial divisions among all women. Emancipation destroyed this traditional form of class distinction and sent elite and middle-class white women searching for new ways to distinguish themselves from their social inferiors. Many young women shared with their mothers a disdain for housework not because of the labor itself, but because they perceived it as the work of black or poor white women. Kate Foster, for example, had learned new domestic skills during the war and continued to care for the home after the war ended. Yet she struggled with the class implications of taking over the duties her slaves once performed, admitting that "it is hard to come down to a level with a servant."[30]

As a result, those who employed African American servants attempted to reestablish traditional lines of power common in the antebellum era. They drew a sense of authority from their insistence on controlling the work hours, pay, and tasks of their hired help. Moreover, they expected their servants to show deference to them, characteristic of white-black relations in slavery. But efforts to establish their authority was met with conflict as former slave women, who tended to fill the ranks of hired domestics in the postwar era, sought to control the terms of their labor. If a servant disliked the tasks, work hours, or pay, she could choose to leave and seek employment elsewhere. Moreover, African American women refused to remain in a home in which their employer insisted on conditions reminiscent of slavery. Fannie Leak was appalled that Katie, a house servant the family hired, refused to concede to her mother's reprimands. On one occasion, Fannie's mother threatened to whip the servant "for some misdemeanor." Fannie was appalled, however, when Katie "sprang from the window, and ran and concealed herself near town some where." Although her servant eventually returned, Leak lamented the loss of white authority over their help, wondering, "what is to become of her [Katie]." When domestics protested or ignored orders, young women saw them as impudent and untrustworthy. Many believed that, as freed people, blacks were dishonest and unwilling to work. Kate Foster distrusted African Americans in freedom and thus advised her peers to refrain from hiring domestics. After a neighbor complained of items missing from her home, Foster blamed the servant, insisting that "the servant has proven what Pa and I felt her to be, a dishonest woman."[31]

Mary Chamberlayne found her servants' freedom troublesome and grew frustrated in trying to establish authority over them. After her marriage to John and the birth of her first child, Mary employed a few servants to oversee the housekeeping and assist in childcare. John Chamberlayne had found steady employment and the family brought in enough income for Mary to hire a regular squad of servants to lighten her workload. Yet, Mary, who had spent her childhood surrounded by household slaves, could only conceptualize her relationship with the servants in terms of the traditional mistress-slave paradigm. In an environment in which Mary demanded complete submission from her employees, her servants rebelled and, on occasion, quit or refused to perform certain tasks. Mary found such behavior troubling and viewed her servants with disdain and distrust. After Abigail, one of her servants, chose to leave, Mary responded with a mixture of relief and anger, noting "I for one am not sorry for she would take the permission anywhere for disagreeable manners." She wrote to her mother that although she intended to hire a replacement for Abigail, she believed she could "not look for anything else but trouble in this department."[32]

Changes in labor relations also occurred outside the home and in the fields as southern whites attempted to define the terms of work for the former slaves who worked their plantations. Some young women, newly married after the war, found themselves in the role of labor manager when their husbands were absent. Eleanore Eulalie Fleming, for one, took charge of recording wages and distributing them to her small labor force. In some cases, they negotiated labor contracts that ensured the power of the landlord over the labor of freedmen and women. Southern daughters, who as adolescents had had little understanding of slave management, also took on the responsibility of overseeing laborers in the fields. Olin Davis, of North Carolina, for example, quickly learned how to give orders to her field workers and thereafter expertly directed them in planting, cultivating, and harvesting the crop.[33]

The political and civic arenas became another setting in which southern whites attempted to restore the traditional racial ordering of society. Former slaveholders perceived the new legal, political, and economic rights of African Americans as a threat to their attempts to reestablish their power after the war. Under Presidential Reconstruction, suffrage was restored to most former Confederates, while black codes and forced labor contracts allowed former slaveholders to retain economic power over African Americans. But, the rising power of Radical Republicans in Congress threatened the South's resurgent elite. In response, southern whites campaigned to limit the newly acquired rights of former slaves. Perhaps the most effective means of promoting white supremacy came from the violence of white terrorist groups coupled with forms of economic coercion that were used to intimidate blacks into relinquishing their political and social liberties. White women especially saw a double meaning in the attempts to suppress blacks: while restoring white supremacy based on the authority of elite men, it would also allow fathers and husbands to restore their masculine identity in the wake of defeat.[34]

Young women understood the reassertion of white supremacy through violence as necessary to restoring the status and reputation of their families. The importance of Reconstruction politics in their lives was evident foremost in their personal letters and diaries. In these intimate writings, they expressed concern over the changing status of African Americans, explained their views on Reconstruction policies, villainized Republican politicians, and lauded southerners who attempted to restore white authority and force former slaves to submit. As they witnessed increasing racial discord and even violence, young women became more vocal in their opposition to radical policies. Like other white southerners, they denounced blacks and white Republican politicians who sought racial equality. Anna Maria Green feared that black suffrage would provoke a race war. "Indeed it seems impossible for the white men to submit to negro rule," she wrote. "It is certainly a distressing state of affairs when negroes hold conventions in our state and indeed have every right of suffrage and civil power."[35]

Southern daughters also enunciated resentment toward Reconstruction policies that they believed subjugated their white male counterparts to the authority of Republican governments. Sarah Chaffin, for example, faulted General Ulysses S. Grant and the Republican Party for denying her brother a position in his administration. "Brother Edwin was grossly deceived by General Grant," she wrote, "when he went finally to get the papers drawn up Grant told him if he would turn Radical he should command the position." In Chaffin's view, Grant's retraction of the position exemplified what she saw as the corrupt nature of Republican politics. Moreover, her brother's loss of potential income in the process seemed to Chaffin to indicate that the Republican governments intended to strip southern white men of their economic power.[36]

As elite white southerners grew increasingly angry at the Republican regimes in Washington and the southern states, they attempted to restore their authority through extralegal means, including terrorism by the Ku Klux Klan, the Red Shirts, and the White Leagues. These armed bodies used violent tactics to keep blacks from voting and to break up Republican political rallies and targeted those who seemed to exercise economic autonomy. The central idea used to justify such methods was the defense of white womanhood. The Klan maintained that they offered protection against the sexualized black man who, without the constraints of slavery, was now free to exploit and demoralize the virtuous, white southern woman. This gendered rhetoric was intended to belie the real reason for targeting African American men: that those who exercised too much economic and political autonomy threatened the efforts to resurrect white supremacy. The ideals of preserving white womanhood thus served a three-fold purpose of excusing the violence of the Klan, reestablishing white male political and economic hegemony, and weakening the social power of freedmen.[37]

Although the federal government passed the Ku Klux Klan Act of 1871 prohibiting the clandestine activities of white terrorist organizations, the violence continued in large-scale assaults upon the political activities of African Americans and white Republicans. In Louisiana, the use of violence to restore Democratic rule proved effective. Whites in Mississippi employed similar tactics in their efforts to ensure Democratic victory during the state elections in 1875. Known as the "Mississippi Plan," Democrats in the state created a campaign to bring all southern whites into the party. The next step was to conduct a relentless campaign of economic coercion and public violence. The use of violence was essential to their plan; Democrats went about causing disturbances at Republican gatherings then using the outbreak of a "riot" to begin firing on the crowd.[38]

South Carolina, like other southern states, followed this model of terror, as whites strove to bring their state back under Democratic control. The most violent outbreak occurred in September of 1876, after a Democratic meeting in which blacks and whites attended. African American Republicans attacked black participants of the gathering, claiming that they had betrayed their race. Violence erupted in what was known as the "King Street" riot between whites and blacks in the city until the mayor called out military forces to squash the fighting. By the end of the day, three people were dead and several others wounded. The white community responded to the riot with alarm, organizing members of rifle clubs to patrol the streets in shifts. Although African Americans, according to the historical record, initiated the violence that led to the King Street riot, white males seized the opportunity to wage an attack on the black community on a much larger scale. Racial tensions continued throughout the remainder of the state election campaigns that pitted Daniel Chamberlain, the Republican governor, against Wade Hampton, the Democratic candidate. During the election season, white members of the rifle clubs used the Mississippi paradigm of violence and economic coercion to keep blacks away from the polls and ensure a Democratic victory.[39]

The tumultuous era of the 1870s brought a retreat from Reconstruction. By 1872, most southern white men had regained the vote. Popular support among northerners for Reconstruction waned in the wake of the economic crisis that began in 1873. With the ratification of the Fifteenth Amendment, furthermore, many advocates of racial equality believed that their work was completed. By the time Grant left office in 1877, Democrats had taken control, or "redeemed," eight of the eleven former Confederate states. When Rutherford B. Hayes assumed the presidency following the Compromise of 1877, he brought about the end of Reconstruction by refusing to intervene any further in the South with military force.[40]

With the end of Reconstruction and the ascendancy of the Redeemer state governments, white southerners increased their efforts to curtail the political and economic power of African Americans in the region. Beginning in the 1880s, various states began to pass segregation laws with regard to public facilities. Challenges to these laws led to the case of *Plessy vs. Ferguson* in 1896 in which the Supreme Court upheld the constitutionality of segregation in public places based on the idea that "separate but equal" facilities did not constitute discrimination. This decision led to the emergence of Jim Crow laws that legalized a separation of the races. The end of the century also witnessed the disfranchisement of African American men through the adoption of voting qualifications, including poll taxes, grandfather clauses, and literacy tests. But the campaign to reassert white supremacy also led to the demonization of African American men as a means to justify the limitations of black rights and increase the authority of white males. Accusations of black men raping white women continued into the 1880s in an effort to define the color line and ensure racial hierarchy. Such extralegal means differed from the earlier Klan attacks. While the Klan operated as an organization and conducted violence in disguise, lynchings involved informal mobs of whites and were public spectacles intended to intimidate the black community and demonstrate white solidarity. In the 1890s, however, Ida B. Wells, a black woman from Memphis, Tennessee, led a campaign against lynching, citing the lack of evidence proving the validity of rape accusations. Yet, by the 1900s, the campaign to return to prewar divisions of racial power waged on the government and community levels had restored white power and limited the political and economic freedoms of African Americans.[41]

Young women of the war era played a key role in the efforts to reassert white authority. Through their published and unpublished memoirs of the Civil War, they promoted an image of African Americans in freedom that upheld the racist ideologies of the New South. Their recollections that lauded slavery as a peaceful time in race relations and portrayed African Americans in freedom as indigent and immoral contributed to the atmosphere of racial antagonism and helped to curtail the advancements in black rights made during Reconstruction. They created a dichotomous image of African Americans in wartime. On one side stood the faithful servant who remained committed to the master and his family throughout the war; on the other side was the slave who abandoned the family for freedom only to find frustration and hardships with the dreaded Yankees. The dichotomous slave image gave way to the villainized representation of African Americans in freedom. Their writings of postwar race relations both in the domestic and community arenas emphasized the detrimental effects of black freedom on the stability of southern society. In some cases, their stories were intended for family members, but others were published in newspapers and by presses in the decades after the war. Either way, young women of the war generation became active agents in creating an atmosphere conducive to white supremacy as a result of their desire to find continuity with the prewar status quo. While the war had torn apart the traditional racial hierarchy, their writings on race would help to restore it.

The recollections of Louisa McCord Smythe exemplify the narrative of racial antagonism that shaped white southern sentiment. Smythe constructed her memoirs to provide a record of the Civil War for future generations of her family. Writing from the standpoint of the late 1890s, however, Smythe's recollections also offered a testimony of how members of her generation came to understand the changing nature of race relations in the New South era. Growing up in South Carolina, Smythe was the member of a slaveholding family and had come to accept the tenets of paternalism. But, emancipation forced her to reassess her relationship with African Americans. While she lamented the loss of household servants with whom she felt particularly close, such as her childhood nanny Marianne, she viewed the majority of freedmen and women through a racist lens. The changing status of African Americans signaled to Smythe a demise of social order. With the control over blacks that slavery had once provided now gone, she saw all African Americans and their white allies as the source of social unrest. It was, in her view, up to southern whites to find some way of reasserting racial hierarchy and thus instilling a sense of order. Smythe and other former slaveholders expressed these attitudes as a means of justifying the racist and often violent methods of ensuring white supremacy.[42]

Smythe, like many of her peers, placed the blame for the racial disorder first on the efforts of northern outsiders. This position served a dual purpose of offering a defense of slavery as a benevolent institution while illustrating the destructive nature of Reconstruction policies, especially those concerning black rights, on southern communities. To demonstrate her position, Smythe turned to early days of Reconstruction in her hometown of Charleston. After Lee's surrender, Union forces occupied the war-ravaged city. It was their presence, Smythe argued, that led hundreds of once faithful and content slaves to abandon the masters and mistresses who had given "plenty" to provide for all their needs. Given the choice, she believed that their servants would have chosen to remain with the family rather than live in freedom. "Deluded, the poor creatures," she wrote, "by false promises, frightened by the site of those to whom they had looked for everything, in such absolute need, and no doubt, feeling themselves the pinching of our poverty, as they had felt the comfort of our plenty; they [the freedmen] one by one began to disappear from the yards of their former owners." She also blamed the presence of Republican "politicians and schoolmarms who came from 'down East'" for instigating the violent confrontations between whites and blacks in her hometown. In tackling the issue of black support for Republican efforts, Smythe argued that newly freed African Americans were pawns of southern white Republicans who, in her view, were bent on retaliation against the old planter elite. When the violence of southern whites escalated in the last year of Reconstruction, Smythe maintained that Republican influences created much of the disturbances, despite evidence that southern whites Democrats had perpetrated the violence in an effort to take back control of the state and local governments. "Poor things they were in a pitiful position between two fires. They knew that their interest and their affections lay with the white people, and yet they were obliged often to pretend to what they didn't feel."[43]

Smythe likewise contended that African Americans fared much worse in freedom in terms of their material and moral conditions. She had little faith that her former servants would lead better lives outside the protective confines of slavery. She depicted freedmen as a sort of nomadic group unable or unwilling to create a stable environment. After the slaves left, she argued, they "would quietly fall into the vacant place, and go on for a day or two with the work of the departed sister or brother, only to depart themselves the moment the notion took them."[44]

Other women of Smythe's age group shared her sentiments concerning the source and consequences of African American freedom. Annie

Jeter Carmouche, whose husband owned a large plantation after the war, wrote in her memoirs that southern white Republicans encouraged African Americans to defy their former masters. The efforts of the Freedmen's Bureau to aid former slaves in negotiating labor contracts and establishing schools signified a transition in race relations that horrified Carmouche and many of her peers. "Some of the atrocities committed by the colored people—generally some low white man at the head—were terrible," she wrote, "especially when they had 'The Freedman's Bureau' to back them." Joachimson blamed the racial instability on the Union forces that occupied her hometown outside Charleston, South Carolina. She argued that it was the influence of northern troops and their promises of "wealth and splendor" that led their slaves to leave the plantation. "Few of them would be able to resist the golden bait," she added, "or suspect that liberty and hard work would soon become for them synonymous terms." In Joachimson's estimation, blacks were far better off as slaves, rather than as freedmen and women facing the uncertainties of freedom. Such assumptions implied that the racial hierarchy benefited blacks as well by alleviating the hardships that she believed were associated with freedom.[45]

Smythe's recollections present a unique understanding of young women's efforts to reestablish racial hierarchy because of her open endorsement of violence as a means of curtailing the political and social freedom of African Americans. Looking back on the riots that took place in South Carolina, she argued that they were necessary actions to promote order. Smythe's husband was among many of those men in Charleston who participated in the violence of King Street and other incidents, and she supported her husband's efforts during the state elections in 1876. Like many of her generation, she blamed blacks and white Republicans in South Carolina for the unrest in her state and praised the formation of "Rifle companies and other military companies" to squash potential uprisings. "The disturbances were quieted by the show of determination made by the whites," she recalled, "the negroes and their instigators knew that if once the fight began there would be no mercy." As a show of her support, Smythe helped her husband and other members of his vigilante group by giving them food and supplies. "Everything was systematized," she wrote, "even to feeding them when on duty but everything was done with the most absolute quiet. I only remember a note would come to me occasionally requesting me to have so many sandwiches and so much coffee ready at such an hour."[46]

Smythe witnessed much of the bloodshed that occurred between blacks and whites in the city. Rather than acknowledge her husband and his peers in the rifle clubs as the aggressors, she laid much of the blame on African Americans and white Republicans, whose political stance directly challenged the power of white Democrats in the state, and who, in her view, had initiated the hostilities. She also held that on occasion blacks in the city had become the attackers. In describing the riot of 1876, she attempted to portray a race war instigated by African Americans whose freedom had destroyed social order:

> Young men of our acquaintance were beaten to death in the streets by negroes. At the slightest alarm, apparently without a word, the streets would be filled by 'our men' each with his gun in his hand and we never knew when the whole city would be bathed in blood. It was only by the greatest coolness that the most awful scenes were prevented.

Smythe's dismal depiction of racial violence in the South reflected the growing sentiment of whites that black freedom created social disorder and only through a resurrection of the racial hierarchy, whether through legal or extralegal means, would order resume.[47]

Sallie Hunt, of Lynchburg, Virginia, chose to romanticize the relationship between slaveholders and their servants to demonstrate the destructive nature of black freedom. Writing for the South Carolina *Weekly News and Courier* in 1885, Hunt details the difficulty for both blacks and whites in accepting the end of slavery. Rather than creating social chaos, she posited, emancipation caused heartache and sadness among former slaves who were better off in slavery. Hunt argued that from their earliest childhood years, southern youth were "slave-holders by the time they could talk." Yet, the master-slave relationship that Hunt and her peers had come to accept was one based on paternalism. By emphasizing the familial bonds, Hunt was erecting a defense of racial hierarchy that portrayed relations between whites and blacks as stable, even affectionate. Freedom, in Hunt's estimation, was a destructive force that tore apart the slave family and stirred social instability. To paint this portrait of race relations in slavery versus in freedom, she turned to her recollections of emancipation day on her plantation. Hunt's father assembled the slaves to announce that they were free. He offered, "any who care to stay with us will meet with the

same treatment they have ever received at their hands." Hunt, however, explained that the news created "the keenest anxiety over certain servants to
whom we were especially attached." But, when presented with the option
to stay with their former masters or leave for freedom, Hunt contended
that most chose to remain with them. "Those who left," she added, "we
were better without." Yet Hunt felt the need to rationalize why some would
choose freedom, arguing that those who left were pawns in the efforts of
"low, debased carpetbaggers" to turn slaves against their former masters.
By downplaying the free will of African Americans while emphasizing
the harmony found in the master-slave relationship, Hunt, in essence, was
attempting to demonstrate the desirability of racial hierarchy.[48]

Another young woman writing from the perspective of the 1880s likewise used the dichotomous image of freed men and women in asserting
an argument to curtail black rights. She recalled that during the war, a
"faithful, trusted head-servant" was charged with hiding the family's valuables. Having sworn to keep the family's hiding place a secret, the servant
refused to turn against his master and mistress and divulge the information to the occupying northern troops. However, another slave, whom
she explained was "an alien without kindred, but recently come among
our slaves, and jealous of the trust imposed in others" learned that the
head-servant knew the hiding place and turned him in to Union soldiers.
Rather than the sad scene painted by Hunt's description of emancipation
day, this young woman, who published her work anonymously in a South
Carolina paper, demonstrated to readers that racial freedom created difficult, even dangerous, predicaments for southern society and that only
through the control of whites over blacks would order be restored.[49]

Race proved a complex issue for southern daughters who found themselves caught between the old paternalistic values of their childhood and
the new freedoms of their former servants. Reconstruction brought about
the transition to a free labor system while constitutional reform opened
the door of citizenship to African Americans. As the daughters of former
slaveholders confronted these changes, they gradually exchanged their
familial sentiments toward their former nurses, cooks, and other domestic
servants for harsher, more racist perceptions of the black race as a whole.
No longer did they see their servants as an extension of the slaveholding
family, but rather subscribed to the sentiment that all African Americans
were part of an indolent and immoral race that, in freedom, created social

chaos and political corruption. This perception was intended to return former Confederates to their place in the political, economic and social structure based upon a new system of racial hierarchy, one that endorsed both legal and extralegal means of limiting black freedom. Southern whites worked to that end by utilizing a variety of methods including changes to voting rights in the state constitutions, use of debt peonage to tie African Americans to the land, and lynching as a means of instilling social fear. Within this context, the memoirs of young white women who came of age in the Civil War became a cultural tool to help gain broader acceptance of the white supremacist agenda in the New South. By reflecting on the relationship between whites and blacks during and after the conflict, this generation hoped to return the South to its traditional racial order.

Young women found their postwar writings a useful psychological tool in reconciling themselves to the defeat of a cause to which they had such personal connections. The loss of the Confederacy meant more than dealing with a return to the Union; it meant dealing with the loss of a future they had hoped to inherit. Gone were the expectations of one day assuming the place of their mothers and grandmothers as slave mistresses reigning over plantation households. Rather, they now had to come to terms with the demise of the master class and the emergence of an industrializing, free labor New South. The generation of women who witnessed the war as teenagers attempted to understand the implications of defeat on their futures. Some dealt with the loss of the Confederacy by focusing on the transitional nature of their wartime experiences. Mary Washington Cabell Early, who wrote about the war in a series of newspaper articles, described how war changed her and her peers:

> They [women] have adapted themselves to their great reverses with the fortitude that belongs to every true woman and the versatility that especially characterizes American women amid their changed circumstances. . . . The changes in their circumstances and surroundings have necessarily modified the characteristics of Virginia women. Not being so closely sheltered from the storms of life as heretofore, contact with its hard realities has rubbed off somewhat of their former shrinking softness, and lessened the pliability of their disposition.

Louisa McCord Smythe also believed that she was among a special group of women who had grown up amid a landscape of turmoil and heartbreak. "I wonder that our generation of women have any nerves left at all," she wrote, "the amount of watching and waiting that we have done seems almost incredible as I look back, and it is so provokingly impossible to give an idea of it to others." Emma Cassandra Riely likewise contended that "the coming generation will never experience the many sad days of trial and suffering we passed through in the South."[50]

Others focused on the outcome of the war and its implications for the future of the South and the Union. Mattie Jarnagin portrayed the end of the war as a positive step toward rebuilding the South, especially in terms of reuniting families. She wrote that when news of surrender reached her home "a dark cloud settled over us" but concluded that "the return of the boys who wore the grey soon made our hearts light again, for we wanted to make happy their short holiday, before they took up life's burdens in earnest." One young woman had a less idyllic view of the postwar period. For her, the Reconstruction years proved to be more of a struggle than the war itself. "The years that come after [the Civil War]," she wrote, "are more replete with tragedy, with heart-stirring sorrows, with 'hope deferred that maketh the heart sick,' with battles fought by women, with hardship, misfortune and distress, than ever stirred the pages of any 'History of the War.'"[51]

Still, some embraced the idea of reuniting with the North and putting the regional strife behind them. One woman who spent her teenage years in Florence, South Carolina, concluded her memoirs with advice to those of her generation still bitter from the struggle. "Those dreadful scenes are now over, and peace reigns in all our land, but many of our Southern women who saw their bravest and best taken from them during those cruel years, still find it hard to say 'Thy will, not mine, be done.'" She offered that northern and southern women, however, shared a bond that had the power to squash any future conflicts. "They too weep over the graves of many loved ones," she argued, "and surely this should prove a bond of sympathy between North and South." When Lelia Morris presented her recollection of the war to the United Daughters of the Confederacy in 1902, she also emphasized the importance of reunion in the South's effort to move forward. She offered an anecdote about a man from the North who married a member of the Nancy Harts. Although the citizens of

La Grange viewed this man skeptically, they eventually accepted him as one of their own. "Thus the blue and the grey have been so united," she wrote, "that the children of this Southland will recognize no North and no South, but all bitterness will be forgotten and all courage remembered for the glory of our country and one flag."[52]

The Confederate belle image constructed in the postwar years provides a window into how southern daughters attempted to shape the Lost Cause narrative, while revealing their reactions to the social landscape of the New South. Notions of self-sacrifice, feminine duty, and white supremacy permeated their writings much like that of the older female generation of their mothers. Those who were teenagers during the war, however, saw age as a distinguishing factor and used it to promote a narrative distinct from other postwar memoirs. As Confederate supporters and slaveholders, these young women had accepted the doctrines of the Lost Cause mythology. They too hoped that by using the imagery of the Confederate belle that they could portray the war as a just mission, glorify the Confederacy, and paint an idyllic picture of the Old South and its "peculiar" institution. The themes of courtship, family, and sacrifice that defined this rhetorical device gave them a voice in the very public battle to shape the memory of the war within the domain of acceptable behavior for southern women of the middling and elite classes. Moreover, their personal and public writings allowed them to navigate the changing environment of the postwar South and come to terms with emancipation. Their recollections of the war and of their relationships with paid servants became the medium through which they could transmit their shifting perceptions of race relations. What emerged was a new basis for white supremacy, one that would remain ensconced in the South until the onset of the Civil Rights movement of the twentieth century.

Conclusion

BY THE EARLY 1900s, southern daughters of the war generation could look to the future with a sense of optimism. Having had children of their own, they saw the torch of southern womanhood passed on to a new generation. Their daughters, born in the postwar era, were now in the throes of adulthood and building their own families. Looking forward, their mothers hoped that a brighter future lay ahead. Those especially affected by the material deprivations of war turned their attention to new forms of financial security and subscribed to the New South boosterism that touted development of industry and diversity of crop production. Mary Washington Cabell Early, for example, believed that the economic future of the South depended on industrial development. "The changes brought about by the war are chiefly noticeable in the agricultural districts of Virginia," Early boasted, "Richmond is built up in much handsomer style than ever before, and has an important element of prosperity in her large milling interests, iron works and tobacco manufactories."[1]

The story of young women told in this book illuminates how age and gender shaped support for the Confederacy. As daughters of slaveholding, secessionist families, they stood to lose everything if the South failed to emerge victorious from the war. From their earliest childhood, their education, church, and parents had indoctrinated them into the ideals of southern womanhood. The cultural script that they inherited trumpeted women as the embodiment of moral fortitude, maternal values, and domesticity. When they reached their adolescence, young women had accepted this ideal as their own and believed that they would one day fill the roles of the generations of southern, slaveholding women before them. Yet, these daughters were born into a unique era, one that would set them apart from their foremothers. The growing regional strife of the

1840s and 1850s signaled to young women an impending threat against their expectations for adulthood. The only hope for preserving the racial and gender traditions that informed their future was to throw their support behind the growing movement for secession. When their respective states left the Union and began to mobilize for battle with the North, they reoriented their lives to help support the Confederate cause and sustain their communities and families through the exigencies of war.

Some historians describe female involvement in the war as a watershed moment after which women entered into new areas of civic activism and paid employment. Others have demonstrated how the war did little to cause a fundamental shift in their lives. This study has taken a different approach to this age-old historiographical debate. Examined in the context of Confederate loyalty and patriotism, young women's experiences in the war produced a conservative outcome in the short term while providing the groundwork for changes in the definition of southern womanhood that would come in the twentieth century. Young women wanted nothing more out of the Confederacy than to maintain continuity with the past and to ensure that their future, one grounded in the antebellum gender and racial hierarchy, would be there for them when they reached adulthood. This desire to preserve the antebellum past provided the motivation, however, for this generation to enter into new worlds of community activism, domestic labor, and paid employment. They also remained committed to a traditional path for women by creating new courtship rituals and adapting old ones to meet the wartime circumstances. This mixture of continuity and change also defined young women's memories of the war, made evident in their personal and published reminiscences. The themes of their recollections, shaped by age, came together to form the Confederate belle image that set their generation's interpretation of the Lost Cause apart from that of their mothers. But this female figure did more than reveal the complexities of gender in Lost Cause mythology. It illuminated their concerns for the future of southern masculinity and racial order in the New South era. They found a solution by trumpeting traditional gender ideals and prewar racist ideologies. Thus, as this generation entered into adulthood, they remained tied to the past while navigating the uncharted waters of the New South.

The events of the war compelled young women to alter their traditional notions of gender roles and shaped their identity as they came of age. This identity, filtered through antebellum notions of feminine duty, incorporated the new attitudes and skills they had gained during the war. Although this self-image failed to undermine traditional notions of southern womanhood, it expanded young women's idea of what it meant to be female and southern. The environment of the postwar South helped sustain this new identity as young women reached adulthood and perpetuated the notion that they were unique from those who came before them and those who would follow. The war had transformed these young women from the protected belles of slaveholding families into self-sufficient managers in the home and civic-minded participants able to confront the changing social, political, and economic landscape of the Civil War and postwar South. Their experiences played an important role in the transformation of southern women, serving to bridge the cultural gap between the Old South and the New.

Appendix

Notes

Bibliography

Index

Appendix

TABLE 1. NUMBER OF SLAVES PER HOUSEHOLD (N=62)

Slaves	Number	Percentage
1–10	26	41.93
11–20	7	11.29
21–50	13	20.96
51–100	8	12.91
More than 100	8	12.91

TABLE 2. RESIDENCY (N=85)

State	Number	Percentage
Alabama	5	5.88
Florida	1	1.18
Georgia	6	7.06
Louisiana	4	4.70
Maryland	1	1.18
Mississippi	7	8.24
North Carolina	6	7.05
South Carolina	15	17.65
Tennessee	12	14.12
Virginia	28	32.94

TABLE 3. YEAR OF BIRTH (N=85)

Year	Number	Percentage
1843	14	16.48
1844	14	16.48
1845	13	15.29
1846	11	12.94
1847	13	15.29
1848	13	15.29
1849	7	8.23

Table 4. Value of Real Property (*N*=51)

Dollar Amount	Number	Percentage
500–10,999	19	37.25
11,000–20,999	9	17.65
21,000–50,999	17	33.34
51,000–100,000	2	3.92
More than 100,000	4	7.84

Table 5. Value of Personal Property (*N*=54)

Dollar Amount	Number	Percentage
500–10,999	17	31.48
11,000–20,999	6	11.11
21,000–50,999	14	25.93
51,000–100,000	11	20.37
More than 100,000	6	11.11

Table 6. Date of First Marriage (*N*=34)

Year	Number	Percentage
1861–63	2	5.88
1864–65	7	20.59
1866–68	9	26.47
1869–70	11	32.35
1871–77	5	14.71

Notes

Abbreviations

ADAH Alabama Department of Archives and History, Montgomery, Alabama

AHC Atlanta History Center, Atlanta, Georgia

Duke Rare Book, Manuscript, and Special Collections Library, Perkins Library, Duke University, Durham, N.C.

GDAH Georgia Department of Archives and History, Atlanta, Georgia

LC Louisiana and Lower Mississippi Valley Collections, Louisiana State University

MDAH Mississippi Department of Archives and History, Jackson, Mississippi

MC Ellen Brockenbrough Library, Museum of the Confederacy, Richmond, Virginia

RWL Robert W. Woodruff Library, Special Collections, Emory University, Atlanta, Georgia

SCHS South Carolina Historical Society, Columbia

SCL South Caroliniana Library, Columbia

SHC Southern Historical Collection, University of North Carolina, Chapel Hill

SL Swem Library, College of William and Mary, Williamsburg, Virginia

TSLA Tennessee State Library and Archives, Nashville

VHS Virginia Historical Society, Richmond

WAM Wesleyan Archives and Museum, University of North Alabama, Florence

Introduction

1. Earl Schenck Miers, ed., *When the World Ended: The Diary of Emma LeConte* (New York: Oxford University Press, 1957), 21–22.

2. Studies of the creation of Confederate nationalism include George Rable, *The Confederate Republic: A Revolution Against Politics* (Chapel Hill: University of North Carolina Press, 1994); Drew Gilpin Faust, *The Creation of Confederate Nationalism: Ideology and Identity in the Civil War South* (Baton Rouge: Louisiana

State University Press, 1988); and Anne Sarah Rubin, *A Shattered Nation: The Rise and Fall of the Confederacy, 1861–1868* (Chapel Hill: University of North Carolina Press, 2005).

3. For a discussion of the origins and course of the sectional debates see David M. Potter, *The South and the Sectional Conflict* (Baton Rouge: Louisiana State University Press, 1968) and Michael F. Holt, *The Political Crisis of the 1850s*, New Ed. edition (New York: W.W. Norton Company, 1983). Eric Foner, in *Free Soil, Free Labor, Free Men: the Ideology of the Republican Party Before the Civil War* (New York: Oxford University Press, 1970) examines the free labor ideals that helped fuel sectionalism.

4. Studies that tie southerners' efforts to preserve the social order with support for the Confederacy include, Lacy K. Ford, *Origins of Southern Radicalism: The South Carolina Upcountry, 1800–1860* (New York: Oxford University Press, 1998). Faust examines the role of gender in the social structure in *Mothers of Invention: Women of the Slaveholding South in the American Civil War* (Chapel Hill: University of North Carolina Press, 1996).

5. The study of Confederate women has undergone dramatic changes since the publication of Ann Firor Scott's *The Southern Lady: From Pedestal to Politics, 1830–1930* (Chicago: University of Chicago, 1970) that brought to light the transformative nature of the war on the image and roles of southern women. Since then George Rable's *Civil Wars: Women and the Crisis of Southern Nationalism* (Urbana: University of Illinois Press, 1989), Faust's *Mothers of Invention* and LeeAnn Whites's *Civil War as a Crisis in Gender: Augusta, Georgia, 1860–1890* (Athens: University of Georgia Press, 1995) have shifted the focus of study to female identity and questioned the watershed nature of the experience in southern women's lives. More recent studies, including Jane Turner Censer, *The Reconstruction of White Southern Womanhood, 1865–1895* (Baton Rouge: Louisiana State University Press, 2003), Alexis Girardin Brown, "The Women Left Behind: Transformation of the Southern Belle, 1840–1880," *Historian* 62 (Summer 2000): 759–79, and Giselle Roberts, *The Confederate Belle* (Columbia: University of Missouri Press, 2003), have included age as a category of analysis, enlarging our understanding of war's effect on identity formation and female roles. Roberts offers an analysis of young women between 15 and 25 who lived in Mississippi and Louisiana during the war. Examining young women's experiences in the context of family honor, Roberts illuminates how and why this age group became participants in the war effort. Censer's study examines three generations of white southern women in the postwar era from North Carolina and Virginia and how they sought to redefine their feminine identity in the changing social, economic, and political landscape of the New South. She argues that white women replaced the traditional notions of femininity, that which emphasized the

search for a perfect marital partner as the fulfillment of women's destiny as well as the ideals of dependence and submission, for the values of "self-reliance and female capability." My study, in part, builds on these earlier works in that I also employ age as a lens of analysis. Yet, my intention is to place these young women in the context of the movement to create a Confederate nationalist identity, thus revealing the intersection of war and female youth culture and its long-term effects on this generation's worldview during and after the war. Moreover, rather than concentrate on a generation, typically spanning fifteen to twenty years, I have narrowed the focus to the developmental stage of adolescence, a period in which identity formation is occurring both in and outside the family setting.

6. Elizabeth Varon, *We Mean To Be Counted: White Women and Politics in Antebellum Virginia* (Chapel Hill: University of North Carolina Press, 1998), 169–70; Rubin, *Shattered Nation*, 53–64.

7. William M. Tuttle, Jr., *Daddy's Gone to War: The Second World War in the Lives of America's Children* (New York: Oxford University Press, 1993), 15, 254; Rebecca E. Klatch, *A Generation Divided: The New Left, the New Right, and the 1960s* (Berkeley: University of California Press, 1999), 3.

8. John and Virginia Demos, "Adolescence in Historical Perspective," *Journal of Marriage and Family* 31 (November 1969): 632–38. Other studies dealing with the distinctions between child and adolescent include Joseph F. Kett, *Rites of Passage: Adolescence in America, 1790 to the Present* (New York: Basic Books, 1977) and Jane Turner Censer, *North Carolina Planters and Their Children, 1800–1860* (Baton Rouge: Louisiana State University Press, 1984).

9. Barbara Welter, *Dimity Convictions: The American Woman in the Nineteenth Century* (Athens: Ohio University Press, 1976).

10. Anya Jabour, "'Grown Girls, Highly Cultivated': Female Education in an Antebellum Southern Family," *Journal of Southern History* 64 (February 1998), 32–34. Other studies that examine female education in the same era include Christie Anne Farnham, *The Education of the Southern Belle: Higher Education and Student Socialization in the Antebellum South* (New York: Oxford University Press, 1994) and Walter J. Fraser, Jr. R. Frank Saunders, Jr., and John L. Wakelyn, eds., *The Web of Southern Social Relations: Women, Family and Education* (Athens: University of Georgia Press, 1985).

11. Susan Bradford Eppes, *Through Some Eventful Years* (Macon: J.W. Burke, Co., 1926), 298–99; Alice Lucas to brother, June 2, 1864, Lucas-Ashley Family Papers, Duke.

12. I verified the number of slaves for sixty-two subjects using information from the United States Seventh (1850) and Eighth (1860) censuses, slave schedules. In determining the real and personal property value for families, I used the United States Eighth (1860) Census, population schedules.

13. For a discussion of male and female concepts of honor see Bertram Wyatt-Brown, *Southern Honor: Ethics and Behavior in the Old South* (New York: Oxford University Press, 1982), Steven Stowe, *Intimacy and power in the Old South: Ritual in the Lives of Planters* (Baltimore: University of Maryland Press, 1987), and Roberts, *Confederate Belle*, 4–5.

14. United States Seventh (1850), Eighth (1860), and Tenth (1880) censuses, population schedules; United States Seventh (1850) and Eighth (1860) censuses, slave schedules.

1. "Our Bright Youth"

1. Eppes, *Through Some Eventful Years*, 95–100.

2. My use of the term "youth culture" is meant to label the concerns and daily activities of young women of the antebellum era. Most historians view this term as a twentieth-century creation linked to the activities of teenagers and young adults in the twenties, fifties, and sixties. While the youth culture that existed in the antebellum South is unlike that of the twentieth century, there were activities that society viewed as solely for young people and excluded older, married adults such as social occasions at school. Moreover, a set of social concerns, namely dress, peer relations, courtships, school life, and social engagements, were particular to youths in the period. Although this youth culture existed in the antebellum era, it was neither on the scale of nor as formally defined as that of twentieth-century youths. Sarah Wadley Diary, January 5, 1861, Sarah Wadley Papers, SHC. For other studies of female youth culture in the Old South, see Anya Jabour, *Scarlett's Sisters: Young Women in the Old South* (Chapel Hill: University of North Carolina Press, 2007).

3. Jabour, "Grown Girls, Highly Cultivated," 32–34.

4. Farnham, *Education of the Southern Belle*, 3–4, 16–18, 89–90; William R. Snell, ed., *Myra Inman: A Diary of the Civil War in East Tennessee* (Macon: Mercer University Press, 2000), chapter one, passim. Between 1850 and 1859 there began in the South a push to offer college classes at female seminaries. Most young women who took college-level courses, however, never intended to work outside the home, and the courses were introductory level. Only in the post-Reconstruction era did the South see the rise of female colleges offering upper-level courses.

5. Farnham, *Education of the Southern Belle*, 72–87; Elizabeth Ridley to William Ridley, March 20, 1861, Ridley Family Papers, VHS; Louisiana Wilson Hankins to Virginia Wilson Hankins, October 21, 1859, Hankins Family Papers, VHS.

6. Sarah Lois Wadley Diary, January 26, 1860; Farnham, *Education of the Southern Belle*, 109–10; Elizabeth Fox-Genovese, *Within the Plantation House-*

hold: Black and White Women of the Old South (Chapel Hill: University of North Carolina Press, 1985) 45–47.

7. Elias Marks, M.D., *Hints on Female Education* (Columbia: A.S. Johnston, 1851), 4–6, Duke.

8. J. Burton, *Lectures on Female Education and Manners* (Baltimore: Samuel Jefferis, 1811), 48–49, 54–55, Duke; James Garnett, *Lectures on Female Education, Comprising the First and Second Series of a Course Delivered to Mrs. Garnett's Pupils, at Elm-Wood, Essex County, Virginia* (Richmond: Thomas W. White, 1825), 130–31, 156–57, Duke.

9. Burton, *Lectures on Female Education and Manners*, 56.

10. Brenda Stevenson, *Life in Black and White: Family and Community in the Slave South* (New York: Oxford University Press, 1996); Eppes, *Through Some Eventful Years*, 84; Snell, *Myra Inman*, 3.

11. Farnham, *Education of the Southern Belle*, chapter 7; Stowe, *Intimacy and Power in the Old South*, 150; Olin Davis to brother, March 25, 1860, Beale-Davis Family Papers, SHC.

12. Fox-Genovese, *Within the Plantation Household*, 110–13; Cynthia Kierner, *Beyond the Household: Women's Place in the Early South, 1700–1835* (Ithaca: Cornell University Press, 1998), 149–51; Martha Anne Davis to John Davis, January 20, 1860, Beale-Davis Family Papers; Louisa Sheppard Recollections, SHC; Sarah Lois Wadley Diary, October 5, 1859; Eppes, *Through Some Eventful Years*, 100; Snell, *Myra Inman*, 8–11, 32, 36.

13. Fox-Genovese, *Within the Plantation Household*, 112–13; Catherine Clinton, *Plantation Mistress: Woman's World in the Old South* (New York: Pantheon Books, 1982) 39–41; Snell, *Myra Inman*, chapter one, passim.

14. Fox-Genovese, *Within the Plantation Household*, 111–13; Clinton, *Plantation Mistress*, 39, 41–44; Eppes, *Through Some Eventful Years*, chapter one, passim; Bettie Alexander to her sister, December 3, 1860, Bettie Alexander Papers, Duke.

15. Eugene Genovese, *Roll Jordon Roll: The World the Slaves Made* (New York: Vintage Books, 1972), 3–7; Fox-Genovese, *Within the Plantation Household*, 100–102.

16. Louisiana Hankins to Virginia Hankins, October 21, 1859, Hankins Family Papers; Burton, *Lectures on Female Education and Manners*, 48–49.

17. Few historians of southern families give much attention to the sisterly bond. Lorri Glover's study of early South Carolina families is one of the first to examine it at some length. See Lorri Glover, *All Our Relations: Blood Ties and Emotional Bonds among the Early South Carolina Gentry* (Baltimore: Johns Hopkins University Press, 2000), 81–85. See also Clinton, *Plantation Mistress*, 54–55; Eppes, *Through Some Eventful Years*, 95–100; Snell, ed., *Myra Inman*, 6–10; Bettie Alexander to sister, December 3, 1860, Bettie Alexander Family Papers.

18. For a discussion of the academic and ideological education of sons of the southern gentry see Lorri Glover, "An Education in Southern Masculinity: The Ball Family of South Carolina in the New Republic," *JSH* 69 (February 2003): 39–70 and Peter S. Carmichael, *The Last* Generation: *Young Virginians in Peace, War, and Reunion* (Chapel Hill: University of North Carolina Press, 2005), 85–86, 101–6. For a discussion of how parents inculcated notions of masculine honor and duty to their sons, see Wyatt-Brown, *Southern Honor*, 149–74. James Hankins to Virginia Hankins, May 20, 1857, May 14, 1860, Hankins Family Papers; Elizabeth Ridley to William Ridley, May 27, 1858, William Ridley to Elizabeth Ridley, February 14, 1859, Ridley Family Papers.

19. James Hankins to Virginia Hankins, July 5, 1857, Hankins Family Papers; William to Elizabeth Ridley, June 18, 1858, Ridley Family Papers; John Davis to Olin Tuberville Davis, March 25, 1860, Beale-Davis Family Papers.

20. Fox-Genovese, *Within the Plantation Household*, 256–59; Clinton, *Plantation Mistress*, 95, 137, 162–63; Rable, *Civil Wars*, 18–19; Jean E. Friedman, *The Enclosed Garden: Women and Community in the Evangelical South, 1830–1930* (Chapel Hill: University of North Carolina Press, 1985), 110–27; Pope, "Preparation for Pedestals: North Carolina Antebellum Female Seminaries" (Ph.D. diss., University of Chicago, 1971), 231–35; Louisiana Hankins to Virginia Hankins, May 2, 1859, Hankins Family Papers.

21. Stevenson, *Life in Black and White*, 121; Clinton, *Plantation Mistress*, 160–61; Snell, *Myra Inman*, xix, 10–11; Olin Davis to brother, April 21, 1860, Beale-Davis Family Papers; James Hankins to Virginia Hankins, May 14, 1860, Hankins Family Papers.

22. Clinton, *Plantation Mistress*, 157–58; Catherine Louisa McLaurin Diary, February 1860, Catherine Louisa McLaurin Collection, SCL, University of South Carolina, Columbia; Sarah Lois Wadley Diary, November 24, 1860.

23. Jabour, *Marriage in the Early Republic: Elizabeth and William Wirt and the Companionate Ideal* (Baltimore: Johns Hopkins University Press, 1998), 1–7.

24. Fox-Genovese, *Within the Plantation Household*, 208–209; Clinton, *Plantation Mistress*, 61–62; Jabour, *Marriage in the Early Republic*, 13; Sarah Lois Wadley Diary, October 2, 1860; E. Susan Barber, "'The White Wings of Eros': Courtship and Marriage in Confederate Richmond," in *Southern Families at War: Loyalty and Conflict in the Civil War South*, Catherine Clinton, ed. (New York: Oxford University Press, 2000), 121; Garnett, *Lectures on Female Education*, 213; Burton, *Lectures on Female Education and Manners*, 55–56.

25. Wyatt-Brown, *Southern Honor*, 149–74; Burton, *Lectures on Female Education and Manners*, 57–59; Garnett, *Lectures on Female Education*, 213.

26. Wyatt-Brown, *Southern Honor*, 207–17; Stowe, *Intimacy and Power in the Old South*, 51–84; Clinton, *Plantation Mistress*, 63–64.

27. Clinton, *Plantation Mistress*, 61–63, 101–2, 113–14; Fox-Genovese, *Within the Plantation Household*, 61–65, 207–208; Elizabeth Dunbar Murray, *My Mother Used to Say: A Natchez Belle of the Sixties* (Boston: Christopher Publishing House, 1959), 64; Elizabeth Morrow Nix, "An Exuberant Flow of Spirits: Antebellum Adolescent Girls in the Writing of Southern Women" (Ph.D. diss., Boston University, 1996), 16–17; Pope, "Preparation for Pedestals," 223.

28. Jabour, *Marriage in the Early Republic*, 13.

29. Burton, Lectures on Female Education and Manners, 56; Garnett, Lectures on Female Education, 221.

30. Fox-Genovese, *Within the Plantation Household*, 208–9; Sarah Lois Wadley Diary, October 2, 1860; Catherine Louisa McLaurin Diary, November 6, 1860.

31. Snell, ed., *Myra Inman*, 6, 10; Clinton, *Plantation Mistress*, 61–62.

32. Kierner, *Beyond the Household*, 146; Fox-Genovese, *Within the Plantation Household*, 61–62; Murray, *My Mother Used to Say*, 63; Sarah Lois Wadley Diary, July 16, August, 9, 14, 1860.

33. Sarah Lois Wadley Diary, August 5, 1860.

34. Farnham, *Education of the Southern Belle*, 133–35; Snell, *Myra Inman*, 11; Murray, *My Mother Used to Say*, 63; Sarah Lois Wadley Diary, January 4, 1861.

35. Fox-Genovese, *Within the Plantation Household*, 112, 243.

36. Eugene Genovese, *Roll, Jordan, Roll*, 3–5.

37. Murray, *My Mother Used to Say*, 70–75; Louisa C. Sheppard Recollections; James Oakes, *The Ruling Race: A History of American Slaveholders* (New York: Alfred Knopf, 1982) and *Slavery and Freedom: An Interpretation of the Old South* (New York: Alfred Knopf, 1990). When it came to young women's devotion to older house slaves and nurses, however, their feelings were not always reciprocated; see, for example, Jacqueline Jones, *Labor of Love, Labor of Sorrow: Black Women, Work, and the Family from Slavery to the Present* (New York: Vintage Books, 1985), 13–29.

38. Fox-Genovese, *Within the Plantation Household*, 111–12, 189; Rable, *Civil Wars*, 33; Eppes, *Through Some Eventful Years*, 95–96, 100–101.

2. The Politicized Belle

1. Daniel E. Sutherland, ed., *A Very Violent Rebel: The Diary of Ellen Renshaw House* (Knoxville, University of Tennessee Press, 1996), 54–55, 113–14.

2. Ibid., 21, 36, 48–50, 127–29, 165–63.

3. Paula Baker, "Domestication of Politics: Women and Ameriocan Political Society," *American Historical Review* (June 1984) 620–47; Linda K. Kerber, "Separate Spheres, Female Worlds, Woman's Place: The Rhetoric of Women's History," *Journal of American History* 75 (June 1988), 9–39; Kierner, *Beyond the Household*, 2; Faust, *Mothers of Invention*, 5–7; Catherine Clinton, *Other Civil*

War, 81–82. See also Catherine Allgor, *Parlor Politics: In Which the Ladies of Washington Helped Build a City and a Government* (Charlottesville: University Press of Virginia, 2000).

4. Lacy K. Ford, *Origins of Southern Radicalism*, 372; McCurry, *Masters of Small Worlds*; Margaret Storey, *Loyalty and Loss: Alabama's Unionists in the Civil War and Reconstruction* (Baton Rouge: Louisiana State University Press, 2004), chapters 1 and 2.

5. James Marten, *Children's Civil War* (Chapel Hill: University of North Carolina Press,1998), 150–51; Daniel W. Crofts, *Reluctant Confederates: Upper South Unionists in the Secession Crisis* (Chapel Hill: University of North Carolina Press, 1989), 90–91, 131, 334–36.

6. Sarah Lois Wadley Diary, August 31, October 26, 1860; Eppes, *Through Some Eventful Years*, 86–87, 125.

7. Paul Finkelman, ed., *His Soul Goes Marching On: Responses to John Brown and the Harper's Ferry Raid* (Charlottesville: University Press of Virginia, 1995); Snell, ed., *Myra Inman*, 97; Louisa McCord Smythe Reminiscences; for a discussion of McCord's travels with her family and her mother's perspective on abolitionism see Leigh Fought, *Southern Womanhood and Slavery: A Biography of Louisa S. McCord* (Columbia: University of Missouri Press, 2003).

8. Eppes, *Through Some Eventful Years*, 119.

9. Rable, *Civil Wars*, 117; Davis, ed., *Requiem for a Lost City: A Memoir of Civil War Atlanta and the Old South* (Macon: University of Mercer Press, 1999), 32–33; Faust, *Mothers of Invention*, 57–60; Snell, *Myra Inman*, 96–97; Ashkenazi, ed., *The Civil War Diary of Clara Solomon: Growing Up in New Orleans, 1861–1862* (Baton Rouge: Louisiana State University Press, 1995), 355; Oranie Virginia (Snead) Hatcher Memoir, VHS.

10. Eppes, *Through Some Eventful Years*, 141–43; Louisa McCord Smythe Recollections, SCL.Crofts, *Reluctant Confederates*, 334–36, 345–46; Cloe Tyler (Whittle) Green Diary, April 15, 1861, SL.

11. Murray, *My Mother Used to Say*, 76–77; Sarah Lois Wadley Diary, October 26, 1860, February 16, 1861.

12. Eppes, *Through Some Eventful Years*, 138; Mrs. D. Giraud Wright, *A Southern Girl in '61: The Wartime Memories of a Confederate Senator's Daughter* (New York: Double Day Press, 1905), 23–24.

13. James Hankins to Virginia Hankins, November 21, 1860, Hankins Family Papers.

14. Louisa McCord Smythe Reminiscences; Sarah Lois Wadley Diary, December 4, 1860; Eppes, *Through Some Eventful Years*, 139–40.

15. Sarah Lois Wadley Diary, October 26, 1860; Cloe Tyler (Whittle) Green Diary, April 15, 1861; Elliott Ashkenazi, ed., *Diary of Clara Solomon*, 334; Snell,

ed., *Myra Inman*, 145; Robert Davis, Jr., ed., "Selective Memories of Civil War Atlanta: The Memoir of Sally Clayton," *Georgia Historical Quarterly*, 82 (Winter 1998): 741; *Charleston Mercury*, November 22, 1864; *Daily Richmond Enquirer*, May 6, 1863.

16. Sarah Lowe Journal, March 22, 24, April 15, May 2, 8, 1861, ADAH; Davis, ed., "Selective Memories of Civil War Atlanta," 741–42.

17. Eppes, *Through Some Eventful Years*, 123; Catherine McLaurin Diary, July 19, 1861; Louisa McCord Smythe Reminiscences; Cordelia Lewis Scales to Loulie, August 17, 1861, Cordelia Lewis Scales Collection, MDAH.

18. Nettie Fondren to Robert Mitchell, May 14, October 9, 1862, Mitchell-Fondren Family Civil War Letters, GDAH.

19. Bettie Alexander to sister, December 3, 1860, Bettie Alexander Papers; Eppes, *Through Some Eventful Years*, 150–52; Annie Jeter Carmouche Memoirs, Annie Jeter Carmouche Papers, LC; Louisa McCord Smythe Recollections.

20. James M. McPherson, *For Cause and Comrades: Why Men Fought in the Civil War* (New York: Oxford University Press, 1997), 22–29; James Hankins to Virginia Hankins, November 21, 1860, Hankins Family Papers; George Whitaker Wills to Mary Wills, June 15, September 17, 1861, June 10, 1864, William Henry Wills Papers, SHC. James McPherson shows that although the rhetoric of honor has been closely associated with Confederate soldiers, Union troops likewise expressed ideals of honor and duty in explaining their military service.

21. Brother to Elizabeth Norfleet (Ridley) Neely, November 19, 1861, Ridley Family Papers; Walter Rundell, Jr., ed., "'If Fortune Should Fail': Civil War Letters of Dr. Samuel D. Sanders," *South Carolina Historical Magazine* 65 (July 1964): 129–31, 135, 133–34.

22. Roberts, *Confederate Belle*, 35–53; Virginia Hankins to James Hankins, undated, Hankins Family Papers; Rundell, ed., "'If Fortune Should Fail,'" 135.

23. Rable, *Civil Wars*, 151–52; Elizabeth Collier Diary, April 11, 1862; Wright, *Southern Girl in '61*, 62; DeAnne Blanton and Lauren M. Cook, *They Fought Like Demons: Women Soldiers in the American Civil War* (Baton Rouge: Louisiana State University Press, 2002), chapter two.

24. Nettie Fondren to Robert Mitchell, September 23, 1863, Mitchell-Fondren Family Civil War Letters; Elizabeth Waties (Allston) Pringle Diary, March 27, 1862, SCHS.

25. *Daily Richmond Enquirer*, August 1, 1861.

26. *Charleston Mercury*, January 3, 1861; *Natchez Daily Courier*, September 24, December 10, 1862.

27. Robert Scott Davis, Jr., ed., *Requiem for a Lost City*, 81–83, 88; Annie Jeter to William Carmouche, September 25, 1861, Annie Jeter Carmouche Papers, LC; Sarah Lois Wadley Diary, July 14, October 7, 1861; Louisa McCord Smythe

Reminiscences; Sutherland, ed., *A Very Violent Rebel*, 48–50; *Daily Richmond Enquirer*, October 30, 1861.

28. *Charleston Mercury*, October 8, 1861.

29. *Charleston Mercury*, January 1, 1861; Judith Ann Robertson Foster Memoir, VHS; Louisa Sheppard Recollections.

30. Whites, *Civil War as a Crisis in Gender*, 57; Ashkenazi, ed., *Diary of Clara Solomon*, 52; Eppes, *Through Some Eventful Years*, 151; Davis, ed., *Requiem for a Lost City*, 44–45; Snell, ed., *Myra Inman*, 96; Mary Fries Patterson Diary, September 9, 1863, SHC; Sarah Lowe Journal, May 1, 4, 5, 14, 1861.

31. Annie Jeter Carmouche Memoirs; Murray, *My Mother Used to Say*, 101; Cordelia Lewis Scales to Loulie, November 24, 1861, Cordelia Lewis Scales Papers; Davis, ed., *Requiem for a Lost City*, 40–41; *Natchez Daily Courier*, November 1, November 7, 1861.

32. Cloe Tyler (Whittle) Green Diary, April 15, 1861; Davis, ed., *Requiem for a Lost City*, 30–31; Sallie McEwen Journal, May 30, 1861, TSLA; Annie Jeter Carmouche Memoirs.

33. *Charleston Mercury*, November 24, 1863; *Natchez Daily Courier*, December 24, 1862.

34. Ibid., February 28, 1862, February 6, 1861; *Natchez Daily Courier*, January 19, 1861.

35. Martha Josephine Moore Diary, May 7, 1863, Frank Liddell Richardson Family Papers, SHC; Ashkenazi, ed., *Civil War Diary of Clara Solomon*, 61; Fannie Lewis Gwathmey Adams, "Reminiscences of a Childhood Spent at 'Hayfield' Plantation Near Fredericksburg, Virginia," Fannie Lewis Gwathmey Adams Papers, MC; Alice Janney Harrison, "Account of Lee's Visit to Leesburg and Harrison Hall," Alice Janney Harrison Papers, VHS.

36. Snell, ed., *Myra Inman*, 93–94; Wright, *Southern Girl in '61*, 57–59.

37. Annie Jeter Carmouche Memoirs; Wright, *Southern Girl in '61*, 150–51; Amanda Worthington Diary, April 13, 1862, MDAH; Kate D. Foster Diary, June 25, 1863, Duke.

38. *Charleston Mercury*, February 8, 1862, May 29, 1861, March 3, 1864.

39. Amanda Worthington Diary, January 5, 29, 1862; Sallie Independence Foster Diary, September 30, 1864.

40. Mary D. Robertson, ed., *A Confederate Lady Comes of Age: The Journal of Pauline DeCaradeuc, 1863–1888* (Columbia: University of South Carolina Press, 1992), 74–75; Kate D. Foster Diary, July 18, 1865; Elizabeth Collier Diary, April 25, 1865.

41. Alice Ready Diary, March 22, 1862, SHC; Amanda Worthington Diary, April 30, 1862; Sarah Lois Wadley Diary, March 2, 1862; Virginia Hankins to James Hankins, July 11, 1864, Hankins Family Papers. Historians have explored

the question of female loyalty in the later years of the war and arrived at varying answers. Historian Drew Gilpin Faust in *Mothers of Invention* argues that women, left alone on the home front to fend for the family and home, eventually came to resent the war as it dragged on. Jacqueline Glass Campbell, in *When Sherman Marched North from the Sea: Resistance on the Confederate Homefront* (Chapel Hill: University of North Carolina Press, 2003), argues that Sherman's march through Georgia and the Carolinas increased the rancor of women toward the Union army and, in turn, strengthened their resolve to support the cause. Campbell is building upon recent studies that argue that while support for the war diminished due to economic and emotional hardships on the home front, loyalty to the cause continued as a result of Union occupation. See Gary Gallagher, *The Confederate War: Popular Will, Nationalism, and Strategy* (Cambridge: Harvard University Press, 1997) and William Blair, *Virginia's Private War: Feeding Body and Soul in the Occupied South, 1861–1865* (New York: Oxford University Press, 1998). For studies of Union policy concerning the Confederate home front see Steven V. Ash, *When the Yankees Came: Conflict and Chaos in the Occupied South, 1861–1865* (Chapel Hill: University of North Carolina Press, 1995) and Mark Grimsley, *The Hard Hand of War: Union Military Policy Toward Southern Civilians, 1861–1865* (New York: Cambridge University Press, 1995).

42. Louisiana Hankins to Virginia Hankins, November 16, 1864, John Henry Hankins to Virginia Hankins, August 21, 1864, Hankins Family Papers; Mother to Jane Sivley, October 22, 1863, William Sivley to Jane Sivley, October 21, 1863, Jane Sivley Papers, SHC.

43. James Hankins to Virginia Hankins, July 11, 1862, Hankins Family Papers; George Whitaker Wills to Mary Wills, June 15, 1861, William Henry Wills Papers.

44. Faust, *Mothers of Invention*, 207–12.

45. Ibid.; Murray, *My Mother Used to Say*, 170–73. For more on southerners' reactions to Union occupation see Ash, *When the Yankees Came*.

46. Emma Cassandra Riely Macon, *Reminiscences of the Civil War* (Cedar Rapids: Torch Press, 1911), 10–12, 32–51, 107–8.

47. Annie Jeter Carmouche Memoirs; Martha Josephine Moore Diary, April 24, 1863.

48. Martha Josephine Moore Diary, May 7, 1863.

49. Cordelia Lewis Scales to Loulie, January 27, 1863, Cordelia Lewis Scales Papers; James M. McPherson, *Battle Cry of Freedom: The Civil War Era* (New York: Oxford University Press, 1988), 578.

50. Sutherland, ed., *Very Violent Rebel*, 145, 163; Snell, ed., *Myra Inman*.

51. Macon, *Reminiscences of the Civil War*, 115–16; Kate D. Foster Diary, September 20, 1863.

52. Henry C. Blackiston, ed., *Refugees in Richmond: Civil War Letters of a Virginia Family* (New Jersey: Princeton University Press, 1989), 60–61, 68–69.

53. Nannie Haskins Journal, July 24, 1863, Nannie Haskins Williams Papers, TSLA; Sutherland, ed., *Very Violent Rebel*, 145; Blackiston, ed., *Refugees in Richmond*, 38.

54. Robertson, ed., *Confederate Lady Comes of Age*, 34; Kate Foster Diary, July 28, 30, 1863; Louisiana Hankins to Virginia Hankins, September 18, 1864.

55. Alice Williamson Diary, May 3, 4, April 26, May 16, August 16, 1864, Duke.

56. Eppes, *Through Some Eventful Years*, 273; Judith Ann Robertson Foster Memoir; Cloe Tyler (Whittle) Greene Diary, July 12, 1863.

57. James C. Bonner, ed., *Journal of a Milledgeville Girl, 1861–1867* (Athens: University of Georgia Press, 1964), 60.

58. Elizabeth Collier Diary, April 25, 1865; Janet Weaver to Andrew Biney Mitchell, July 12, 1865, Randolph Family Papers, VHS.

59. Robertson, ed., *Confederate Lady Comes of Age*, 74–75, 76.

3. The Self-Sufficient Daughter

1. Daniel E. Huger Smith, Alice R. Huger Smith, and Arney R. Childs, eds., *Mason Smith Family Letters* (Columbia: University of South Carolina Press, 1950) xx-xxii.

2. Henry Walker, "Power, Sex, and Gender Roles: The Transformation of an Alabama Planter Family During the Civil War," in *Southern Families at War*, ed. Clinton, 175–188; Faust, *Mothers of Invention*, 51–52, 248–53; Joan Cashin, "'Since the War Broke Out'": The Marriage of Kate and William McClure," in *Divided Houses: Gender and the Civil War*, eds. Clinton and Nina Silber (New York: Oxford University Press, 1992), 200–212; Scott, *Southern Lady*, 100–102; Laura F. Edwards, *Scarlett Doesn't Live Here Anymore: Southern Women in the Civil War Era* (Urbana: University of Illinois Press, 2000), 71–84.

3. Sallie Walker Boone Memoirs, Civil War Collection, TSLA; Sallie Independence Foster Diary, August 20, 22, 1862; Smith, et. al., eds., *Mason Smith Family Letters*,19; Sarah Lois Wadley Diary, December 17, 18, 1861; Elizabeth Waties (Allston) Pringle Diary, May 20, 1864.

4. Sallie Walker Boone Memoirs; Lucy Blackwell Malone Reminiscences, Thompson Family Papers, SHC.

5. Ellen Cooper Johnson Memoirs; mother to Jane Sivley, February 26, 1864, Jane Sivley Papers.

6. Mary E. Massey, *Refugee Life in the Confederacy* (Baton Rouge: Louisiana State University Press, 1964),15; Faust, *Mothers of Invention*, 37–39; Louisa Shep-

pard Recollections; Anna Cagdell (Howell) Hollowell Diary, February 27, 1862; Sue Montgomery to Moultrie Wilson, undated (1865), Moultrie Wilson Papers.

7. Massey, *Refugee Life*, 28–29; Macon, *Reminiscences of the Civil War*, 21–23; Mary Rawson Diary, September 8, 1864, Rawson-Collier-Harris Family Papers, AHC; Sarah Lois Wadley Diary, September 22, 23, 1863.

8. Massey, *Refugee Life*, 67; Sarah Lois Wadley Diary, September 23, 1863; Mary Rawson Diary, September 17, 18, 1864; Blackiston, ed., *Refugees in Richmond*, 25; Louisa McCord Smythe Reminiscences; Mary Rawson Diary, September 20, 1864; Macon, *Reminiscences of the Civil War*, 21–23.

9. Massey, *Refugee Life*, 132–33; Anna Cagdell (Howell) Hollowell Diary, February 27, 1862; Sue Montgomery to Moultrie Wilson, undated (1865), Moultrie Wilson Papers; Mother to Jane Sivley, April 19, 1864, Jane Sivley Papers; Massey, *Refugee Life*, 125–26; Macon, *Reminiscences of the Civil War*, 32–51.

10. Farnham, *Education of the Southern Belle*, 182; Faust, *Mothers of Invention*, 39; Mary Rawson Diary, September 3, 1864; Davis, ed., *Requiem for a Lost City*, 66; Massey, *Refugee Life*, 30–31.

11. Mother to Jane Sivley, April 19, 1864, Jane Sivley Papers.

12. Farnham, *Education of the Southern Belle*, 182; Lucy Blackwell Malone Reminiscences; Faust, *Mothers of Invention*, 39; Ellen Cooper Johnson Memoirs.

13. Farnham, *Education of the Southern Belle*, 3–4; Davis, ed., "Selective Memories of Civil War Atlanta," 85.

14. Cordelia Lewis Scales to Loulie, August 17, 1861, Cordelia Lewis Scales Papers; Judith Ann Robertson Foster Memoir.

15. Sue Richardson Diary, October 13, 20, 21, 22, 23, 1863, RWL; Frances James (La Rue) Dorsey Diary, September 14, 1863, VHS; Sarah Lois Wadley Diary, July 19, 1864; Sallie Walker Boone Memoirs; Smith, et. al., eds., *Mason Smith Family Letters*, 159, 160–61; Sarah Lois Wadley Diary, December 7, 1861; Wright, *Southern Girl in '61*, 201.

16. Ash, *When the Yankees Came*, 157; Lucy Blackwell Malone Reminiscences; Sarah Lois Wadley Diary, April 11, 1864.

17. Sally Independence Foster Diary, August 11, 22, 23, 25, 26, 1862; Amanda Worthington Diary, June 10, 1863; Sarah Lois Wadley Diary, April 11, 1864; Louisiana Hankins to Virginia Hankins, October 18, 1864.

18. Bettie Alexander to sister, January 13, 1862, Bettie Alexander Papers; Sarah Lois Wadley Diary, April 15, 1864, July 13, 1862; Alice Ready Diary, April 30, 1862.

19. Miers, ed., *When the World Ended*, 53–54; Robertson, ed., *Confederate Lady Comes of Age*, 67; Elizabeth Waties (Allston) Pringle Diary, March 27, 1862.

20. Leon F. Litwack, *Been in the Storm So Long: The Aftermath of Slavery* (New York: Knopf, 1979), 180–81; Snell, ed., *Myra Inman*, xiii, 341–46, 214.

21. Snell, ed., *Myra Inman*, 249–50, 265, 331, 231; Campbell, *When Sherman Marched North From the Sea*, 4, 17, 45.

22. Miers, ed., *When the World Ended*, 41; Sue Richardson Diary, October 11, 1864; Bonner, ed., *Journal of a Milledgeville Girl*, 65.

23. Rable, *Civil Wars*, 118–19; Faust, *Mothers of Invention*, 72–73; Alice Ready Diary, March 22, 1862; Mary D. Robertson, ed., *Lucy Breckinridge of Grove Hill: The Journal of a Virginia Girl, 1862-1864* (Columbia: University of South Carolina Press, 1994), 35–36; Kate Foster Diary, July 28, 1863.

24. Sarah Lois Wadley Diary, August 29, 1863; mother to Jane Sivley, February 26, 1865, Sivley Family Letters; Sue Richardson Diary, December 3, 1863, January 2, November 2, 1864.

25. Rable, *Civil Wars*, 118–19; Miers, ed., *When the World Ended*, 54; Macon, *Reminiscences of the Civil War*, 57; Sue Richardson Diary, April 21, 1864; Louisa McCord Smythe Reminiscences.

26. Rable, *Civil Wars*, 118–19; Macon, *Reminiscences of the Civil War*, 57; Louisa McCord Smythe Reminiscences; Smith, et. al. eds., *Mason Smith Family Letters*, 159–61.

27. Snell, ed., *Myra Inman*, 260, 263.

28. Sarah Wadley Diary, December 7, 17, 1861, July 19, 1864.

29. Faust, *Mothers of Invention*, 198–201, 207–14; Sarah Lois Wadley Diary, August 31, 1863; Cordelia Lewis Scales to Loulie, October 29, 1862, Cordelia Lewis Scales Papers; Alice Ready Diary, March 11, April 30, 1862; Ellen Cooper Johnson Memoirs.

30. Emmeline Allmand Crump Lightfoot, "The Evacuation of Richmond," Emmeline Allmand Crump Lightfoot Reminiscences; Louisa McCord Smythe Reminiscences; Snell, ed., *Myra Inman*, 114; Ellen Cooper Johnson Memoirs.

31. Smith, et. al., eds., *Mason Smith Family Letters*, 80–81, 86–87, 117–18.

32. Mother to Jane Sivley, October 22, 1863, Sivley Family Papers; Rundell, ed., "'If Fortune Should Fail,'" 131,133, 223–24.

33. Willie to Jane Sivley, October 12, 1863, Sivley Family Papers; Richard H. Wills to Mary Wills, June 10, 1861, George Whitaker Wills to Mary, September 28, 1862, William Henry Wills Papers; Smith, et. al., eds., *Mason Smith Family Letters*, 117–18.

34. McPherson, *Battle Cry of Freedom*, 437–42; Faust, *Mothers of Invention*, 45–51; Rable, *Civil Wars*, 92–95; Robertson, ed., *A Confederate Lady Comes of Age*, 28, 38; Miers, ed., *When the World Ended*, 47.

35. Ellen Cooper Johnson Memoirs; Sarah Lois Wadley Diary, August 23, 1864; Louisa Sheppard Recollection; Margaret (Ridley) Gooch Memoirs.

36. Eppes, *Through Some Eventful Years*, 179; Ellen Cooper Johnson Memoirs;

Susan "Livie" Olivia Fleming to Lalie, January 25, 1865, Eleanor Eulalie (Cay) Fleming Papers; Macon, *Reminiscences of the Civil War*, 117–18.

37. McPherson, *Battle Cry of Freedom*, 437–42; Rable, *Civil Wars*, 121–35; Faust, *Mothers of Invention*, 80–113.

38. Faust, *Mothers of Invention*, 88, 90–91; Rable, *Civil Wars*, 131–32; reported in the *Charleston Mercury*, November 22, 1864.

39. *Daily Richmond Enquirer*, January 13, 1864.

40. Faust, *Mothers of Invention*, 86–88; *Daily Richmond Enquirer* August 10, 1863.

41. Pharis Shearer to Jane Sivley, March 12, 1863, Mother to Jane Sivley, April 19, 1864; Rundell, ed., "'If Fortune Should Fail,'" 221, 220.

42. Smith, et. al. eds., *Mason Smith Family Letters*, 164–65; Eppes, *Through Some Eventful Years*, 182; Louisa Sheppard Recollections; Ellen Cooper Johnson Memoirs.

43. Sarah Lois Wadley Diary, February 4, June 5, 1863; Faust, *Mothers of Invention*, 86–88; Rable, *Civil Wars*, 131; Louisa Sheppard Recollections.

4. The Perfect Woman

1. Janet Weaver composition, Andrew Biney Mitchell to Janet Henderson Weaver, January 12, 1865, Randolph Family Papers.

2. Fox-Genovese, *Within the Plantation Household*, 207–8; Clinton, *Plantation Mistress*, 61–63.

3. Scholarship on courtship and marriage in the Confederacy emphasizes the diversity of women's experiences. Historians such as Drew Faust and E. Susan Barber argue that the availability of suitors was usually greater in the cities and towns, where troops often passed through or were stationed. Those in the rural, plantation districts of the South were more likely to experience a sharp decline in the male population and troops were less likely to spend lengthy visits. For studies on courtships on the southern home front see Faust, *Mothers of Invention*, 139–41; E. Susan Barber, "White Wings of Eros: Courtship and Marriage in Confederate Richmond," in *Southern Families at War: Loyalty and Conflict in the Civil War South*, ed. Catherine Clinton (New York: Oxford University Press, 2000), 119–20; Roberts, *Confederate Belle*, 87–93. Case studies of courtships include George M. Anderson, S.J., "The Civil War Courtship of Richard Mortimer Williams and Rose Anderson of Rockville," *Maryland Historical Magazine* 80 (Summer 1985), 119–38, Sidney Hovey Wanzer and Anna Bradford Agle, eds., "Dearest Braddie: Love and War in Maryland, 1860–61," *Maryland Historical Magazine* 88 (Spring 1993), 337–58, and Chris Fordney, ed., "Letters from the Heart," *Civil War Times Illustrated* 34 (September-October 1995), 28, 73–82.

4. Elizabeth Collier Diary, June 28, 1862; Janet Weaver composition, Randolph Family Papers.

5. Annie Jeter Carmouche Memoirs; Mary C. Bell Claytor, "Personal Recollections of Hunter's Raid, VHS; Barber, "White Wings of Eros," 119–32; Margareta Ellen Wise Mayo Reminiscences, VHS; Robertson, ed., *A Confederate Lady Comes of Age*, 72–73; Mary Fries Patterson Diary, September 9, November 6, 1863; Alice Ready Diary, February 13, 1862; Sarah Lois Wadley Diary, April 8, May 16, 1863.

6. Sarah Lowe Journal, May 4, 1861; Faust, *Mothers of Invention*, 146–47; Amanda Worthington Diary, September 23, 1863, January 19, 1865.

7. Daniel W. Stowell, "A Family of Women and Children: The Fains of East Tennessee," in Clinton, *Southern Families at War*, 158; Eppes, *Through Some Eventful Years*, 219; Sarah Lois Wadley Diary, December 21, 1863; Virginia Wilson Hankins Diary, June 27, 1863; Nannie Haskins Diary, February 27, 1863.

8. Faust, *Mothers of Invention*, 145–52; Bettie Alexander to sister, August 2, 1861, Bettie Alexander Papers; Snell, ed., *Myra Inman*, 110; Robertson, ed., *Confederate Lady Comes of Age*, 19; Nannie Haskins Diary, March 23, 1863.

9. Barber, "White Wings of Eros," 121. Calculations of marriage patterns come from archival records of thirty-two members of the subject group. Information on when they married comes from their personal papers. Foster Diary, December 12, 1862; Anna Cagdell (Howell) Hollowell Diary, September 2, 1862; Ashkenazi, ed., *Diary of Clara Solomon*, 50.

10. Ellen K. Rothman, *Hands and Hearts: A History of Courtship in America* (New York: Basic Books, 1984), 103–7, 111–13; Faust, *Mothers of Invention*, 147–50; Rable, *Civil Wars*, 52–53; Barber, "White Wings of Eros," 120–22; Sutherland, ed., *Very Violent Rebel*, 168; Elizabeth Collier Diary, September 2, 1863; Cordelia Lewis Scales to Loulie, November 24, 1861, Cordelia Lewis Scales Papers; Bonner, ed., *Journal of a Milledgeville Girl*, 46–47.

11. Annie Jeter Carmouche Memoirs; Catherine McLaurin Diary, July 5, 1862.

12. Carroll Smith-Rosenberg, "The Female World of Love and Ritual: Relations Between Women in Nineteenth-Century America," *Signs* 1 (Autumn 1975), 1–29; Faust, *Mothers of Invention*, 142; Bonner, ed., *Journal of a Milledgeville Girl*, 16; Robertson, ed., *Confederate Lady Comes of Age*, 28–29; Sally Independence Foster Diary, passim; Robertson, ed., *Lucy Breckinridge of Grove Hill*, 177.

13. Patricia L. Richard, "'Listen Ladies One and All': Union Soldiers Yearn for the Society of Their 'Fair Cousins of the North,'" in *Union Soldiers and the Northern Home Front*, eds. Paul A. Cimbala and Randall M. Miller (New York: Fordham University Press, 2002), 143–81; Snell, ed., *Myra Inman*, 156; Sally Independence Foster Diary, December 5, 12, 1862; Cordelia Lewis Scales to Loulie, February 9, 1862, Cordelia Lewis Scales Papers.

14. Robert Mitchell to Nettie Fondren, July 28, October 12, December 16, 1861, Mitchell-Fondren Family Civil War Letters; Blackiston, ed., *Refugees in Richmond*, 35.

15. Stephen W. Berry II, *All That Makes a Man: Love and Ambition in the Civil War South* (New York: Oxford University Press, 2003), 173–92; Nettie Fondren to Robert Mitchell, April 2, 1862, Mitchell-Fondren Family Civil War Letters; John Vaughn Willcox to Virginia Hankins, December 2, 1864, Hankins Family Papers.

16. Fordney, ed., "Letters from the Heart," 73, 78–79, quotes on pages 80–81, 76.

17. Nettie Fondren to Robert Mitchell, May 24, 1862, Robert Mitchell to Nettie Fondren, July 28, October 24, 1861, Nettie Fondren to Robert Mitchell, October 5, 1863, Mitchell-Fondren Family Civil War Letters.

18. Faust, "Christian Soldiers: The Meaning of Revivalism in the Confederate Army," *Journal of Southern History* 53 (February 1987), 63–90; Nettie Fondren to Robert Mitchell, April 2, May 18, 1862, Mitchell-Fondren Family Civil War Letters; Blackiston, ed., *Refugees in Richmond*, 35–36, 50, 70–71.

19. Louisa McCord Smythe Reminiscences; Robert Mitchell to Nettie Fondren, August 26, 1861, Nettie Fondren to Robert Mitchell, May 20, 1862, Mitchell-Fondren Family Civil War; Fordney, ed., "Letters from the Heart," 73–82.

20. John Vaughn Willcox to Virginia Hankins, December 2, 1864, Hankins Family Papers.

21. John Vaughn Willcox to Virginia Hankins, March 29, 1866.

22. Judith Ann Robertson Foster Memoir; Robert Mitchell to Nettie Fondren, December 22, 1861, Mitchell-Fondren Family Civil War Letters; Anderson, "Civil War Courtship of Richard Mortimer Williams and Rose Anderson of Rockville," 129–30; Fordney, ed., "Letters from the Heart," 74.

23. Fordney, ed., "Letters from the Heart," 74; Judith Ann Robertson Foster Memoirs; Anderson, "Civil War Courtship of Richard Mortimer Williams and Rose Anderson," 129–30.

24. Rable, *Civil Wars*, 51–52; Mother to Jane Sivley, January 21, December 5, 1864, Sivley Family Papers.

25. Ashkenazi, ed., *Diary of Clara Solomon*, 137; mother to Jane Sivley, November 4, 1863, Sivley Family Papers.

26. Rundell, ed., "'If Fortune Should Fail'" 133, 219

27. Sue Montgomery to Moultrie Reid Wilson, November 11, 1864, Moultrie Reid Wilson Papers, SCL; Robertson, ed., *Lucy Breckinridge of Grove Hill*, 34–35, 41, 63, 42, 88, 104; Anderson, "Civil War Courtship of Richard Mortimer Williams and Rose Anderson of Rockville," 119–20.

28. Nettie Fondren to Robert Mitchell, November 21, 1862, Mitchell-Fondren Family Civil War Letters; Annie Jeter Carmouche Memoirs; Mary Fries

Patterson Diary, May 2, 1864, Patterson Family Papers; Clara Bowen to Alice (Bailey) Boozer, December 24, 1864, Alice Boozer Letters, SCL; Sarah Lois Wadley Diary, December 25, 1862.

29. Robertson, ed., *Lucy Breckinridge of Grove Hill*, 91, 16, 175, 178.

30. Mary Washington (Cabell) Early Recollections, Early Family Papers, VHS; Mollie Simpson to sister, January 4, 1862, Simpson-Brumby Family Papers, SHC; Louisa McCord Smythe Reminiscences; Clara Bowen to Alice Boozer, December 24, 1864, Alice Boozer Letters.

31. Scott, *Southern Lady*, 106–7; Faust, *Mothers of Invention*, 242–54; Rable, *Civil Wars*, 242–44; Elizabeth Waties (Allston) Pringle Diary, December 31, 1865, January 1, 1866; Snell, ed., *Myra Inman*, 332; Drew Gilpin Faust, "Christian Soldiers," 83–85; Eric Dean, *Shook Over Hell: Post-Traumatic Stress, Vietnam, and the Civil War* (Cambridge: Harvard University Press, 1999), 8, 202–7; John E. Talbott, "Combat Trauma in the American Civil War," *History Today* 46 (March 1996), 41–47.

32. Whites, *Civil War as a Crisis in Gender*, 134–36; Edwards, *Gendered Strife and Confusion*, 107–44.

33. Smith, et. al., eds., *Mason Smith Family Letters*, 238–40.

34. Dean, *Shook Over Hell*, 202–7; Faust, *Mothers of Invention*, 252; Bonner, ed., *Journal of a Milledgeville Girl*, 4; Clara Bowen to Alice Boozer, December 24, 1864, Alice Boozer Letters; Ellen Cooper Johnson Memoirs, SCL.

35. Smith, et. al., eds., *Mason Smith Family Letters*, 238–40; Eppes, *Through Some Eventful Years*, 286–87; Sallie Independence Foster Diary, August 31, 1868.

36. Bonner, ed., *Journal of a Milledgeville Girl*, 116; Kate D. Foster Diary, April 8, 1866, December 7, 1871.

37. Carmichael, *The Last Generation*, 120; Mary Walker Gibson to John Chamberlayne, February 10, 1873, July 11, September 8, September 2, 1873, Chamberlayne Family Papers, VHS.

38. Carmichael, *The Last Generation*, 215–14, 217; Mary Walker Gibson to John Chamberlayne, January 13, 1873, Chamberlayne Family Papers.

39. Mary Walker Gibson to John Chamberlayne, February 12, March 7, 1873, January 13, 1873, Chamberlayne Family Papers.

40. Whites, *Civil War as a Crisis in Gender*, 149–50; Judith Ann Robertson Foster Memoir; Eppes, *Through Some Eventful Years*, 319; Ellen Cooper Johnson Memoirs; Sarah Chaffin to Harriot Wight, March 11, 1867, Chaffin Family Papers.

41. Sallie Independence Foster Diary, September 24, 1866, August 31, 1868.

42. Barber, "White Wings of Eros," 128; Rable, *Civil Wars*, 271; information on the year of marriage for the subject group is drawn from archival records and the United States Bureau of the Census, Tenth U.S. Census, 1880; Eppes,

Through Some Eventful Years, 336; Ellen Cooper Johnson Memoirs; Bonner, ed., *Journal of a Milledgeville Girl*, 4; Fordney, ed., "Letters from the Heart," 82; Sarah Chaffin to Harriot Wight, February 22, 1868, Chaffin Family Papers.

43. Sarah Chaffin to Harriot Wight, February 22, 1868, Chaffin Family Papers; Judith Ann Robertson Foster Memoirs; Mary Washington (Cabell) Early Diary, September 28, 1876.

44. Judith Ann Robertson Foster Memoirs; Louisa McCord Smythe Reminiscences; Eppes, *Through Some Eventful Years*, 319; Mary Washington (Cabell) Early Diary, September 28, 1876; Louisa McCord Smythe Reminiscences.

45. Lucy Ball to unknown, May 13, 1870, William Henry Wills Papers.

46. Rable, *Civil Wars*, 271–72; Censer, *Reconstruction of White Southern Womanhood*, 138–148. Historians, who examine the persistence of the plantation ideal after the war, posit that the southern gentry continued in the postwar era. Censer, however, argues that for many the attempt to maintain their antebellum lifestyle lasted but briefly. For studies of plantation life after the war see, Jonathan Wiener, "Planter Persistence and Social Change: Alabama, 1850–1870," *Journal of Interdisciplinary History* 7 (Autumn 1976): 235–60.

47. Blackiston, ed., *Refugees in Richmond*, 81, 92.

48. Sarah Chaffin to Harriot Wight, March 11, 1867, Chaffin Family Papers; Chaffin Family Papers Gus Vaughn to Mary (Brumby) Vaughn, October 31, 1866, Simpson and Brumby Family Papers.

5. The Confederate Belle Ideal

1. Caroline Joachimson, "Just One Family," *Our Women in the War: the Lives they Lived; the Deaths they Died* (Charleston: News and Courier Book Presses, 1885), 30–31.

2. Other historians have examined the significance of age in shaping one's memory of war. William Tuttle argues in his study of children during World War II that the events of one's childhood shape one's views of politics, society, and family in adulthood. Times of crisis, such as economic depression and war, leave an especially lasting impression on a generation. Like Tuttle, James Marten examines how the experiences of children in wartime shape their worldview as adults, but he shows also how children became important figures in the public remembrance of the Civil War. In the rhetoric of the Lost Cause, children, especially the orphans of soldiers killed in battle, exemplified the sacrifices southerners made in their fight for independence; see Tuttle, *Daddy's Gone to War*, 15, 254 and Marten, *Children's Civil War*, 187–242; Whites, *Civil War as a Crisis in Gender*, 200–9; Faust, *Mothers of Invention*, 252–53.

3. For discussion of the creation and definition of the Lost Cause see Charles Reagan Wilson, *Baptized in Blood: The Religion of the Lost Cause, 1865–1920*

(Athens: University of Georgia Press, 1983), 140, 147, Gaines M. Foster, *Ghosts of the Confederacy: Defeat, the Lost Cause, and the Emergence of the New South* (New York: Oxford University Press, 1987), and David W. Blight, *Race and Reunion: The Civil War in American Memory* (Cambridge: Belknap Press, 2001); Alan T. Nolan, "The Anatomy of a Myth," in Gary W. Gallagher and Nolan, eds., *The Myth of the Lost Cause and Civil War History*, (Bloomington: Indiana University Press, 2000).

4. Sarah Gardner, *Blood and Irony: Southern White Women's Narratives of the Civil War, 1861–1937* (Chapel Hill: University of North Carolina Press, 2004), 39–73.

5. Nina Silber, *The Romance of Reunion: Northerners and the South, 1865–1900* (Chapel Hill: University of North Carolina Press, 1993), quote on page 7, 39–65; Censer, "Reimagining the North-South Reunion: Southern Women Novelists and the Intersectional Romance, 1876–1900" *Southern Cultures* (Summer 1999): 64–91; Gardner, *Blood and Irony*, 61–66.

6. Gardner, *Blood and Irony*, 115–31; Karn Cox, *Dixie's Daughters: The United Daughters of the Confederacy and the Preservation of Confederate Culture* (Gainesville: University Press of Florida), 1, 93–117.

7. For studies of women's literary efforts see Gardner, *Blood and Irony*; Censer, *Southern White Womanhood*; Wright, *A Southern Girl in '61*, 216–17.

8. Ellen Cooper Johnson Memoirs; Judith Ann Robertson Foster Recollections.

9. No author, *Our Women in the War*, quote from front cover; Wright, *A Southern Girl in '61*, 3.

10. Louisa McCord Smythe Reminiscences; Mary Washington (Cabell) Early, "Society in War Times," Early Family Papers; Oranie Virginia (Snead) Hatcher Memoir; Joachimson, "Just One Family," 30–31; Florida Saxon, "Unto the Bitter End," *Our Women in the War*, 70.

11. Unknown author, "In the Cradle of the War," *Our Women in the War*, 281; unknown author, "Village Life in the South," *Our Women in the War*, 454.

12. Lelia C. Morris, "Personal Recollections of the War: Girl Confederate Soldiers," MC.

13. Ellen Cooper Johnson Memoirs; Mary Washington (Cabell) Early, "Home Life in War Times," Early Family Papers; unknown author, "Village Life in the South," 453–55.

14. Mary C. Bell Claytor, "Personal Recollections of Hunter's Raid"; Macon, *Reminiscences of the Civil War*, 115; Louisa McCord Smythe Reminiscences; Joachimson, "Just One Family," 31–32, 36.

15. Saxon, "Unto the Bitter End," 71; Joachimson, "Just One Family," 41.

16. Studies of postwar efforts to reconstruct southern white masculinity include Whites, *Civil War as a Crisis in Gender*; Laura Edwards, *Gendered Strife*

and Confusion: The Political Culture of Reconstruction (Urbana: University of Illinois Press, 1997). Peter Carmichael in *The Last Generation* touches on how Confederate defeat affected southern white men, 216.

17. Mrs. Mattie H. Jarnagin, "Ravages of the Federals," *Our Women in the War*, 321–22; Esther Alden, "Fun in the Fort," *Our Women in the War*, 355.

18. Saxon, "Unto the Bitter End," 71.

19. Ellen Cooper Johnson Memoirs; Sallie Walker Boone Memoirs; Saxon, "Unto the Bitter End," 70.

20. The connection between racial violence toward freed people and white, southern womanhood is well documented in recent works including those by Glenda Elizabeth Gilmore, *Gender and Jim Crow, Women and the Politics of White Supremacy in North Carolina, 1896–1920*; Martha Hodes, *White Women Black Men: Illicit Sex in the Nineteenth-Century South* (New Have: Yale University Press, 1997); and Lisa Cardyn, "Sexual Terror in the Reconstruction South" in *Gender and Sexuality in the American Civil War*, Clinton and Silber, eds. (New York: Oxford University Press, 2006), 140–67.

21. For discussions of former slaveholding women's class identity in flux after emancipation see Whites, *Civil War as a Crisis in Gender*, chapter 4; Faust, *Mothers of Invention*, 249–50; and, Edwards, *Scarlett Doesn't Live Here Anymore*, chapter 9.

22. Sue Richardson Diary, May 12, 14, 1865; Smith, et. al., eds., *Mason Smith Family Letters*, 225–26; Eppes, *Through Some Eventful Years*, 284–85.

23. Whites, *Civil War as a Crisis in Gender*, 128; Edwards, *Scarlett Doesn't Live Here Anymore*, 173; Litwack, *Been in the Storm So Long*, 255.

24. Smith, et. al., eds., *Mason Smith Family Letters*, 187–88, 225–26; Robertson, ed., *Confederate Lady Comes of Age*, 79; Blackiston, ed., *Refugees in Richmond*, 72.

25. Miers, ed., *When the World Ended*, 55.

26. Litwack, *Been in the Storm So Long*, 255; Eppes, *Through Some Eventful Years*, 286, 333–34.

27. Eppes, *Through Some Eventful Years*, 279–80.

28. Ibid., 284–85; Louisa McCord Smythe Reminiscences; Sally Independence Foster Diary, August 31, 1868.

29. Virginia Hankins to William Hankins, October 1, 1869, Hankins Family Papers.

30. Edwards, *Scarlett Doesn't Live Here Anymore*, 173; Kate D. Foster Diary, March 12, 1868.

31. Fannie Leak Diary, January 14, 1870. For a discussion of how African Americans shaped the conditions of work and their resistance to employment terms resembling slavery in the post-emancipation South see Tera Hunter, *To 'Joy My Freedom: Southern Black Women's Lives and Labors after the Civil War*

(Cambridge: Harvard University Press, 1997); Jones, *Labor of Love, Labor of Sorrow*, 44–78; and Leslie Schwalm, *Hard Fight For We: Women's Transition from Slavery to Freedom in South Carolina* (Urbana: University of Illinois Press, 1997), part III. Kate D. Foster Diary, February 5, 1872.

32. Mary Walker Gibson Chamberlayne to mother, January 19, 1874., Chamberlayne Family papers.

33. Rable, *Civil Wars*, 252–54; Censer, "Changing World of Work," 38; Susan "Livie" Olivia Fleming to Lalie, August 29, 1872, Eleanore Eulalie (Cay) Fleming Papers; Olin Davis to mother, April 16, 1874, Beale-Davis Family Papers.

34. Eric Foner, *Reconstruction: America's Unfinished Revolution* New York: Harper and Row, 1988), 183–84, 199–201, 342–43; Edwards, *Gendered Strife and Confusion*, 184–217.

35. Smith, et. al., eds., *Mason Smith Family Papers*, 252, 254, 263; Harrie Hale Patton to Mollie (Simmons) Patton, October 8, 1865, Harrie Hale Patton Papers, Virginia Historical Society; Louisa McCord Smythe Reminiscences; Bonner, ed., *Journal of a Milledgeville Girl*, 126–27.

36. Foner, *Reconstruction*, 171–84; Sutherland, ed., *Very Violent Rebel*, 190; Maria Smith Peek to Daniel Marrow, May 21, 1865, Marrow Family Papers; Sarah Chaffin to Harriot Wight, March 22, 1874, Chaffin Family Papers.

37. Hodes, *White Women Black Men*, 147–48.

38. Foner, *Reconstruction*, 342–43, 558–61, 574–75; Allen W. Trelease, *White Terror: The Ku Klux Klan Conspiracy and Southern Reconstruction* (New York: Harper and Row, 1971), xx-xxi, 136.

39. Foner, *Reconstruction*, 570–75; Charles J. Holden, *State of Rebellion: Reconstruction in South Carolina* (Columbia: University of South Carolina Press, 1996), 174–75, 188–205; Richard Zuczek, *In the Great Maelstrom: Conservatism in Post-Civil War South Carolina* (Columbia: University of South Carolina Press, 2002), 51.

40. William Gillette, *Retreat from Reconstruction, 1869–1879* (Baton Rouge: Louisiana State University Press, 1979); Foner, *Reconstruction*, 575–601; Edwards, *Scarlett Doesn't Live Here Anymore*, 181–82; Whites, *Civil War as a Crisis in Gender*, 211–12.

41. For a discussion of the evolution of segregation in the South see C. Vann Woodward, *The Strange Career of Jim Crow* (New York: Oxford University Press, 1955). The issue of rape and lynching is discussed in Hodes, *White Women, Black Men*, Gilmore, *Gender and Jim Crow*, 82–89, 91–92, and Lisa Cardyn, "Sexual Terror in the Reconstruction South." A good history of Ida B. Wells and the anti-lynching campaign is Jacqueline Jones Royster, ed., *Southern Horrors and Other Writings: The Anti-Lynching Campaign of Ida B. Wells, 1892–1900*, The Bedford Series in History and Culture (Boston: Bedford/St. Martin's, 1997).

42. Rable, *Civil Wars*, 252–54; Louisa McCord Smythe Reminiscences.

43. Louisa McCord Smythe Reminiscences.

44. Ibid.

45. Annie Jeter Carmouche Memoirs; Joachimson, "Just One Family," 38.

46. Edwards, *Gendered Strife and Confusion*, 216–17; Louisa McCord Smythe Reminiscences.

47. Louisa McCord Smythe Reminiscences.

48. Sallie Hunt, "Boys and Girls in the War," *Our Women in the War*, 45–46.

49. Unknown author, "Village Life in the South," 458.

50. Mary Washington (Cabell) Early, "The Women of New Virginia," Early Family Papers; Louisa McCord Smythe Reminiscences; Macon, *Reminiscences of the Civil War*, 135.

51. Jarnagin, "Ravages of the Federals," 325; Hunt, "Boys and Girls in the War," 46.

52. Mrs. R. R., "Potter's Raid," *Our Women in the War*, 295; Morris, "Personal Recollections of the War."

Conclusion

1. Mary Washington (Cabell) Early, "A Glimpse of New Virginia," Early Family Papers.

Bibliography

Primary Sources

MANUSCRIPT COLLECTIONS

Alabama Department of Archives and History

Sarah Lowe Journals
Mary D. Waring Diary

Atlanta History Center

Mary Rawson Diary

Rare Book, Manuscript, and Special Collections, Perkins Library, Duke University

Bettie Alexander Papers
Kate D. Foster Diary
Gertrude Jenkins Papers
Lucas-Ashley Family Papers
Alice Williamson Diary

Georgia Department of Archives and History

Mitchell-Fondren Civil War Papers

Louisiana and Lower Mississippi Valley Collections, Louisiana State University

Annie Jeter Carmouche Papers

Mississippi Department of Archives and History

Cordelia Lewis Scales Papers
Worthington and Stone Family Papers
Worthington Family Papers

Museum of the Confederacy, Ellen Brockenbrough Library

Fannie Lewis Gwathmey Adams Papers
Mary C. Bell Claytor Memoirs
Janet Weaver Papers

South Carolina Historical Society, Columbia

Elizabeth Waties (Allston) Pringle Diary

South Caroliniana Library

Alice Boozer Letters
Mrs. Albert Rhett Heyward Papers
Ellen Cooper Johnson Memoirs
Catherine Louisa McLaurin Diary
Louisa McCord Smythe Reminiscences
Moultrie Reid Wilson Papers

Southern Historical Collection, University of North Carolina, Chapel Hill

Beale and Davis Family Papers
Elizabeth Collier Diary
Eleanore Eulalie (Cay) Fleming Papers
Leak-Wall Family Papers
Lucy Blackwell Malone Reminiscences
Mary E. Fries Patterson Diary
Alice Ready Diary
Frank Liddell Richardson Family Papers
Sally Rowan Saufley Papers
Louisa Sheppard Recollections
Simpson and Brumby Family Papers
Jane Sivley Letters
Thompson Family Papers
Sarah Lois Wadley Papers
William Henry Wills Family Papers

Swem Library, College of William and Mary

Cloe Tyler (Whittle) Greene Diary

Tennessee State Library and Archives

Mary Walker Meriwether Bell Letters, Civil War Collection
Sallie Walker Boone Memoirs
Margaret (Ridley) Gooch Memoirs
Anna Cagdell (Howell) Hollowell Family Papers
Sallie McEwen, Civil War Collection
Nannie Haskins Williams Papers

Virginia Historical Society

Bailey Family Papers

Chaffin Family Papers
Chamberlayne Family Papers
Frances James La Rue Dorsey Diary
Early Family Papers
Finney Family Papers
Judith Ann Robertson Foster Memoir
Goodwin Family Papers
Jeannette Garnett (Ryland) Gwathmey Diary
Hankins Family Papers
Alice Janney Harrison Papers
Oranie Virginia (Snead) Hatcher Memoir
Emmeline Allmand Crump Lightfoot Reminiscences
Marrow Family Papers
Margaretta Ellen Wise Mayo Family Papers
Ridley Family Papers
Janet Weaver Papers

Wesleyan Archives and Museum, University of North Alabama

Sallie Independence Foster Diary

Robert W. Woodruff Library, Special Collections, Emory University

Sue Richardson Diary

NEWSPAPERS

Charleston Mercury
Daily Richmond Enquirer
Natchez Daily Courier

CENSUS RECORDS

U.S. Bureau of the Census. Manuscript Census Schedules. Seventh (1850), Eighth (1860), and Tenth (1880) Censuses.
———. Slave Schedules. Seventh (1850) and Eighth (1860).

PUBLISHED WORKS

Anderson, George M. "The Civil War Courtship of Richard Mortimer Williams and Rose Anderson of Rockville." *Maryland Historical Magazine* 80 (Summer 1985): 119–38.
Anderson, John Q. *Brokenburn: The Journal of Kate Stone, 1861–1868.* Baton Rouge: Louisiana State University Press, 1955.
Ashkenazi, Elliott, ed. *The Civil War Diary of Clara Solomon: Growing Up in New Orleans, 1861–1862.* Baton Rouge: Louisiana State University Press, 1995.

Blackiston, Henry C. *Refugees in Richmond: Civil War Letters of a Virginia Family*. New Jersey: Princeton University Press, 1989.

Bonner, James C., ed. *The Journal of a Milledgeville Girl, 1861–1867*. Athens: University of Georgia Press, 1964.

Burr, Virginia Ingraham, ed. *The Secret Eye: The Journal of Ella Gertrude Clanton Thomas*. Chapel Hill: University of North Carolina Press, 1990.

Burton, J. *Lectures on Female Education and Manners*. Baltimore: Samuel Jefferis, 1811.

Davis, Robert Scott. "Selective Memories of Civil War Atlanta: The Memoir of Sally Clayton." *Georgia Historical Quarterly* 82 (Winter 1998): 735–50.

———, ed. *Requiem for a Lost City: A Memoir of Civil War Atlanta and the Old South*. Macon: Mercer University Press, 1999.

Davis, Varina Howell. *Jefferson Davis: A Memoir by His Wife*, reprint edition. Vol. 1. Baltimore: Nautical and Aviation Publishing of America, 1990.

Eppes, Susan Bradford. *Through Some Eventful Years*. Macon: J.W. Burke Co., 1926.

Fordney, Chris, ed. "Letters from the Heart." *Civil War Times Illustrated* 34 (September-October 1995): 28, 73–82.

Garnett, James. *Lectures on Female Education, Comprising the First and Second Series of a Course Delivered to Mrs. Garnett's Pupils, at Elm-Wood, Essex County, Virginia*. Richmond: Thomas W. White, 1825.

Longstreet, Helen Dortch. *Lee and Longstreet at High Tide: Gettysburg in the Light of the Official Record*. Published by author, 1905.

Macon, Emma Cassandra Riely. *Reminiscences of the Civil War*. Cedar Rapids: The Torch Press, 1911.

Marks, Elias, M.D. *Hints on Female Education*. Columbia: A.S. Johnston, 1851.

Miers, Early Schenck, ed. *When the World Ended: The Diary of Emma LeConte*. New York: Oxford University Press, 1957.

Mitchell, Margaret. *Gone With the Wind*. New York: Scribner, 1936.

Murray, Elizabeth Dunbar. *My Mother Used to Say: A Natchez Belle of the Sixties*. Boston: Christopher Publishing House, 1959.

Our Women in the War: the Lives they Lived; the Deaths they Died. Charleston: News and Courier Book Presses, 1885.

Robertson, Mary D., ed. *A Confederate Lady Comes of Age: The Journal of Pauline DeCaradeuc, 1863–1888*. Columbia: University of South Carolina Press, 1992.

———. *Lucy Breckinridge of Grove Hill: The Journal of a Virginia Girl, 1862–1864*. Columbia: University of South Carolina Press, 1994.

Royster, Jacqueline Jones. *Southern Horrors and Other Writings: The Anti-Lynching Campaign of Ida B. Wells, 1892–1900*. The Bedford Series in History and Culture. Boston: Bedford/St. Martin's, 1997.

Rundell, Walter, Jr., ed. "'If Fortune Should Fail': Civil War Letters of Dr. Samuel D. Sanders." *South Carolina Historical Magazine* 65 (July 1964): 129–44, 218–32.

Smith, Daniel Huger, Alice R. Huger Smith, and Arney R. Childs, eds. *Mason Smith FamilyLetters,1860–1868*. Columbia: University of South Carolina Press, 1950.

Snell, William R. *Myra Inman: A Diary of the Civil War in East Tennessee*. Macon: Mercer University Press, 2000.

Sutherland, Daniel E., ed. *A Very Violent Rebel: The Diary of Ellen Renshaw House*. Knoxville, University of Tennessee Press, 1996.

Wanzer, Sidney Hovey and Anna Bradford Agle. "Dearest Braddie: Love and War in Maryland, 1860–61." *Maryland Historical Magazine* 88 (Spring 1993): 337–58.

Wright, Mrs. D. Giraud. *A Southern Girl in '61: The Wartime Memories of a Confederate Senator's Daughter*. New York: Doubleday Press, 1905.

Secondary Sources

BOOKS

Ash, Stephen V. *When the Yankees Came: Conflict and Chaos in the Occupied South, 1861–1865*. Chapel Hill: University of North Carolina Press, 1995.

Allgor, Catherine. *Parlor Politics: In Which the Ladies of Washington Help Build a City and a Government*. Charlottesville: University Press of Virginia, 2000.

Berringer, Richard, Herman Hattaway, Archer Jones, and William N. Still, Jr. *Why the South Lost the Civil War*. Athens: Georgia University Press, 1986.

Berry, Stephen W. *All That Makes a Man: Love and Ambition in the Civil War South* (New York: Oxford University Press, 2003).

Blair, William. *Virginia's Private War: Feeding Body and Soul in the Confederacy, 1861–1865*. New York: Oxford University Press, 1998.

Blanton, DeAnne and Lauren M. Cook *They Fought Like Demons: Women Soldiers in the American Civil War*. Baton Rouge: Louisiana State University Press, 2002.

Blassingame, John. *The Slave Community: Plantation Life in the Antebellum South*. New York: Oxford University Press, 1972.

Blight, David W. *Race and Reunion: The Civil War in American Memory*. Cambridge: Belknap Press, 2001.

Bynum, Victoria E. *Unruly Women: The Politics of Social and Sexual Control in the Old South*. Chapel Hill: University of North Carolina Press, 1992.

Campbell, Jacqueline Glass. *When Sherman Marched North from the Sea: Resistance on the Confederate Homefront*. Chapel Hill: University of North Carolina Press, 2003.

Carmichael, Peter S. *The Last Generation: Young Virginians in Peace, War, and Reunion.* Chapel Hill: University of North Carolina Press, 2005.

Censer, Jane Turner. *North Carolina Planters and Their Children, 1800–1860.* Baton Rouge: Louisiana State University Press, 1984.

———. *The Reconstruction of White Southern Womanhood, 1865–1895.* Baton Rouge: Louisiana State University Press, 2003.

Chambers-Schiller, Lee Virginia. *Liberty, a Better Husband: Single Women in America: The Generations of 1780–1840.* New Haven: Yale University Press, 1984.

Channing, Steven A. *Crisis of Fear: Secession in South Carolina.* New York: Simon and Schuster, 1970.

Cimprich, John. *Slavery's End in Tennessee.* Tuscaloosa: University of Alabama Press, 1986.

Clinton, Catherine. *The Other Civil War: American Women in the Nineteenth Century.* New York: Hill and Wang, 1984.

———. *Plantation Mistress: Woman's World in the Old South.* New York: Pantheon Books, 1982.

———. *Tara Revisited: Women, War, and the Plantation Legend.* New York: Abbeville Press, 1995.

Cox, Karen. *Dixie's Daughters: The United Daughters of the Confederacy and the Preservation of Confederate Culture.* Gainesville: University Press of Florida, 2003.

Crofts, Daniel W. *Reluctant Confederates: Upper South Unionists in the Secession Crisis.* Chapel Hill: University of North Carolina Press, 1989.

Dean, Eric. *Shook Over Hell: Post-Traumatic Stress, Vietnam, and the Civil War.* Cambridge: Harvard University Press, 1999.

Delfano, Susanna and Michelle Gillespie, eds. *Neither Lady nor Slave: Working Women of the Old South.* Chapel Hill: University of North Carolina Press, 2002.

Edwards, Laura F. *Gendered Strife and Confusion: The Political Culture of Reconstruction.* Urbana: University of Illinois Press, 1997.

———. *Scarlett Doesn't Live Here Anymore: Southern Women in the Civil War Era.* Urbana: University of Illinois Press, 2000.

Escott, Paul D. *After Secession: Jefferson Davis and the Failure of Confederate Nationalism.* Baton Rouge: Louisiana State University Press, 1978.

Farnham, Christie Anne. *The Education of the Southern Belle: Higher Education and Student Socialization in the Antebellum South.* New York: New York University Press, 1994.

Faust, Drew Gilpin. *The Creation of Confederate Nationalism: Ideology and Identity in the Civil War South.* Baton Rouge: Louisiana State University Press, 1988.

————. *Mothers of Invention: Women of the Slaveholding South in the American Civil War.* Chapel Hill: University of North Carolina Press, 1996.

Finkelman, Paul, ed. *His Soul Goes Marching On: Responses to John Brown and the Harper's Ferry Raid.* Charlottesville: University Press of Virginia, 1995.

Foner, Eric. *Free Soil, Free Labor, Free Men: the Ideology of the Republican Party Before the Civil War.* New York: Oxford University Press, 1970.

————. *Reconstruction: America's Unfinished Revolution.* New York: Harper and Row, 1988.

Ford, Lacy K. *Origins of Southern Radicalism: The South Carolina Upcountry, 1800–1860.* New York: Oxford University Press, 1991.

Foster, Gaines M. *Ghosts of the Confederacy: Defeat, the Lost Cause, and the Emergence of the New South.* New York: Oxford University Press, 1987.

Fought, Leigh. *Southern Womanhood and Slavery: A Biography of Louisa S. McCord.* Columbia: University of Missouri Press, 2003.

Fox-Genovese, Elizabeth. *Within the Plantation Household: Black and White Women of the Old South.* Chapel Hill: University of North Carolina Press, 1985.

Fraser, Walter J., Jr., R. Frank Saunders, Jr., John L. Wakelyn, eds. *The Web of Southern Social Relations: Women, Family and Education.* Athens: University of Georgia Press, 1985.

Friedman, Jean E. *The Enclosed Garden: Women and Community in the Evangelical South, 1830–1900.* Chapel Hill: University of North Carolina Press, 1985.

Gallagher, Gary. *The Confederate War: Popular Will, Nationalism, and Strategy.* Cambridge: Harvard University Press, 1997.

Gallagher, Gary, and Alan T. Nolan, eds. *The Myth of the Lost Cause and Civil War History.* Bloomington: Indiana University Press, 2000.

Gardner, Sarah E. *Blood and Irony: Southern White Women's Narratives of the Civil War, 1861–1937.* Chapel Hill: University of North Carolina Press, 2004.

Genovese, Eugene D. *Roll, Jordan, Roll: The World the Slaves Made.* New York: Vintage Books, 1974.

Gillette, William. *Retreat From Reconstruction, 1869–1879.* Baton Rouge: Louisiana State University Press, 1979.

Gilmore, Glenda Elizabeth. *Gender and Jim Crow: Women and the Politics of White Supremacy in North Carolina, 1896–1920.* Chapel Hill: University of North Carolina Press, 1996.

Glover, Lorri. *All Our Relations: Blood Ties and Emotional Bonds Among the Early South Carolina Gentry.* Baltimore: Johns Hopkins University Press, 2000.

Green, Elna C. *Southern Strategies: Southern Women and the Woman Suffrage Question.* Chapel Hill: University of North Carolina Press, 1997.

Grimsley, Mark. *The Hard Hand of War: Union Military Policy Toward Southern Civilians, 1861–1865.* New York: Cambridge University Press, 1995.

Hadden, Sally. *Slave Patrols: Law and Violence in Virginia and the Carolinas.* Cambridge: Harvard University Press, 2001.

Hodes, Martha. *White Women, Black Men: Illicit Sex in the Nineteenth-Century South.* New Haven: Yale University Press, 1997.

Holden, Charles J. *State of Rebellion: Reconstruction in South Carolina.* Columbia: University of South Carolina Press, 1996.

Holt, Michael F. *The Political Crisis of the 1850s,* New Ed. edition. New York: W.W. Norton Company, 1983.

Hunter, Tera W. *To 'Joy My Freedom: Southern Black Women's Lives and Labors after the Civil War.* Cambridge: Harvard University Press, 1997.

Jabour, Anya. *Marriage in the Early Republic: Elizabeth and William Wirt and the Companionate Ideal.* Baltimore: Johns Hopkins University Press, 1998.

———. *Scarlett's Sisters: Young Women in the Old South.* Chapel Hill: University of North Carolina Press, 2007.

Jones, Jacqueline. *Labor of Love, Labor of Sorrow: Black Women, Work, and the Family from Slavery to the Present.* New York: Vintage Books, 1985.

Kett, Joseph F. *Rites of Passage: Adolescence in America, 1790 to the Present.* New York: Basic Books Publishing, 1977.

Kierner, Cynthia. *Beyond the Household: Women's Place in the Early South, 1700–1835.* Ithaca: Cornell University Press, 1998.

Klatch, Rebecca E. *A Generation Divided: The New Left, the New Right, and the 1960s.* Berkeley: University of California Press, 1999.

Lebsock, Suzanne. *The Free Women of Petersburg: Status and Culture in a Southern Town, 1784–1860.* New York: W. W. Norton Company, 1984.

Litwack, Leon F. *Been in the Storm So Long: The Aftermath of Slavery.* New York: Knopf, 1979.

McArthur, Judith N. *Creating the New Woman: The Rise of the Southern Women's Progressive Culture in Texas, 1893–1918.* Urbana: University of Illinois Press, 1998.

McCurry, Stephanie. *Masters of Small Worlds: Yeomen Households, Gender Relations, and the Political Culture of the Antebellum South Carolina Low Country.* New York: Oxford University Press, 1995.

McMillen, Sally G. *Motherhood in the Old South: Pregnancy, Childbirth, and Infant Rearing.* Baton Rouge: Louisiana State University Press, 1990.

McPherson, James M. *Battle Cry of Freedom: The Civil War Era.* New York: Oxford University Press, 1988.

———. *For Cause and Comrades: Why Men Fought in the Civil War.* New York: Oxford University Press, 1997.

Marten, James. *The Children's Civil War.* Chapel Hill: University of North Carolina Press, 1998.

Massey, Mary Elizabeth. *Bonnet Brigades.* New York: Knopf Press, 1966.

———. *Refugee Life in the Confederacy*. Baton Rouge: Louisiana State University Press, 1964.

Mohr, Clarence L. *On the Threshold of Freedom: Masters and Slaves in Civil War Georgia*. Athens: University of Georgia Press, 1986.

Oakes, James. *The Ruling Race: A History of American Slaveholders*. New York: Alfred Knopf, 1982.

———. *Slavery and Freedom: An Interpretation of the Old South*. New York: Knopf Press, 1990.

Potter, David M. *The South and the Sectional Conflict*. Baton Rouge: Louisiana State University Press, 1968.

Ransom, Roger L. and Richard Sutch. *One Kind of Freedom: The Economic Consequences of Emancipation*. Second edition. New York: Cambridge University Press, 2001.

Rable, George. *Civil Wars: Women and the Crisis of Southern Nationalism*. Urbana: University of Illinois Press, 1989.

Ripley, Peter C. *Slaves and Freedmen in Civil War Louisiana*. Baton Rouge: Louisiana State University Press, 1976.

Roark, James L. *Masters Without Slaves: Southern Planters in the Civil War and Reconstruction*. New York: Norton, 1977.

Roberts, Giselle. *The Confederate Belle*. Columbia: University of Missouri Press, 2003.

Rothman, Ellen K. *Hands and Hearts: A History of Courtship in America*. New York: Basic Books, 1984.

Rubin, Sarah Anne. *A Shattered Nation: The Rise and Fall of the Confederacy, 1861–1868*. Civil War America. Chapel Hill: University of North Carolina Press, 2005.

Schwalm, Leslie. *Hard Fight For We: Women's Transition from Slavery to Freedom in South Carolina*. Urbana: University of Illinois Press, 1997.

Scott, Ann Firor. *The Southern Lady: From Pedestal to Politics, 1830–1930*. Chicago: University of Chicago Press, 1970.

Silber, Nina. *The Romance of Reunion: Northerners and the South, 1865–1900*. Chapel Hill: University of North Carolina Press, 1993.

Simkins, Francis Butler and Patton, James Welch. *The Women of the Confederacy*. Richmond: Garrett and Massie, 1936.

Sterkx, H.E. *Partners in Rebellion: Alabama Women in the Civil War*. Rutherford: Fairleigh Dickinson University Press, 1970.

Stevenson, Brenda. *Life in Black and White: Family and Community in the Slave South*. New York: Oxford University Press, 1996.

Stowe, Steven M. *Intimacy and Power in the Old South: Ritual in the Lives of the Planters*. Baltimore: Johns Hopkins University Press, 1987.

Trelease, Allen W. *White Terror: The Ku Klux Klan Conspiracy and Southern Reconstruction.* New York: Harper and Row, 1971.

Tuttle, William M., Jr. *Daddy's Gone to War: The Second World War in the Lives of America's Children.* New York: Oxford University Press, 1993.

Varon, Elizabeth R. *We Mean to be Counted: White Women and Politics in Antebellum Virginia.* Chapel Hill: University of North Carolina Press, 1998.

Walser, Richard. *Literary North Carolina: A Brief Historical Survey.* Raleigh: State Department of Archives and History, 1970.

Weiner, Marli F. *Mistresses and Slaves: Plantation Women in South Carolina, 1830–80.* Urbana: University of Illinois Press, 1998.

Welter, Barbara. *Dimity Convictions: The American Woman in the Nineteenth Century.* Athens: Ohio University Press, 1976.

Wheeler, Marjorie Spruill. *New Women of the New South: The Leaders of the Woman Suffrage Movement in the Southern States.* New York: Oxford University Press, 1993.

Whites, LeeAnn. *The Civil War as a Crisis in Gender: Augusta, Georgia, 1860–1890.* Athens: University of Georgia Press, 1995.

Wiener, Jonathan M. *Social Origins of the New South: Alabama, 1860–1885.* Baton Rouge: Louisiana State University Press, 1978.

Wiley, Bell Irwin. *Confederate Women.* Westport: Greenwood Press, 1975.

Wilson, Charles Reagan. *Baptized in Blood: The Religion of the Lost Cause, 1865–1920.* Athens: University of Georgia Press, 1983.

Woodward, C. Vann. *The Strange Career of Jim Crow.* 3rd ed., rev. New York: Oxford University Press, 1974.

Wright, Gavin. *Old South, New South: Revolutions in the Southern Economy Since the Civil War.* Baton Rouge: Louisiana State University Press, 1979.

Wyatt-Brown, Bertram. *Southern Honor: Ethics and Behavior in the Old South.* New York: Oxford University Press, 1982.

Zuczek, Richard. *In the Great Maelstrom: Conservatism in Post-Civil War South Carolina.* Columbia: University of South Carolina Press, 2002.

ARTICLES

Baker, Paula. "The Domestication of Politics: Women and American Political Society." *American Historical Review* 89 (June 1984): 620–47.

Barber, E. Susan. "'The White Wings of Eros': Courtship and Marriage in Confederate Richmond." In *Southern Families at War: Loyalty and Conflict in the Civil War South,* ed. Catherine Clinton, 119–32. New York: Oxford University Press, 2000.

Brown, Alexis Girardin. "The Women Left Behind: Transformation of the Southern Belle, 1840–1880." *Historian* 62 (Summer 2000): 759–79.

Cashin, Joan. "'Since the War Broke Out'": The Marriage of Kate and William McClure." In *Divided Houses: Gender and the Civil War*, eds. Catherine Clinton and Nina Silber, 200–12. New York: Oxford University Press, 1992.

Censer, Jane Turner. "A Changing World of Work: North Carolina Elite Women, 1865–1895." *North Carolina Historical Review* 73 (January 1996): 28–55.

———. "Reimagining the North-South Reunion: Southern Women Novelists and the Intersectional Romance, 1876–1900." *Southern Cultures* (Summer 1999): 64–91.

Demos, John and Virginia Demos, "Adolescence in Historical Perspective." *Journal of Marriage and Family* 31 (November 1969): 632–38.

Faust, Drew Gilpin. "Christian Soldiers: The Meaning of Revivalism in the Confederate Army." *Journal of Southern History* 53 (February 1987): 63–90.

———. "Altars of Sacrifice: Confederate Women and the Narratives of War." *Journal of American History* 76 no. 4 (March 1990): 1200–28.

Glover, Lorri. "An Education in Southern Masculinity: The Ball Family of South Carolina in the New Republic." *Journal of Southern History* 69 (February 2003): 39–70.

Jabour, Anya. "Grown Girls, Highly Cultivated": Female Education in an Antebellum Southern Family." *Journal of Southern History* 64 (February 1998); 23–64.

Kerber, Linda K. "Separate Spheres, Female Worlds, Woman's Place: The Rhetoric of Women's History." *Journal of American History* 75 (June 1988): 9–39.

McGerr, Michael. "Political Style and Women's Power, 1830–1930." *Journal of American History* 77 (December 1990): 864–85.

Richard, Patricia L. "'Listen Ladies One and All': Union Soldiers Yearn for the Society of Their 'Fair Cousins of the North.'" In *Union Soldiers and the Northern Home Front*, eds. Paul A. Cimbala and Randall M. Miller, 143–81. New York: Fordham University Press, 2002.

Smith-Rosenberg, Carroll. "The Female World of Love and Ritual: Relations Between Women in the Nineteenth-Century America." *Signs* 1 (Autumn 1975): 1–29.

Stowe, Steven. "The Rhetoric of Authority: The Making of Social Values in Planter Family Correspondence." *Journal of American History* 73 (March 1987): 916–33.

Stowell, David W. "A Family of Women and Children: The Fains of East Tennessee." in *Southern Families at War: Loyalty and Conflict in the Civil War South*, ed. Catherine Clinton, 155–73. New York: Oxford University Press, 2000.

Talbott, John E. "Combat Trauma in the American Civil War." *History Today* 46 (March 1996): 41–47.

Walker, Henry. "Power, Sex, and Gender Roles: The Transformation of an Alabama Planter Family During the Civil War." In *Southern Families at War:*

Loyalty and Conflict in the Civil War South, ed. Catherine Clinton, 175–91. New York: Oxford University Press, 2000.

Wiener, Jonathan M. "Female Planters and Planters' Wives in Civil War and Reconstruction Alabama, 1850–1870." *Alabama Review* 30 (April 1977): 135–49.

———. "Planter Persistence and Social Change: Alabama, 1850–1870." *Journal of Interdisciplinary History* 7 (Autumn 1976): 235–60.

UNPUBLISHED DISSERTATIONS AND THESES

Nix, Elizabeth Morrow. "An Exuberant Flow of Spirits: Antebellum Adolescent Girls in the Writings of Southern Women." Ph.D. diss., Boston University, Boston, 1996.

Pope, Christie Farnham. "Preparation for Pedestals: North Carolina Antebellum Female Seminaries." Ph.D. diss., University of Chicago, 1977.

Index

Victoria E. Ott is an assistant professor of American history at Birmingham-Southern College.